THE WELFARE STATE EAST AND WEST

CONTRIBUTORS

Erik Allardt, *University of Helsinki*
Shmuel Eisenstadt, *Hebrew University of Jerusalem*
Nathan Glazer, *Harvard University*
Naomi Maruo, *Chuo University, Tokyo*
Yukio Noguchi, *Hitotsubashi University, Tokyo*
Richard Rose, *University of Strathclyde, Glasgow*
Rei Shiratori, *Dokkyo University, Tokyo*
Wolfgang Zapf, *University of Mannheim*

The Welfare State
East and West

Edited by
Richard Rose
and Rei Shiratori

New York · Oxford
Oxford University Press
1986

Oxford University Press

Oxford   New York   Toronto
Delhi   Bombay   Calcutta   Madras   Karachi
Petaling Jaya   Singapore   Hong Kong   Tokyo
Nairobi   Dar es Salaam   Cape Town
Melbourne   Auckland

and associated companies in
Beirut   Berlin   Ibadan   Nicosia

Copyright © 1986 by Oxford University Press, Inc.

Published by Oxford University Press, Inc.,
200 Madison Avenue, New York, New York 10016

   Papers derived from meetings held at the University of Strathclyde, Scotland
and at Nikko, Japan, and Tokyo, and produced under the auspices of
the Institute for Political Studies in Japan.

Library of Congress Cataloging-in-Publication Data
Main entry under title:
The Welfare state East and West.

   1. Welfare state—Congresses.   I. Rose, Richard, 1933–
II. Shiratori, Rei, 1937–   .   III. Nihon Seiji Sogo Kenkyujo.
HN3.W2   1986   361.6′5   86-697
ISBN 0-19-503956-4 (alk. paper)

9 8 7 6 5 4 3 2 1

Printed in the United States of America
on acid-free paper

ACKNOWLEDGMENTS

The production of a book about welfare on three continents inevitably requires the assistance of people in many lands. Appropriately enough, the initial idea was first discussed at a colloquium of the Research Committee on Political Sociology of the International Political Science Association and the International Sociological Association at the Werner-Reimers Stiftung, Bad Homburg, near Frankfurt. The volume has been produced under the auspices of the Institute for Political Studies in Japan (IPSJ), a consortium of Japanese scholars interested in encouraging comparative research involving Japan with other advanced industrial societies, thus widening the intellectual horizons of American and European as well as Japanese students of society.

Water unites what cultures divide. The contributors to this volume first met to explore the extent of intellectual similarities and differences beside the shores of Loch Lomond, Scotland, at the Ross Priory conference center of the University of Strathclyde. We discovered that there was a clear common focus, and that the differences among economists, political scientists, and sociologists were as significant as those among nationalities. The second meeting was held by Lake Yu at Nikko, a setting as idyllic as the drive from Tokyo was reminiscent of Japan's urban problems. Themes from this discussion were also presented at a seminar in Tokyo on the future of the welfare state opened by the incumbent Minister for Social Welfare, Mr. Kozo Watanabe.

In addition to the efforts of the authors represented here, Dr. Graham Healey of the Centre for Japanese Studies, University of Sheffield, made a particularly helpful contribution as a bilingual interlocutor. Special assistance with the organization of meetings was given by the Japanese Embassy in London, and the Japan Foundation.

Richard Rose
Centre for the Study of Public Policy
University of Strathclyde

Rei Shiratori
Institute for Political Studies
in Japan and Dokkyo University

CONTENTS

THE WELFARE STATE EAST AND WEST

Welfare in Society: Three Worlds or One?

Richard Rose and Rei Shiratori

Every country is unique—or is it? Certainly, Americans like to think that the United States is different from every other country. Patriotic Americans proclaim that the country is a unique success story, whereas alienated Americans have attributed to the United States a unique moral inferiority. Yet the assertion of America's uniqueness rejects the equally familiar idea that America is the prototypical nation, pioneering institutions that other societies will emulate in future. Historically, the United States had a vanguard role as a pioneer of democratic institutions. It has also been a leader in industrial and postindustrial innovation, a role confirmed by the export of technology and consumer goods by multinational corporations. However, proponents of welfare policies see the United States as marching at a slower tempo, lagging behind European nations in the development of a welfare state (Rose, 1985a).

Europeans have historically considered each society to be different from all others, including America. The first half of this century saw two world wars that reflected divisions within Europe. The decades since have seen a grand rapprochement, politically, economically, and socially. The creation of the European Community, bringing together victors and defeated from past wars, gives tangible political recognition of common concerns. Travel on holiday as well as business makes people familiar with places once thought distant. Television demonstrates a common pop culture, and the European Broadcasting Union disseminates football matches across a continent. The spread of Coca Cola, Levi's, Japanese cars, and transistor radios demonstrates that the most common market today is not within Europe but global, responding to tastes that are much alike on many continents. In intellectual activities, America's culture cannot be ignored as irrelevant by Europeans, whether it is seen as desirable or debilitating. Only in one field—the institutions of the welfare state—can Europeans, particularly on the Left, argue that the United States is both different and backward.

Even if the Atlantic has now been narrowed to just one more river to cross, the Pacific spans a vast distance, culturally as well as geographically. Whereas Americans and Europeans may think that they are different, Japanese *know* that they are different. By contrast with Britain, another island nation, the Japanese for more than a thousand years successfully resisted the penetration of foreign cultures and migrants. When Britain led the world in creating the Industrial Revolution, Japan forbade foreign commerce, and was still in a handicraft age. The Japanese society that emerged from defeat in World War II was predominantly agricultural, without a tradition of high-technology industries, such as Germany used as the basis for its post-1945 reconstruction.

During the lifetime of a majority of its citizens, Japan has undergone a great economic transformation. The pervasiveness of its exports, nearly all products of modern technology, demonstrates Japan's integration in the world economy. Economic strength is shown by the fact that even though Japan must import all of its oil, it has continued to maintain an expanding economy even after the 1973 oil crisis. Democratic political institutions—free elections, freedom of the press, a government accountable to Parliament, and the freedom of oppositions to demonstrate—have made Japan more like the United States or European governments than like its Asian neighbors in Korea, Singapore, the Philippines, Taiwan, or the People's Republic of China. The long dominance of the Liberal Democratic party (LDP) is comparable to that of the Social Democrats in Sweden or Christian Democrats in Italy.

By conventional material measures, Japanese citizens today enjoy a very high level of welfare. The current life expectancy of a Japanese baby is 77 years, higher than that of United States, of Britain, or of most European countries. Two-fifths of Japanese proceed to college after leaving secondary school; that is nearly as high a proportion as in the United States, and double what is normal in Europe. Job security is high; during the troubled 1980s Japanese unemployment has been averaging 3 percent, a rate half that of the United States, and one-quarter that of the European Community overall. Retirement is possible as early as age 55, and pension arrangements guarantee security in old age. Moreover, family solidarity remains high: divorce rates are half that of England and one-quarter that of the United States. Notwithstanding the tensions that a very competitive education system creates for young people, juvenile crime rates in Japan are far below those of Europe or the United States.

To say that Japan has caught up with (or surpassed) America and Europe presupposes that we live in a world in which people's desires vary little, whether they are raised in Sweden, Italy, or Israel, in the American Frost Belt or the Sun Belt, or in Japan. The "good" goods that people seek—health, education, and income security, and such intangibles as political freedom—are common wants and, in contemporary postindustrial societies, common achievements.

Yet both Occidentals and Orientals would hesitate to assert that a society that can successfully compete in the international economy is like other countries in every important respect. Material goods may be similar across international boundaries, but cultural values are not so readily exported. The United States has time and again seen its foreign policy frustrated by the fact that people in other nations often think and act differently than Washingtonians. European history is a record of conflicts between neighboring countries. Within the United Kingdom the British have found that cultural differences have prevented a peaceful solution to the problem of Northern Ireland.

Whereas the goods that Japan produces for export have a value independent of national culture, welfare goods and services must be produced in ways consistent with Japanese culture. Differences are most striking in the role of the family. In Europe and the United States, homes that once produced much welfare by generations caring for each other have been replaced by the nuclear family, which is likely to be distant from its parents. Many children now live in a single-parent home. In Japan the linkage between generations is strong; most elderly Japanese try to live with one or more of their children, and help care for the grandchildren. The value placed upon elderly parents living with their married offspring and grandchildren makes Japan more like a traditional Asian society, such as India, than like the United States or a European country (Economic Planning Agency, 1983, p. 225).

The meaning of work has changed too. European socialists proclaim that their ethic of mutual care through the state is a better form of organization than the conventional capitalist economy. In the United States, pundits and pollsters wonder whether the work ethic is in decline, and postmaterialist values becoming dominant. The Protestant ethic, claimed to provide the original cultural impetus to capitalism, cannot be used to explain Japan's productivity, for Shintoism is not the same as Protestantism. Nor could Japan's emphasis upon group solidarity be considered like the American value of individualism, or the more conflict-oriented European emphasis upon collective class action. Japanese group solidarity—which affects industrial relations and government as well as family life—is a cultural artifact that is definitely *not* for export. Even when material living standards are similar, there remain important differences between the East, as represented by Japan, and the West, as represented by Europe.

Where does the United States fit in? Geographically, it is only from the vantage point of Moscow or Peking that the United States and Europe constitute the West, and Japan the East. European civilizations, as in the days of Marco Polo and Christopher Columbus, are halfway between the United States and Japan. When New York or Los Angeles is made the center of civilization, then it is Europe that is the East and Japan the West.

Culturally, the United States and Japan are alike in having origins different from European civilizations. The American attitude toward Europe was initially ambivalent. Today the United States is no longer burdened with the inferiority complex of an ex-colonial nation, nor does Japan any longer have such a complex. Yet contemporary American civilization is indigenous; insofar as it borrows from abroad it is syncretic, making use of Latin American, African, and now Asian importations, as well as European. Moreover, European borrowings span a far wider variety of cultures—from Italy and Greece through Eastern Europe to Scandinavia, Britain, and Ireland—than would be found within a single European country. Japanese borrowings are also syncretic: in the Ginza, an American hamburger stand, a Chinese restaurant, a Viennese coffeehouse, a French restaurant, and a Japanese noodle shop all promise to satisfy the appetites of Japanese.

In political economy America and Japan have common differences from Europe. Both countries have big economies, with a great displacement in the world economy. Among members of the Organization for Economic Cooperation and Development (OECD), the club of rich nations, America has the largest gross domestic product (GDP), greater than that of the 10 nations of the European Community combined. Japan ranks second, with a GDP greater than Britain, Germany, and France combined. Together, America and Japan have a GDP that is larger than that of the whole European Community. Whereas European societies often have a high per capita standard of living, most countries are small in population. The total GDP of Scandinavia is only 11 percent of that of the United States, and one-quarter that of Japan. Whereas fluctuations in the economies of small nations have only a small impact upon the world economy, fluctuations in Japan's exports or in the value of the American dollar have a big impact.

America and Japan are also alike in *not* accepting premises of socialism or social democracy that are pervasive throughout European mixed-economy welfare states. In Europe, the state is expected to be an active participant in the direction of the economy, owning as well as coordinating activities of major industries. By contrast, in the United States and Japan private enterprise is meant to reap the benefits and run risks. In Europe, the state is regarded as having a major responsibility to provide welfare for all its citizens through public education, a national health service, and the generous provision of pensions and income maintenance payments to the unemployed. The strength of this commitment has been shown by the fact that, notwithstanding ideological predispositions, even Margaret Thatcher's government has been unable to cut back Britain's expenditure on social programs. In the United States, the individual, supplemented by the family, community, ethnic, and other communal groups, is still regarded as having the primary responsibility for personal welfare (Klass, 1985). In Japan the family and, for those working in large organizations, the employer, undertake responsibilities that supplement individual effort, and substitute for the state provision of welfare.

Many Americans accustomed to think of Japan as alien may nonetheless find the dominant political values of the right-of-center Liberal Democratic party government more familiar than left-of-center values often dominant in christian democratic as well as social democratic Europe. An ideological map would locate Japan as the westernmost of the "Sun Belt" states, to the right of Texas and California, and a few centers of ideas on America's Atlantic Coast might even appear closer to Europe than to California. Ronald Reagan's 1980 and 1984 election victories, like Jimmy Carter's win in 1976, emphasize that American voters do not endorse the European welfare state. Like Japan, the United States still emphasizes the limits of state provision for popular welfare. A Japanese politician would find himself ideologically more at home in Texas than in Sweden or Germany, and a Texas politician would be more at home in Kobe than in Copenhagen.

THE OBJECT OF THE BOOK

This study of the welfare state East and West considers how the provision of welfare differs in societies that are similar in their high standard of material wealth—the United States, Japan, Scandinavia, Britain, Germany, and Israel. Each chapter is written by an internationally recognized social scientist, who has devoted years to studying the welfare state in his or her particular society, and who pays for its benefits as a taxpayer. Pooling the knowledge and outlooks of eight authors living in three different continents is a good way to test for similarities and differences between societies.

Comparing the welfare state across the continents is not meant to imply that what is being studied is the same in every country. Rather, it is to explore whether and under what circumstances public policies for welfare—and private provision as well—are similar or different. Comparison starts with a set of common questions; research tests whether or not the answers are the same.

The first question to address is the nature of state and society. Definitions of welfare—good health, education, and security of income—do not vary greatly across national boundaries. The basic concerns of individuals and families are not derived from political values, but from more pervasive human values (cf. Stoetzel, 1983; Rose, 1984, Chapter 8). But the institutional mechanisms for delivering welfare, whether by government or independent of government, differ greatly.

The United States and Scandinavia present marked contrasts in the extent to which society is seen as a single community with common concerns and responsibilities. As Nathan Glazer's chapter about the United States emphasizes, Americans tend to see social relationships in terms of individual concerns and individual responsibilities. Only those who cannot look after themselves are expected to rely upon the state to look after them. As Erik Allardt shows, in Scandinavia there is a great sense of social solidarity; welfare is a collective responsibility of society, undertaken by the state, acting collectively on behalf of the citizenry. In Japan, as Naomi Maruo's chapter emphasizes, the family often retains primary responsibilities for welfare.

The nature of the state differs greatly across national boundaries too. Israel is an extreme case, for the Jewish Agency, Histadrut, and other Zionist bodies began to provide welfare in the Palestine Mandate prior to the creation of the State of Israel. As Shmuel Eisenstadt's contribution shows, the "pre-state" responsibilities of these institutions for welfare remain important in Israel today. Germany and Japan have suffered the trauma of dictatorship, invasion, and defeat in war. People cannot so readily assume a caring, "user-friendly" state in what was not so long ago an authoritarian, repressive state (Rose, 1985b).

Japanese share with Europeans the concept of the state as an overarching institution, responsible for the good and ill of society. Israelis, thanks to the Zionist impetus, derive individual identity from their collective commitment to the State of Israel. By contrast, neither Americans nor English have a strong sense of the state as an active agent in society (cf. Nettl, 1968). Americans may still see the state as somehow "outside" society; to speak of government intervention would puzzle many Europeans or Japanese, who see the state as naturally involved in the provision of welfare. In England, the tendency is to muddle the distinction between state and society. As Richard Rose's study of the welfare mix emphasizes, it is an open empirical question whether govermental or nongovernmental institutions make a greater contribution to total welfare in society.

National differences are readily recognized when the second question is posed: What was the process of evolution creating the contemporary provision of welfare? As early industrial nations, Britain and Germany each began to develop welfare institutions before World War I. The United States, also an early-industrializing nation, did not begin a similar process until the New Deal of the 1930s. Further developments in state welfare in Europe were confirmed in immediate postwar reconstruction; they did not commence in the United States until the 1960s, and were challenged by an antiwelfare backlash in the 1970s. Societies that are today bywords for modernity—Scandinavia and Japan—were later modernizers. When continental Europe and the United States were industrializing in the late nineteenth century, Scandinavians were emigrating in search of industrial employment, or facing life in relatively poor rural societies. Most Japanese were living at little better than the level of subsistence peasants as late as the 1950s.

Politics accounts for many of the differences in the evolution of welfare institutions. The German Chancellor, Bismarck, in a semiauthoritarian regime engaged in defensive modernization, convinced the Kaiser to endorse the provision of welfare benefits *instead of* democracy (Flora & Heidenheimer, 1981). In Britain, by contrast, the development of the welfare state was brought forward by the gradual broadening of the right to vote, receiving a particular impetus from the return of a Liberal government in 1906. In Israel, government provision of welfare could commence only after the creation of the state in 1948; today it is dependent upon Israel maintaining defense forces that guarantee national security, yet leave fiscal scope for welfare expenditure as well.

What we refer to as historical differences often reflect persisting differences in national values. Cultural values are the living embodiment of past experiences and choices. This is very evident in the United States, where the promotion of welfare by the national government has been more the exception than the rule, occurring during limited but important presidencies, such as the first two terms of Franklin D. Roosevelt and a few years in the 1960s under Presidents Kennedy and Johnson.

Posing questions about political values within the context of a single nation usually concentrates attention upon the differences between political parties and partisan ideologies, whether left or right, catholic, agrarian, or bourgeois liberal. But international comparison stimulates an awareness of values that differentiate one nation from others. This is most evident in Japan, where one political coalition, now known as the Liberal Democratic party, has won almost every postwar election. LDP governments have greatly increased expenditure on welfare during their thirty years in office, and also expanded social expenditure as a proportion of the national product. But the LDP has paid more attention to encouraging growth in the national product than to growth in welfare expenditure. Parties that pay lip service to European welfare state values, such as the Democratic Socialist party and Komei party, are not popular with the electorate. At the other extreme, the antisocialist bourgeois coalition of parties in Scandinavia accepts the primary institutions of the Scandinavian welfare state. What appears a normal social market economy to German politicians of all parties would appear like socialism to many American Democrats as well as Republicans.

When attention is shifted from political values to public programs, then major similarities begin to appear. The contrast is partial, not complete between state provision of welfare in Europe as against the United States and Japan. In health insurance, the U.S. government, through Medicare, Medicaid, and other programs, accounts for a substantial fraction of total health expenditure, and the state health schemes of Europe and Japan require recipients to make payments for some services. In education, there are many functional imperatives creating common practices everywhere: for example, computers can be used the same in every modern society. Even in languages, Japanese and Europeans today have one thing in common: English (or American) is the normal language for use in international travel, business, and politics, and it is often the language of pop culture too.

The objectives of welfare are common to all societies in the modern world. The fact that many German, British, or Scandinavian welfare state programs are now spread worldwide demonstrates that many features of welfare transcend national boundaries. This is true of the nonstate provision of welfare—for example, of housing and food through the market, or of care for the elderly and sick within the home—as well as of state provision. Just as the cultural approach to welfare emphasizes national differences, so the program approach emphasizes cross-national similarities. What differs, as the first chapter emphasizes, is the way in which the state, the market, and the household each contributes to the welfare mix. We do not characterize Japan by education aspirations that it shares with the United States but by what is uniquely Japanese.

The final concern of this book—the future of welfare in society—addresses a fundamental question: To what extent are the United States, Japan, and Europe beginning to converge in the provision of welfare, and in the problems that this presents? The chapter by Yukio Noguchi on Japanese pension commitments in the decades ahead shows that not everything is as secure as it seems in Japan. It is also evidence that an increased expenditure on pensions in consequence of an increase in the number of elderly in the population follows a common logic unaffected by national values. Noguchi's concerns are shared by fiscal experts in almost every OECD country.

A volume that considers the experience of Americans, Japanese, and Europeans presents a standing caution against facile generalizations about postcapitalist society. Even more, it provides the basis for considering the possibility that modern societies may become *more* different rather than more similar.

The history of Japan in the past century is ambiguous evidence of convergence and divergence among societies. The opening of Japan to the West was followed by an extraordinary period of Japanese efforts to learn from the United States and Europe. The Japanese imported technology wholesale and, in the wake of U.S. occupation in 1945, many Western mass culture values and practices. Initially, efforts to learn from the West were confined to an elite. But the elite was acting as a trustee for the nation as a whole. Equally important, national culture meant that Japanese who borrowed ideas from the West did not themselves become westernized. Today, a visitor to Tokyo can see juxtaposed in the streets evidence of both Japanese and non-Japanese culture.

The conventional approach to industrialization sees it as a unilinear path that all nations must follow sooner or later. Woodrow Wilson's dream that the whole world was ripe for conversion to democracy is now seen to be vain. But it is possible to argue that there is a tendency toward the homogenization of welfare standards, within Europe at least. This is important, insofar as it indicates that economic growth is more important than cultural differences based upon contrasting Catholic and Protestant heritages. But in the United States and Japan, economic wealth can substitute for the growth of welfare from the state (Rose, 1985a). The provision of a high standard of welfare by the market as well as the state requires a high standard of living. Otherwise, most people would not be able to depend upon their own earnings or their employer for welfare benefits that in Europe are financed by the taxing power of the state (cf. Appendix).

The effects of the worldwide slowing down of economic growth pose basic challenges to conventional ideas of welfare production. In fiscal terms governments are forced to run harder to stand still; they must collect more taxes in order to fund existing spending commitments. Old programs, not new, are the primary cause of increased social expenditure. As the population ages, more money must be spent on pensions and on health care. And as unemployment rises, more money is spent on cash payments to the unemployed and others without a sufficient regular income (OECD, 1985; *Journal of Public Policy,* 1985). Concurrently, the slowing down of the rate of national economic growth means that tax revenues may not increase public revenue painlessly through economic growth.

Higher taxes are not paid voluntarily, but public opinion evidence indicates that in Europe most people are prepared to pay high taxes to maintain high levels of welfare benefits. The United States and Japan, however, show more resistance to high taxes. This is a function of national political values, rather than of the actual level of taxes, for taxes in both countries claim a lower share of the national product than the average for OECD countries. When spending goes up faster than taxation, the inevitable consequence is that the public deficit rises—and this has notably been the case in the United States and in Japan.

Examining welfare on three continents guards against the fallacious assumption that a reduction in state provision of welfare is necessarily a reduction in welfare in society. If Scandinavia is a model of what the state can do to provide welfare (and what citizens will pay taxes for), then Japan is a counterexample of how a society can do without high levels of public provision, yet have a population that is educated, healthy, and secure in old age. In terms of the goals of welfare, the 700 million people living in advanced industrial societies are broadly at one in the welfare they desire, and expect to obtain in their lifetime. As for the means of welfare, the world is varied; notwithstanding similarities, there remain major national differences in what the state, the market, and the family contribute to the welfare mix. Comparative analysis can guard against the facile assumption that there is one best way to secure welfare. The records of Japan, or the United States, and of European countries emphasize that the state's role in maintaining welfare in contemporary society is variable, not constant. While welfare is a common concern, the contrasting outlooks of government in the United States and Japan, as against Europe, show, in the words of an old Japanese proverb, that people can be "in the same bed but with different dreams."

REFERENCES

Economic Planning Agency, *Annual Report on the National Life for 1983.* Tokyo: Japanese Government, 1983.

Flora, Peter and Heidenheimer, A. J., *The Development of Welfare States in Europe and America.* New Brunswick, N.J.: Transaction, 1981.

Journal of Public Policy, "Social Expenditure, 1960–1990: A Symposium." 5:2, 1985.

Klass, Gary, "Explaining America and the Welfare State: An Alternative Theory." New Orleans, La.: American Political Science Association Annual Meeting, 1985.

Nettl, J. P., "The State as a Conceptual Variable." *World Politics* 20:559–581, 1968.

Organization for Economic Cooperation and Development, *Social Expenditure, 1960–1990.* Paris: OECD, 1985.

Rose, Richard, *Understanding Big Government: The Programme Approach.* Beverly Hills, Calif. and London: Sage Publications, 1984.

Rose, Richard, "How Big is American Government? And How Distinctive?" New Orleans, La.: American Political Science Association Annual Meeting, 1985a.

Rose, Richard, "National Pride in Cross-National Perspective," *International Social Science Journal* 37 (1):85–96, 1985b.

Stoetzel, Jean, *Les Valeurs du Temps Present.* Paris: Presses Universitaires de France, 1983.

1

Common Goals but Different Roles: The State's Contribution to the Welfare Mix

RICHARD ROSE

The welfare state is a familiar phrase, yet also misleading. The familiarity of the term reflects the recognition that the state has a major role in providing major welfare goods desired in every modern society, such as health, education, and security of income in old age and distress. Yet the term is misleading, for it reduces welfare solely to the actions of government. The state's role in producing welfare is important, but the state has no monopoly in welfare production.

Welfare is the product of the whole of society. The market also produces welfare; employers can provide pensions, health care, and training for their workers, and families can purchase education, health care, and pensions. Defining welfare solely as a product of the market and the state remains limiting, because it assumes that welfare must be measured in money. Yet households provide all manner of nonmonetized services for children, the sick, and the elderly. The care that family members provide for each other is primarily altruistic; no money changes hands. To argue that there is no scope for the household or market to produce welfare is to adopt a totalitarian position that makes the state responsible for everything that happens in society.

The state is not the chief institution to which most people turn for their welfare, even though the major family concerns identified by opinion surveys—employment, health, education, and income—are the subject of

Written as part of a program of research on the growth of government sponsored by British Economic and Social Research Council grant HR 7849/1. Useful comments were made on the paper in draft at seminars of the Fiscal Affairs Division of the International Monetary Fund, and at the Brookings Institution, Washington, D.C.

13

public policies. When people are asked who can help them most to deal with their problems, the great majority look to their own actions, to other members of their family, or to friends and neighbors, and not to the state (Rose, 1980a; see also Sniderman and Brody, 1977: 520).

Nor is welfare the primary concern of the state. Historically, the first concern of the state has been the maintenance of public order and the defense of its territory against foreign attack. The second concern has been the provision of transport and communication services required to create a modern economy. Welfare came later as a policy commitment of the modern state (Rose, 1976). Today, health, education, and income maintenance programs make major claims upon public expenditure and public employment, but not to the exclusion of other older concerns. Transfer payments to pensioners are growing rapidly, but so too are transfer payments to those from whom government borrows to finance its deficit. The major welfare programs of government account for half, not the whole, of government's resources (OECD, 1985).

From the perspective of a family, its total amount of welfare is more important than the particular sources of that welfare. Therefore, we must think in terms of the *welfare mix,* that is, the contribution that each of three very different social institutions—the household, the market, and the state—makes to total welfare in society. The state today is the most prominent producer of welfare, but it is not the sole source. The market is also a major source of welfare, insofar as individuals and households purchase welfare services, and many workers receive welfare benefits as a condition of employment (Titmuss, 1958: Chapter 2; Rein, 1982). Historically, the household has been the primary source of welfare, and a substantial amount continues to be provided within the family (Goldschmidt-Clermont, 1982).

The welfare mix is logically independent of the amount of welfare produced in society. When peasants shift from producing their own food to buying food in the market, they do not necessarily eat more or better just because they buy what they eat. The creation of a national health service immediately alters the effective demand for health care, but it does not initially alter supply. Producers of health care are simply paid by the state rather than by the private sector. An increase in the state's contribution to the welfare mix may substitute for another source of welfare; it does not necessarily produce a net increase.

The market, the state, and households are imperfect providers of welfare; the strengths of each sector can compensate for limitations of the others. Public finance theorists see state provision of welfare services as correcting failures of the market (e.g., Musgrave and Peacock, 1967; Lane, 1985). In a complementary fashion, the state production of welfare can be criticized because of failures of nonmarket institutions of government (Wolf, 1979; Peacock, 1982). The welfare state and the market can correct for what might be called failure in the family (Flora, 1981), and family and voluntary resources may compensate for failures of both market and state (Badelt, 1984).

Total welfare in society is likely to be greater if there are multiple sources rather than a single monopoly supplier. But the distribution of welfare is likely to be different too. Insofar as the family is the primary source, then single persons, widows, and divorced persons will be handicapped, and much welfare will be produced by nonwaged housewives without a money reward. Insofar as the market is the primary source of welfare, access to welfare depends on income as well as need. Insofar as the state is the primary source, access depends on entitlement according to bureaucratic regulations, and allocating services without charge may create inefficiencies resulting in higher costs.

To understand welfare in society we must understand what the state does *and does not* contribute to the welfare mix. This is important in political as well as social terms. Most politicians believe that their continued electoral success depends on their ability to maintain or increase an already high level of state provision of welfare. Neo-Marxist writers assert that a high level of welfare provision is a necessary condition for maintaining the legitimacy of the state (Gough, 1979; Offe, 1984; but see Rose, 1984a: Chapter 8). Policymakers responsible for managing the national economy are anxious, because welfare expenditure now accounts for the largest share of the national product and its share is growing (OECD, 1985). Citizens have reason to be anxious too, for even if government is not the sole source of welfare, it is indubitably a major provider of services for nearly everyone at important stages in their lives.

An understanding of the conjoint importance of the household, the market, and the state is particularly important in international comparisons. This is most evident in the comparison of First and Third World societies, for a characteristic of the Third World is that most production and consumption is *not* monetized; the household is of primary importance. In First World countries, money is important but not all-important, as the role of the family in Japan demonstrates. Nor is the state all-important, as is demonstrated by the role of the market in selling welfare services in America. To argue that Americans have less health care than Europeans simply because the United States does not have a British-style national health service is to ignore the role of marketed medicine. When state and market are added together, the United States spends a higher proportion of the national product on health than many European countries.

Whereas the welfare goals of individuals and families are much the same whatever their citizenship, the means to achieve these goals differ significantly from country to country. The state is but one institution for converting popular demands into welfare products. Therefore, this chapter sets out a model of the production of total welfare in society, considers variations in the dynamics of welfare provision, and considers what difference it makes whether welfare is produced by the state, the market, or the household.

THE PRODUCTION OF WELFARE IN SOCIETY: A SIMPLE MODEL

A societywide approach to welfare adopts the bottom-up perspective of the individual family as consumer. By contrast, a policymaker has a top-down perspective on welfare, concentrating on large aggregates recorded in money terms in government budgets. By a process of goal condensation, what is closest at hand, public expenditure, tends to become most important. However, from the perspective of the household, the welfare of its individual members is of first concern.[1] In the extreme case of health care, no news is good news, for a person in good health needs no money spent for medical treatment.

Primary welfare products are here defined as those necessarily affecting everyone on a continuing basis (e.g., the need for housing) or at a given stage in the life cycle (e.g., the need for education). The contingent needs of minorities such as the blind or single-parent families do not detract from universal and certain needs. In a modern economy, every individual has a continuing need for money, food, housing, and mobility, and during a lifetime a major need for education, health, and personal care by others.[2] Each welfare product has distinctive properties. The state need not produce all of them. It is an open empirical question *whether* provision is made by the state, the market, and/or the household, and how different are the sources on opposite sides of the Atlantic or the Pacific.

The welfare products of concern to most people can be readily identified empirically. Income, food, housing, health care, education, transportation, and personal social services are far more easily measured than such abstract welfare goals as community or equity. The approach thus avoids empirically empty definitions of welfare that have tended to turn pure welfare economics into "an uninterpreted system of logical deductions which would not be about anything at all" (Little 1950: 81f). The approach also excludes such important intangible concerns as affection, happiness, and life satisfaction, for which subjective social psychological measures are more appropriate (Easterlin, 1974; Allardt, 1977; Stoetzel, 1983).

To concentrate on the production of welfare is to focus on exchangeable goods and services that one individual is able to provide another. Exchangeable goods and services exclude important self-services that each person necessarily must provide for himself and herself, such as sleeping or eating. By definition, welfare products are capable of being exchanged, whether or not an exchange takes place; for example, a meal can be bought in a restaurant, prepared by another member of a household, or prepared by the person who eats it. This broad definition is consistent with the practice of including nonmonetized as well as monetized labor in measures of output in Third World countries (Hill, 1979).

The production of welfare goods and services can be monetized *or* non-monetized, that is, not involving any cash payment to the producer. A farmer does not need to buy food to have a meal. Nor does a child need to buy a parent's affection to receive child care. Conventional national income accounts include only the cost of preparing meals outside the home, but not the meals prepared for children within the home. Time–budget studies emphasize that a large portion of time is spent in unpaid work producing welfare within the home. In OECD nations the total number of unpaid hours worked within the home is roughly equal to the total hours devoted to producing the goods and services recorded in the national income accounts (Szalai et al., 1972; Young and Willmott, 1973; Gershuny, 1981).

Consumption can be monetized *or* nonmonetized independently of its mode of production. Welfare produced within the home is not sold to the consumer; it is given freely. It is thus "priceless" from both a production and a consumption point of view. Welfare produced and sold in the market, such as private education, is fully monetized, involving consumer and producer payment. Many state welfare services are mixed; the public provision of welfare goods without charge to the consumer does not mean that they are produced without cost. For example, the British National Health Service is called free because users do not pay for it. But is is not free at the point of production, claiming 10 percent of total public expenditure.

There are four different ways of providing a given welfare service (Figure 1.1), depending on whether or not the service is monetized at the point of production, and whether it is sold at the point of consumption: the *market* (production and consumption of services monetized, as with private education); the *state* (production monetized, but consumption on a nonmarket basis, as with public education); the *household* (neither production nor consumption monetized, as when a father teaches his son how to use a saw); and *barter* (a market exchange without money, as in a teacher giving tuition to a plumber's child in return for household repairs). Barter quickly leads to the need to reinvent money, if only in some form of scrip or labor tokens. Therefore, it is not further explored here.

A careful specification of the conditions of producing and consuming welfare services shows that the nonprofit production of welfare in schools, hospitals, day-care centers, and other places is only a variant of market provision. The fact that these organizations are not making a profit does not mean that their employees work for nothing. Professors, doctors, and service workers in universities and in hospitals expect to be paid for their labor. Since profit is a small portion of the total cost of producing a service, the cost per beneficiary is virtually the same in these organizations as elsewhere. The cost may be met by the family or by a

Figure 1.1. Alternative sources of welfare in the mixed society.

Monetized in Production	Monetized to Consumers	
	Yes	*No*
Yes	Market	State
No	Barter	Household

third party (e.g., payment of hospital charges by private insurance or by the state). The state can fund nonprofit organizations as an alternative or supplement to providing welfare services itself (Smith and Rosenbaum, 1981; Thompson, 1983). In the United States, Weisbrod (1977) estimates that 70 percent of all revenue of nonprofit organizations comes from the charges made for the provision of goods and services; philanthropic gifts account for a limited portion of income (White, 1981). Nonmonetized voluntary services rendered to recipients who pay nothing pale in importance when compared with fully monetized, nonprofit activities (Kramer, 1981; Central Statistical Office, 1985: Tables 11.1–7).

Total welfare in society (TWS) can be described by a simple identity, in which H equals the household production of welfare, M equals welfare bought and sold in the market, and S equals welfare produced by the state.

$$TWS = H + M + S$$

The welfare mix of a given society is characterized by the proportion of goods and services produced by each of the three sectors. The mix can take many different forms; the two extremes are monopoly provision by one source, or each source providing one-third of goods and services.

In order to understand changes in total welfare, we must understand three principal changes in the sources of production: changes in the traditional role of the household, the monetization of welfare production by the Industrial Revolution, and the fiscalization of welfare production by the state.

The household was the original economy, *producing without money* virtually all the goods required by its members. The word economy is derived from the Greek *oikonomia,* "management of the household." Until comparatively recently the domestic economy of a peasant family emphasized household production and consumption outside the realm of market exchange. In a village the concept of the household could be extended to include solidarity with all who lived in the community.

The household economy has been the chief source of most welfare goods and services for most of the history of the world. Health care was provided at home. The needs of the elderly were looked after by younger members of a family; a weekly money income in retirement meant little when very little money changed hands. While children might not learn much reading, writing, or arithmetic from parents, they gained vocational training, and a would-be artisan was apprenticed to a craftsman, living within his extended household. The household economy remains of fundamental importance today. In many member states of the United Nations, the bulk of goods and services produced are not provided by the state or by the marketplace; they are the product of work within the household.

The Industrial Revolution brought about large-scale *monetization.* Paid employment became the norm rather than work in exchange for shelter, food, and other services. In rural communities family-oriented peasants gradually turned into market-oriented farmers (Franklin, 1969). As the Industrial Revolution monetized the national product, it made possible the monetization of welfare provision. The farmworker who received food and a cottage in a nonmoney exchange for labor was superseded in importance by the millworker or miner, who rented a home and bought food from a local shop. Welfare goods and services were now bought and sold in the market by those who could afford it. The level of wages constituting a living wage was related to the cost of staple foods and cheap housing, both allocated through the market in industrial towns.

Because families in towns needed a weekly money income, mutual benefit and friendly societies for the poor developed in the nineteenth century to insure families against the risks of sickness, old age, and death. In the late nineteenth century a major role of many British unions was the provision of benefits to dues-paying members. By contrast with German trade unions, which sought to influence the state to provide welfare services, British unions jealously guarded their friendly societies, opposing state intervention in nonprofit market activities (Heidenheimer, 1969: Table 7; cf. Olson, 1965). In every Western nation, insurance companies expanded, selling sickness benefits and pensions to millions who now had money to save. A rising standard of living led those who had discretionary income to spend money to educate their children and, because labor was plentiful, to hire domestic servants to look after their family. Industrial technology offered new opportunities for geographical as well as social mobility.

The provision of welfare by the state requires *fiscalization,* that is, the development of the state's capacity routinely to collect large sums of money from its citizens. This capability was lacking in preindustrial societies, where taxes were often levied in labor or kind rather than money, or not collected at all (Ardant, 1975; Braun, 1975). Fiscal capability is still weak in many Third World countries today (Goode, 1984). Substantial tax revenue is a significant supply-side cause of the growth in state provision of welfare, and increasing fiscalization of the national product is a necessary condition for the growth of welfare programs.

The nineteenth-century development of state welfare provision involved public health, a collective good that could not be sold in the marketplace because beneficiaries could not be excluded if they did not pay. Given the threat of epidemic diseases in cities, the state undertook this public health responsibility, but it did so without simultaneously underwriting private health care, which was left to the market. Elementary education was normally the first private benefit provided citizens without charge by the state. Income maintenance programs followed later, offering a safety net for those not covered by private insurance and needing money to live in a money economy.

In the twentieth century the state provision of welfare has grown greatly. In 1961 Peacock and Wiseman argued that a major cause was the enhanced fiscal capacity resulting from mobilization for war. While relevant to Britain and the United States, the explanation is not suitable for defeated or occupied nations. In the subsequent decades of peace, welfare provision has continued to grow, financed by the additional revenues generated by the growth of the national product, resulting in the enhancement of established programs and the launching of new programs (Rose and Karran, 1984).

State welfare programs have broken the cash nexus between supply and demand. While welfare products are private goods and services that could be marketed, they are usually supplied without charge, being regarded as merit goods suitable for all citizens. Access to state welfare services is thus fundamentally different from access to such public services as electricity or the post office, or to the products of profit-making companies. Changing the basis of entitlement from consumer demand to citizenship is done in the name of civic equity. But the entitlements of citizens are not unlimited. An elderly person's pension is intended to provide enough money to buy nourishing food, but not enough to buy meals at expensive restaurants.

Even though supply is not charged, the production of welfare remains monetized. Richard Titmuss's (1970) famous interpretation of blood donation as a gift relationship, in which altruism replaced economic calculus, was only *half* correct. While blood is usually given free by altruistic donors, health service workers, whose labor is necessary to transfer the blood to patients, are not similarly motivated. They are unionized employees who work for money wages. If altruism represents the idealized vision of the proponents of state-provided welfare, then a strike for higher wages by workers administering blood transfusion services is the nightmare vision of its critics.

Monetization and its concomitant, economic growth, have first of all led to an *expansion* in total welfare in society. This is true by definition, insofar as economic growth increases per capita income in society, and money income is taken as the measure of welfare. It is also true inasmuch as growth has involved a process in which industrialization and affluence have greatly diffused money incomes throughout society, as well as increasing national wealth in aggregate. Individuals today have far more income, education, health care, and security in old age, and these advantages are more widely distributed. There has been a fundamental transformation of society since the mid-nineteenth century, very great increases in welfare since before World War I, and substantial changes since World War II.

A second important consequence of change has been the *substitution* of one source of welfare for another. To a significant extent monetization substituted for the nonmoney provision of goods and services in kind by farmers and peasants. Substitution has meant that the increased contribution by one source of welfare has been partly offset by a decline in welfare from another source. In the long term, monetization produces a net expansion of welfare, for the additional resources of the money economy are greater than those substituted for in the household economy. But net increases are substantially less than gross (Sametz, 1968: 84ff).

Fiscalization also involves an element of substitution. Insofar as the provision of a welfare service is taken over from the market (e.g., a health service) or from the household (e.g., child day-care centers), then an increase in state provision is more or less counterbalanced by a decrease in provision from other sources. Only when a state welfare service is created *ex nihilo* does fiscalization immediately lead to an expansion of welfare. When a state welfare benefit is provided without charge to the consumer, there is a prima facie case for assuming that the shift in the burden of finance from the consumer to the fisc will increase demand. But since these services must be paid for by tax increases, there is an opportunity cost that may slowly lead to a decrease in the provision of other welfare services. If increased welfare is financed by the fiscal dividend of economic growth, total welfare in society expands, but the primary cause is economic growth rather than public policy.

The process of growth is destabilizing. As more and more of society's activities become monetized, the household provision of welfare will be expected to decline in significance. As the fiscal capacity of the state grows, the state's share should increase, with state provision of welfare without charge tending to reduce greatly welfare services that the market must charge for.

In the long run, state provision of welfare services can have one of two consequences. *Monopoly* will result if the state becomes the sole source of welfare production; this is assumed in reductionist discussions of the welfare state. Household activities are dismissed as irrelevant either because they are considered premodern or on the spurious ground that they cannot be observed because they are not monetized. Provision of welfare by the market is assumed to be taken over by the state, or swamped by state provision of services without charge. There are a priori grounds for assuming that the more welfare the state produces, the more it is likely to crowd out the market and the household, or gain a hegemonic influence.

Alternatively, a *mixed society* results if the growth in state provision of welfare does not completely crowd out welfare produced in the market and household. A mixed society accepts the importance of fiscalized welfare, but it emphasizes that the market and the household also make important contributions to total welfare in society. Insofar as total welfare is the product of a plurality of sources, then the household, the market, and the state are not so much competing as complementary. Yet insofar as a plurality of sources provide welfare, then an increase in welfare from one source may simply substitute for rather than increase total welfare in society.

THE DYNAMICS OF TOTAL WELFARE IN SOCIETY

The longer the time perspective, the greater the expansion in the total welfare of industrial societies. This is true not only of the transformation from the nineteenth century to the mid-twentieth century but also of the great explosion in the production of welfare in four decades since World War II. Why has this happened?

Economic growth provides the simplest and most pervasive theory to explain the increase in welfare. While welfare goods and services can be assumed to reflect universal wants, meeting these wants often costs money. While education is universally desired, much more is spent on education in First World countries than in Third World countries because the latter have less money to spend. Third World countries do not value education less; it could even be argued that because it is scarcer, they value education more. An increase in the national product increases the resources that can be used to purchase education or other welfare products. Without economic growth, total welfare in society can hardly increase. Even after discounting for this substitution of monetized for nonmonetized welfare, the doubling or quadrupling of the national product over a generation or two invariably results in a substantial net increase in welfare.

Materialist conceptions of the growth of welfare tend to be neutral as between market or state provision of welfare. If the money is not there, then the market will not produce welfare, nor can the fisc finance it. From a materialist perspective, the expansion of market or state production of welfare requires more money. This materialist assumption is shared by market-oriented liberals and by state-oriented Marxists.

The materialist approach to welfare production is most important in distinguishing between First World nations, Soviet-style East European countries, and poor Third World nations. A defining attribute of Third World countries is that a limited portion of their national product is monetized; income often comes from production within the household, and a substantial fraction of the population subsists outside the market economy. Within the money economy, the state may be the chief provider of income, but it employs only a small fraction of the adult population in a Third World country (Heller and Tait, 1983). The limited size of the money national product means that the state lacks the fiscal resources to pay for education, health care, and pensions for all families in society. The immediate and palpable constraint on welfare production is a shortage of money; nonmonetized household production is the prinicpal source of welfare.

Industrial nations have material resources that are magnitudes greater than those of largely premonetized Third World economies. OECD nations differ from Soviet bloc countries in being mixed economies; producers are free to offer welfare services in the market, and citizens have money to buy services. In communist states of Eastern Europe, the national product per capita is high relative to the past history of these nations, now surpassing or approaching the level necessary for establishing comprehensive welfare state programs at the level of Western Europe in the 1950s. Given that East Germans have many welfare needs identical to West Germans, and Poles and Russians have needs like Finns or English people, then we would expect to find a substantial portion of the national product of industrialized Soviet bloc systems spent on welfare production. This is in fact the case (Pryor, 1968; Estes, 1984: 68ff). The welfare mix is very different as between Eastern and Western Europe, for market provisions of goods and services on a large scale is inconsistent with communist doctrines. Yet citizens in the Soviet system can augment food bought in the market by household production, and obtain other services by bribery, barter, or the use of party or personal contacts (Grossman, 1977; Katsenelinboigen, 1977).

Because the national product per capita is higher in OECD than in Soviet bloc countries, total welfare in society should be higher too. Moreover, this hypothesis should hold whatever the particular mix of provision of welfare by the market or the state. Both *étatiste* Sweden and the "antistate" United States can be expected to produce more welfare than Eastern bloc countries such as the Soviet Union or Bulgaria, because of having a higher gross domestic product (GDP) per capita.

Among OECD nations, what accounts for similarities or differences in the welfare mix? Several different types of explanations can be identified. An economic approach hypothesizes that the household production of welfare is reduced to a very low level by pervasive *monetization*. Political economy theories see democratic politicians intimidated by voters pressing for something (welfare benefits) for nothing (merit goods available without charge). Both theories hypothesize that the democratization of government inevitably leads to the *fiscalization* of welfare. Instead of providing bread and circuses, contemporary politicians are expected to provide health care and inflation-proof pensions.

Political theories propose two different and partially overlapping reasons why the welfare mix should vary from country to country. One explanation is that national values differ: the Swedes are said to have a more positive and trusting evaluation of state activity than Americans, and the Japanese to value the family more. These values are assumed to be so pervasive within each nation that the government of the day, whatever its political color, must respect the national consensus (King, 1973).

The emphasis on national values implies that all welfare products within a country will have much the same mix. It also comes dangerously close to inferring causation from consequences, assuming that the welfare mix of Americans, Swedes, English, or Japanese must be what citizens want, because it is what they get.

An alternative political theory is that the particular mix of state and market is determined by the values of the dominant party within a country. If a government is normally socialist, as in Sweden, then the state will have a bigger role, but will have a smaller role if the government is predominantly nonsocialist, as with the Christian Democrats in Italy or the Liberal Democratic party in Japan. The idea that "parties matter" (Castles, 1982) implies that the state's contribution to the welfare mix will alter with the swing of the electoral pendulum. If parties do make a difference, then education, health, and social security spending will vary with election outcomes (but see Rose, 1984b). In countries where coalition government is the norm, then more stability may be found, albeit the consensus about a welfare mix will depend on the terms of the political coalition. For example, where a Catholic party is of central importance in a coalition, as in Belgium, then the role for nonstate agencies (particularly the welfare activities of the Catholic church) will be different from that in a country such as Denmark, where it is absent. If the alternation of power is between two similar antisocialist parties, as in the United States, then the market's role will be bigger.

The program approach to public policy hypothesizes that the state's contribution to the welfare mix will tend to vary from program to program *within* a country (Rose, 1985a). Everywhere the state spends more on education, which cannot be provided within the family in a modern society, and less on personal social services, for which the household is a natural unit of production. The household, the market, and the state each can have a comparative advantage in the production of one or more welfare services, and a comparative disadvantage in producing others. The comparative advantage of different sectors is derived from intrinsic characteristics of each. For example, the state has the capacity to levy taxes upon all citizens to pay for expensive merit goods. But the household can provide personal services in ways that an impersonal state bureaucracy cannot, and the market can organize the sale of food to suit individual tastes.

By contrast with economic approaches postulating a progressive crowding out of the household, and of the market as well, the program approach hypothesizes the persistence of a mixed society, however high the level of the state's material provision, because of intrinsic differences between major welfare goods and services.

Of the seven major welfare concerns—income, food, housing, personal social services, education, health, and transportation—some appear well suited to monopoly provision by a single source, and others can be produced by a combination of household and market, or household and state, or by all three. Intrinsic differences suggest different sources of production of the welfare mix as follows:

1. *Household monopoly* (personal social services). Caring for the young and the elderly occurs in the home as a by-product of family relationships. The family, rather than institutional or communal care, remains the basic household unit in every OECD nation. Even in Israel, the *kibbutz* ideal of collective communal responsibility for care has been falling by the wayside.

2. *State monopoly* (education). The provision of education came first among the responsibilities assumed by the modern state in the late nineteenth century. Industrialization and democratization required a literate population. In the twentieth century the growing complexity of subject matter requires more sophisticated and experienced instructional facilities, reducing the potential input from the household and making marketed education increasingly expensive. Concurrently, secularization has removed the church, the chief organizational alternative to the state as a source of education.

3. *Household and market* (food). In OECD societies food is sold by the market; it is not treated as a merit good to be supplied without charge by the state. Preparing meals in the household is the norm. The most basic of individual needs, food, is only a primary state responsibility in the very exceptional circumstances of wartime, when the state rations food as part of mobilizing resources for total war. Exceptionally, the United States has a Food Stamp program that gives some low-income families vouchers to exchange for specified foods. But this program is more an outgrowth of the need to dispose of surplus crops generated by subsidies to farmers than it is an expression of government intent to regulate diet.

4. *Household and state* (health care). To a substantial extent an individual's health is not a product of social services; it reflects the way in which a person looks after himself or herself. Insofar as health care is provided by others, throughout Europe and Japan there is state provision of specialized medical and hospital services. But care for minor illnesses of children and the elderly is often provided in the home. A person visiting a doctor for treatment is more likely to return home for recuperation than to enter a hospital.

5. *Household, market, and state* (income, housing, and transportation). Within OECD societies, families draw income from a mixture of sources. About half of all persons receiving a regular money income are either public employees or else receive an income maintenance grant such as a pension; the other half work in the private sector. Another substantial bloc of the population—children and housewives—receive money through transfers within the household (cf. Rose, 1985b: Table 1.17). As for housing, it is bought and sold in the market, but tax subsidies for interest payments affect costs, and some housing may be publicly owned. A substantial fraction of housing maintenance is produced by

unpaid do-it-yourself household labor. Transportation too reflects a mix of inputs: the market sells motor cars; the state provides roads and usually operates railways, buses, and airlines; and individuals drive themselves about or walk to many destinations.

To emphasize cross-national similarities in the production of particular welfare goods is not to deny the existence of some differences between nations. But for national differences to be thorough, they would have to persist across all dimensions of welfare. Claims about national differences are usually based not on systematic comparison but on casual generalization from particular observations.

Differences in degree or detail do not constitute differences in kind. While the concept of the welfare mix allows for an infinite range of possible permutations in welfare production, intrinsic characteristics of programs result in limited differences. Even in two countries as distant and seemingly different as Japan and Britain, there are many similarities. For example, Japan, like Britain, has a comprehensive state pension program. In Japan there is great reliance on public transportation, but like Britain, it also has millions of private motorists, and pedestrian travel is common too. Even the distinctive emphasis placed on the family as a source of social services is not unique to Japan. In Britain family members look after each other, albeit not with the same degree of cohesion as in Japan.

Major differences *do* exist in the state provision of welfare among industrial nations. There is a very substantial variation in the proportion of the national product devoted to public expenditure, ranging from 62 percent in Sweden to 33 percent in Switzerland, which has a similarly high national product. When social expenditure is examined, the differences are also substantial. In Sweden, public spending on social programs is 33.4 percent of the national product, more than double the level in Switzerland, where it is 14.9 percent. Among the larger OECD nations Germany ranks highest, spending 31.5 percent of its national product on social expenditure, and Japan ranks lowest, spending 17.5 percent (OECD, 1985: Table 1).

An *étatiste* definition of welfare, which assumed that the only welfare in society was that produced by the state, would credit the average Swede with more than twice as high a standard of health, income, food, housing, social services, and education and transportation as the average Swiss. This inference is false, because it ignores the contribution that the market and the household make to the production of total welfare in society. Where the national product is high, then welfare in aggregate is likely to be high, whatever the distribution of provision among the state, the market, and the household.

Contrasting the state, the market, and the household as competing sources of welfare is misleading; for the concept of the welfare mix emphasizes interdependencies between the three sources, which are often complementary rather than competitive. Because the household provides nonmonetized care for people with minor ills, the state can concentrate its resources on providing professional care for major illnesses. Because a great deal of house maintenance can be done by residents on a do-it-yourself basis and because tax relief is given on mortgage interest payments, it is easier for an individual to buy a house in the market.

State, market, and household recognize the existence of a mixture of resources substituting welfare from one sector for another. Where social security provides only a flat-rate benefit on retirement, the market and household savings are expected to provide supplements. Where the state provides a generous earnings-related pension on retirement, less provision need be made through the market or the household. The state may mandate safety-at-work regulations as a form of preventive health care, and employers can make use of state vocational education to train their employees.

From an overall societal perspective, the existence of interdependencies blurs distinctions between the state, the market, and the household. But this does not eliminate a fundamental precondition of interdependence, the prior recognition of separate entities based on exchange (the market), power (the state), or affection (the family). Interdependencies occur because of differences between the parties involved.

The distinctions between the three sources of welfare is most evident in time of troubles. An individual or family unable to produce the welfare services that they need within the home can turn to the market, if their income permits (employing people to care for an aged relative) or to the state (securing an elderly relative a place in a public nursing home) or both (using the social security income of an elderly person to buy a place in a private nursing home). An employer facing difficulty in financing welfare services for employees may reduce the number of employees, transfer production abroad, or in the extreme case go bankrupt. Government cannot go bankrupt. The commitments of the modern state to provide health care, education, and income security go on and on; they are open-ended and continuing entitlements of citizens.

A distinctive feature of the state's provision of welfare services is that the costs are met not by unwaged labor or by selling services, but by taxation. State-produced welfare must be paid for; it is a product of a money economy, even though it is supplied according to nonmarket criteria. Political decisions have made citizenship rather than consumer purchasing power or kinship the crucial determinant of access to major state welfare services. Every individual who is a citizen receives without charge such welfare services as education, health care, or income maintenance grants.

Economists sometimes describe welfare goods provided without charge by the state as merit goods, intrinsically so desirable that everyone should have access as of right (Musgrave, 1959: 13). But economists have no rationale for the identification of particular products as merit goods. It is a political not an economic decision whether public services are provided without charge to the consumer. In most OECD countries charges are made for public transportation, but not for education. Merit goods are hybrid products. Political decisions make them free of charge at the point of consumption, but they nonetheless cost government money to produce.

In a high-income society, citizens want to spend a significant portion of their income on health care, education for their children, and savings for old age. From a societal perspective, one can ask: What difference does it make whether welfare is provided through the state or the market? The cost is more or less the same, for marginal efficiencies or inefficiencies of government are small compared to the total cost of production. The greatest potential inefficiency—the increase of supply and demand because no charge is made for merit goods—can be significant. But it does not mean that twice or three times as much health care, education, or state pensions are provided as people would otherwise wish to consume at their own expense.

One necessary consequence of the state provision of major welfare services is that the cost must be borne by the fisc. The contemporary welfare state puts a big front-end load upon the national treasury. In order to meet this cost, government must annually collect taxes equal to about one-quarter of the GDP—and rising each year as the cost of these services tends to grow faster than the national product itself. There is a risk to the fisc that the costs of welfare may grow faster than the political capacity of the state to meet these costs by taxation.

For the first three decades of the postwar era, politicians were able to enjoy what Heclo (1981: 397) has described as "policy without pain," funding the rising cost of welfare programs from the fiscal dividend of economic growth. A buoyant economy produced more tax revenue without requiring any increase in tax rates, and an economy subject to inflation saw tax revenues increase at an accelerating rate. Thanks to the fiscal dividend of growth, the state could spend more on education, health, and income maintenance programs and, consistent with the philosophy of a mixed society, individual citizens could also enjoy an increase in take-home pay.

In the 1980s the risk to the fisc is immediate, not contingent. Rates of economic growth have slowed down greatly, and in bad years the economies of Western nations contract. The cost of social programs has continued to grow. But in the changed circumstances of less buoyant economies, there is less additional revenue at hand from the fiscal dividend of economic growth (Rose and Karran, 1984). If the market rather than the state had been selling health, education, and pensions, then the economic slowdown since 1974 would have put the brakes on demand, and forced adjustments in supply.

Given the fiscalization of these programs, the structural problem facing government today is how to raise the revenue needed to finance the substantial and rising costs of welfare programs, without upsetting the balance of the mixed economy by cutting the take-home pay of the ordinary worker. This problem did not exist prior to the world recession that began in 1973. The period from 1952 to 1960 was one of treble affluence (Table 1.1A). In the seven major industrial nations, the economy grew on average by 5.2 percent a year. Because the costs of public policy grew at nearly the same average rate, this meant that the proportion of the national product allocated through public expenditure remained virtually the

Table 1.1. The Consequences of the Inertia Growth of Public Spending[a]

A. Treble Affluence 1952–60

	CPP/GDP 1952 (%)	GDP 1952–60	CPP 1952–60	CPP/GDP 1960	Front-end load,[b] 1960 (%)
		(% annual change)			
United States	25.1	2.8	2.7	25.0	24
Britain	31.7	3.2	2.2	29.3	20
France	30.0	4.8	4.9	30.2	31
Germany	29.1	8.2	7.8	28.2	27
Italy	22.8	5.6	7.7	26.6	36
Sweden	23.9	3.7	6.1	28.7	47
Japan	14.6	8.5	7.3	13.6	12
Average	25.3	5.2	5.5	25.9	28

B. Changing Mix, Continuing Affluence, 1961–72

	1961	1961–72	1961–72	1972	1972
United States	26.6	4.1	5.4	30.3	40
Britain	30.0	2.7	4.0	34.4	50
France	31.2	5.5	6.4	34.2	40
Germany	28.8	4.5	6.4	35.1	50
Italy	25.5	5.5	8.6	35.0	55
Sweden	28.5	4.4	7.8	40.8	73
Japan	12.9	9.7	11.6	15.5	18
Average	26.2	5.2	7.2	32.2	47

C. The Reversal of Fortunes, 1973–82

	1973	1973–82	1973–82	1982	1982
United States	29.7	1.7	4.0	36.3	85
Britain	34.3	0.7	3.7	44.6	222
France	34.8	2.4	6.0	47.5	118
Germany	36.1	1.7	4.2	44.8	108
Italy	34.4	2.1	6.1	48.5	138
Sweden	40.2	1.4	6.4	62.2	283
Japan	15.7	3.8	10.4	27.3	75
Average	32.2	2.0	5.8	44.5	147

Sources: OECD definition of current disbursements of general government. *National Accounts of OECD Countries* (Paris: OECD, annual).

[a]GDP, Gross domestic product at market prices; CPP, costs of public programs.

[b]The proportion of growth in the national product claimed by the costs of public programs, given the preceding rates of change in both terms.

same, rising an average of only 0.6 percent from the 25.3 percent base in 1952. In four countries—the United States, Britain, the Federal Republic of Germany, and Japan—the costs of public policy actually fell as a proportion of the national product. In every country, both take-home pay and spending on public programs grew, and grew substantially. As of 1960, little more than one-quarter of an average year's growth was needed to meet the front-end load imposed by another year's growth in public spending.

In the 1960s the mix changed between growth in take-home pay and public policies, but affluence continued. The economies of major nations continued to grow at the same rate as in the 1950s. However, the cost of public policies grew at a faster rate, 7.2 percent a year. The percentage increase was greatest in Japan, 11.6 percent (Table 1.1B). But because Japan's public spending base was so low, a very small proportion of its rapidly growing national product was allocated through the fisc. As of 1970, Japan was more like a nineteenth-century industrializing nation than a late twentieth-century welfare state. In major nations the proportion of the national product allocated through the state on average grew to nearly one-third by 1972. But the front-end load of financing another year's growth claimed only half the expected fiscal dividend of economic growth.

A reversal of fortune came with world recession in 1973. Since then there as been a fall of 1.4 percent in the rate at which public spending has grown, but this is much less than the 3.2 percent fall in the annual rate of growth in the national product.The effect of compounding these differences for a decade has been to push up public spending by nearly two-fifths. The costs of public policy claimed an average of 44.5 percent of the national product in 1982. In Sweden, the fisc now claims 62 percent of the national product to meet the costs of public policy, and in France and Italy nearly half the national product. The United States spends more through the fisc than did most major European welfare states at the start of the 1970s, and Japan has virtually caught up with the U.S. position then. Moreover, in Japan the costs of public policy have been growing at nearly double the average for major nations since 1973, and at two and one-half times the rate of the Japanese economy.

Because public spending is growing much faster than the national product today, and because governments everywhere now have a much higher level of spending commitments, the front-end load upon the economy now exceeds the annual rate of growth in every European country examined (Table 1.1C). In Sweden, the costs of public spending have been growing at an average rate of 6.4 percent a year while the Swedish economy has been growing at a rate of only 1.4 percent annually. To finance this, the Swedish government has been spending more than double the annual fiscal dividend of economic growth. This can be done—but only by cutting take-home pay. Doing this has produced labor unrest and difficulties with business for both Social Democratic and bourgeois governments of Sweden. In Britain, the fisc has had public spending grow by twice as much as the economy; inflation, low rates of investment, high level of unemployment, a breakdown of consensus within the trade unions, and a Labour party split have followed. So great has been the inertia force of "uncontrollable" spending commitments that an antistate Thatcher government failed to reverse continuing pressures to reduce take-home pay in its first term of office.

The United States and Japan are outstanding today because pressures of public spending have not yet produced a sustained fall in take-home pay. In the United States, the chief reason for this is that public spending grows more slowly than in most major nations. The front-end load of public spending has nonetheless doubled in a decade, because the U.S. economy has also been growing at less than the average rate. The threat to take-home pay in the United States could thus be met by a moderate increase in economic growth. In Japan, by contrast, the problem is that public spending has grown at a rate far higher than that of the Japanese economy. To prevent take-home pay from falling, the Japanese need to reduce the rate of expenditure growth to that of Sweden, the fastest expanding European welfare state. This would be sufficient to guarantee an indefinite continuation of double affluence, given the dynamic of the Japanese economy.

The "underfunding" of welfare by the state in the United States and Japan has long been criticized by proponents of the European-style welfare state. But the identification of the European norm as the only way to secure welfare in society is based on the fallacy that the state is the sole provider of welfare. The state has no monopoly on the production of welfare. A high rate of expansion in state welfare has also been based on a gamble, namely, that there is no risk to the fisc in guaranteeing costly open-ended entitlements to all citizens. This hope now appears to be false.[3]

DYNAMICS OF TOTAL WELFARE IN THE FAMILY

Turning from macroeconomic problems of public finance to the household is both necessary and desirable, for in a democracy welfare production ought to satisfy individuals and household. Moreover, the household is capable of dealing with financial problems in a way not available to the state or the market, namely, by the nonmonetized production of welfare.

Household welfare is just as much a social product as welfare produced by the market or the state. By definition, it consists of goods and services that can be exchanged; the family is distinctive because affectionate personal ties rather than the cash nexus are the basis of such exchanges. Individuals who live by themselves have fewer obligations to produce nonmonetized welfare services for others, but they also receive fewer services in kind.

Total welfare in the family (TWF) is the sum of goods and services obtained from the state and on the market, and produced within the household.

$$TWF = H + M + S$$

The analysis of the welfare of a family cannot be confined solely to welfare from the state. To emphasize that every family has multiple sources of welfare is not to deny the importance of the state's role. Contemporary proponents of privatizing welfare, whether to the market or to nonmonetized household production, often commit the same fallacy as proponents of the state provisions of welfare, namely, assuming that monopoly must characterize the production of welfare. This is contrary to reality.

Analysts of public policy often treat pensions as if pensioners' welfare depended solely on social security and related welfare programs. In fact, this is not the case. The pensions paid elderly persons are only one source of household income. A substantial proportion of the elderly can derive an income from occupational pension schemes, or savings. Japanese firms that pay large lump sums upon retirement encourage recipients to become capitalists, investing their cash retirement benefit in the market. Another example of mix is health care in the United States. Government now underwrites medical care for the elderly and indigent, but personal care for the elderly continues to be produced primarily in the home, by spouses caring for each other, and by care from children, friends, and neighbors. Employers and employees pay the market cost for health care for most families in work.

From the perspective of the family, the primary concern is to maintain welfare consumption at a level deemed satisfactory. Total welfare is more important to a family than are the particular sources. When there are difficulties—whether because of a loss of market income, a marginal reduction in public benefits, or a contraction of family resources—another source may substitute to maintain welfare.

Massive public outgoings on health, income security, and education appear as income in the family welfare budget. Even though citizens express concern about the tax cost of programs, they are not anxious to dispense with the benefits financed by their taxes. As between reducing both welfare programs and taxes or maintaining and increasing both, the great majority of Europeans prefer high tax–high benefit welfare state programs (cf. Hadenius, 1985; Rose, 1985C: Table IV.5; ACIR, 1983). Insofar as public expenditure on welfare programs is not growing as fast as it once did, the change will be marginal or even imperceptible to most people. The electoral calculus threatens political extinction in consequence of cutting programs benefiting majorities. So-called squeezes on spending do not reduce public spending in total, because they leave the majority of families unaffected. Any cuts in welfare programs are likely to be concentrated upon those with few beneficiaries, as a corollary of protecting benefits for majorities.

Media publicity can generate a revolution of falling expectations by publicizing threats of reduction in public welfare spending, and a slowing down in the growth of welfare expenditure can be misreported or misperceived as if it were an absolute cut (Rose, 1980b). If families then maintain their welfare at a constant level, they may be satisfied in doing better than they had been led to expect by "scare" stories in the media.

The market puts welfare at risk when families suffer a loss of income through unemployment, or a low income is insufficient to meet all family needs. Public programs are designed to insure against such risks as unemployment and exceptional medical expenses. Tax allowances and children's allowances provide for needs routinely arising in the life cycle. But the provision of these programs is not meant to preempt individuals working or seeking employment at above-subsistence wages.

For most people in OECD nations, the market provides an income sufficient to meet major welfare needs that must be met through the market (e.g., food, housing, and transportation). Statements about millions in poverty or in unemployment deserve attention, but the tens of millions in work and not in poverty should be remembered.[4] By definition, half the families in society will have an income above the median. An average income assures a far higher material standard of living than a generation or two ago. In an era of economic growth, even people whose income is falling relative to the workforce as a whole may have a higher absolute standard of living, as average income rises.

The family has a unique resource for maintaining welfare, namely, production of welfare without money changing hands. When a family's cash income is not adequate to meet all its spending commitments, it can cut down expenditure by substituting meals prepared in the home for meals prepared in restaurants or cafes. When a person's income drops through retirement or unemployment, the expense of journeys to work also stops. When costs of painting a house or maintaining a garden rise, a family can do the work themselves at much less cash cost. In some cases, such as personal social services, family care may be preferred to care purchased through the market or received from state agencies. There are limits to what can be produced in the home. Education uses specialized facilities, and so too do illnesses requiring hospitalization. But at the margin—and it is at the margin that welfare problems are most likely to arise today—the nonmonetized production of welfare offers much scope to substitute for market and state, and thus to maintain total welfare in the family.

Every individual has an additional resource for welfare, his or her own efforts. The welfare goods and services produced by the state, the market, and others in the household are but inputs to the lives of individuals. Outcomes require individual effort as well; for example, a pupil must make an effort to learn if the school's input of teaching is to be effective. An increase in individual effort can substitute at the margin for a reduction in monetized welfare production. A deterioration in the pupil:teacher ratio does not mean less learning if pupils make compensating efforts in a slightly enlarged class. In some fields, individual effort is superior to paid assistance by others. If individuals made more effort to keep themselves physically fit through exercise and a better diet, then monetized health care would decline and simultaneously the positive health of the population improve.

What difference does it make whether welfare products are provided through the state, the market, or the household? The differences are partial, not total: a money income remains a sum of money, whatever the source. A house is a roof over one's head, whoever maintains it; a meal can have the same amount of calories, whether prepared at home or bought in a restaurant; and a bus ride is a bus ride, whoever owns the bus.

Differences between sources of welfare involve benefits *and* costs. The distinctive characteristic of state provision of welfare is that it makes access depend on political status (citizenship) rather than market status (purchasing power) or family status (household). Anyone who meets the entitlement qualifications laid down in a public law is able to claim such merit goods as education, health care, or income maintenance grants. The rationale is political. Citizens are conceived as being members of a single national community, deserving statutorily guaranteed benefits by virtue of their citizenship. In a democracy such benefits are considered an expression of mutual regard; in a dictatorship, benefits are given by the state in order to extract more services from subjects.

Whatever the philosophy of collective care by public servants, the state provision of welfare benefits is necessarily legalistic, bureaucratized, and—at the point of production—monetized. State welfare services require authorization by public law. The access of individual citizens is not simply on demand but also by virtue of statutory entitlement. Just as an individual needs money to generate effective demand in the marketplace, so a recipient of a state welfare benefit needs eligibility according to legal criteria. In order for a benefit to be available nationwide and available at the same standard, public officials administering programs must impersonally apply rules to those whom they meet. Bureaucratic rules are necessary to ensure standardization at the point of delivery. Public providers of welfare services have a pecuniary interest in what they do, and usually belong to unions that seek to maximize their pay (Rose, 1985b). In education and health, money is spent principally on salaries to public employees. A salary increase for service providers is an extra charge on the fisc. But it is arguable under what circumstances and to what extent an increase in expenditure on salaries is immediately translated into an increase in welfare outputs (Heller, 1981).

The distinctive characteristic of the market provision of welfare is that you can get what you pay for. The food a family eats is not dictated by law or by bureaucratic directives but by prices in the market. At a given level of expenditure, people can satisfy their tastes for food, housing, and transportation in many different ways. State-funded health care often leaves the choice of doctor to the patient, and public enterprises provide citizens with services that they choose to buy.

The limitation of the market provision of welfare is that you *only* get what you can pay for. Choice is effective insofar as a family has the income to pay for what it wants. Whereas the incomes of families are unequal, their status as citizens is equal. Each citizen can stand as tall as the next in claiming benefits, and those whose need is greatest, whether because of financial or physical handicaps, can claim most. A rationale for the state provision of welfare is to compensate for income inequalities by providing benefits to those with low incomes, and to promote equality of access by providing benefits without any test of income. This is done in public education, in a national health service, and in a variety of income maintainence programs.

The distinctive feature of the family is that its capacity to produce and consume welfare varies greatly through the life cycle. Whereas cross-national comparison calls attention to differences in citizen entitlements according to nationality, and comparisons across incomes call attention to differences in the market between classes, comparison across families emphasizes differences within the life cycle. Of the seven major domains of welfare examined here, four—education, health, pension income, and personal social services—reflect a life cycle bias in the incidence of need.

The welfare services consumed in the family are distributed unequally across time, because need is differential. A graph of family needs across time is likely to show a W-shaped line of welfare consumption (Figure 1.2). The need is high in childhood for education and preventive health care. It falls when a young person leaves school to go out to work, and is in good health. The need rises again when a person settles in marriage; housing becomes more important, and a couple's children require edu-

Figure 1.2. The W-shaped distribution of welfare.

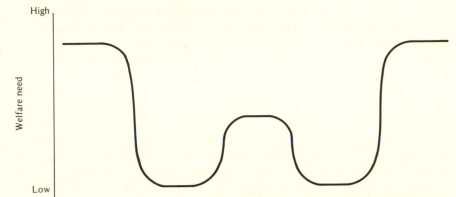

Family life cycle

cation. Once children leave school, the welfare needs of a middle-aged couple in good health tend to fall. In old age, needs rise again to complete the W; elderly couples require a pension to assure a regular income, and health care is important too.

When individuals are viewed from a life cycle perspective, inequalities are a function of differences in family structure. A single-parent family cannot produce as much welfare in the home as a two-parent family, and a widow or widower will not receive as many personal social services as will an elderly married couple. A single person in ill health will have no one to care for him or her at home, whereas most persons rely on their families to do so.

Fiscal stress in the state need *not* lead to family stress, because of the multiple resources of families through the life cycle. For individuals who are at the bottom of the W-shaped need for welfare products, a temporary freeze in the level of state provision of welfare will be virtually unnoticed, for they will be making no demands for state services at that time. For those working—and the great majority of the labor force remains employed—the market, supplemented by household services, can offset marginal shortfalls in state-produced welfare.

When state provision of welfare does not expand proportionately to the expansion of needs, then families at a peak of the W-shaped life cycle can seek more from the market (working more hours, earning more, or altering expenditure on nonwelfare goods) or from increased household efforts. Insofar as these are successful, then total family welfare will be maintained. Unemployed persons need not rely solely on low levels of state benefits, for there is often an employed person in the same household. Unemployment benefits are a second or even third income in many families; for example, a youth's unemployment benefit supplements parental wages.

While important, the state is not the monopoly producer of welfare in society; thus, a crisis of the welfare state is not a crisis of welfare in society. In mixed societies, families have a multiplicity of ways to maintain their welfare. The means of producing welfare, and therefore the mix, vary as among the United States, Europe, and Japan; the goal of maintaining or increasing total welfare in the family remains the same.

NOTES

1. The distributional approach often used by sociologists tends to follow the top-down model too. It is not concerned with the welfare of individuals or households. It compares the welfare of such aggregates as classes. Moreover, there is a persisting tendency for distributional analyses to concentrate exclusively on state expenditure for welfare provision, ignoring both the market and the household.

2. The definition includes all five welfare products identified as central by Wilensky (1975: 1), albeit he does not analyze them all. It adds personal social services and transportation. Clothing is omitted, because of the large element of taste and style in clothing; its

provision is similar to food, being bought in the market or made in the household rather than provided free by the state. Leisure is excluded because of its complexities; state provision is visible but relatively limited by comparison with leisure provision by the market and the household. Including clothing and leisure would not change the overall substantive conclusions.

3. The emphasis here differs from OECD (1985), because this review also includes non-social expenditure, which is substantial and can be fast growing (e.g., interest payments on the debt); for an informed critique of OECD social expenditure analysis, see "Social Expenditure" (1985).

4. To define poverty in terms of "relative deprivation"—that is, an income lower than the national average—is to stipulate by definition that the bottom quarter of Swedish or Japanese society is necessarily poorer than the middle quarters of society in Africa or India, an assertion that cannot be sustained by material evidence.

REFERENCES

ACIR, *Changing Public Attitudes on Government and Taxes.* Washington, D.C.: Advisory Commission on Intergovernmental Relations S-12, 1983.

Allardt, Erik, "Public Policy and Dimensions of Welfare." in *Comparing Public Policies* (R. Rose and J. Wiatr, eds.). Warsaw: Polish Academy of Sciences, 1977, pp. 95–112.

Ardant, G., "Financial Policy and Economic Infrastructure of Modern States and Nations," in *The Formation of National States in Western Europe* (C. Tilly, ed.) Princeton, N.J.: Princeton University Press, 1975, pp. 164–242.

Badelt, Christoph, "New Concepts for the Supply of Government Services," in *Public Finance and the Quest for Efficiency* (Horst Hanusch, ed.). Detroit: Wayne State University Press 1984, pp. 267–278.

Braun, Rudolf, "Taxation, Sociopolitical Structure and State-Building: Great Britain and Brandenburg-Prussia," in *The Formation of National States in Western Europe* (C. Tilly, ed.). Princeton, N.J.: Princeton University Press, 1975, pp. 243–372.

Castles, Francis G. ed., *The Impact of Parties: Politics and Policies in Democratic Capitalist States.* London and Beverly Hills, Calif.: Sage Publications, 1982.

Central Statistical Office, *Social Trends.* London: Her Majesty's Stationery Office, No. 15, 1985.

Easterlin, Richard, "Does Economic Growth Improve the Human Lot? Some Empirical Evidence," in *Nations and Households in Economic Growth* (P. A. David and M. W. Reder, eds.). New York: Academic Press, 1974.

Estes, Richard J., *The Social Progress of Nations.* New York: Praeger, 1984.

Flora, Peter, "Solution or Source of Crises? The Welfare State in Historical Perspective," in *The Emergence of the Welfare State in Britain and Germany* (W. J. Mommsen, ed.). London: Croom-Helm, 1981, pp. 343–383.

Flora, P. and Heidenheimer, A. J., eds., *The Development of Welfare States in Europe and America.* New Brunswick, N.J.: Transaction, 1981.

Franklin, S. H., *The European Peasantry.* London: Methuen, 1969.

Gershuny, J. I., "Changement des Modeles de Loisir, Royaume Uni, 1961–1974/5." *Temps Libres* 4:115–134, 1981.

Goldschmidt-Clermont, L., *Unpaid Work in the Household.* Geneva: International Labour Office, Women Work and Development, 1, 1982.

Goode, Richard, *Government Finance in Developing Countries.* Washington, D.C.: Brookings Institution, 1984.

Gough, Ian, *The Political Economy of the Welfare State.* London: Macmillan, 1979.

Grossman, Gregory, "The Second Economy of the USSR." *Problems of Communism,* September–October, pp. 25–40, 1977.

Hadenius, Axel, "Citizens Strike a Balance: Discontent with Taxes, Content with Spending," *Journal of Public Policy* 5:3, 349–364, 1985.

Heclo, Hugh, "Toward a New Welfare State?" in *Development of Welfare States in Europe and America* (P. Flora and A. J. Heidenheimer, eds.), 1981, pp. 383–406.

Heidenheimer, A. J., "Trade Unions, Benefit Systems and Party Mobilization Styles." *Comparative Politics* 1(3):313–342, 1969.

Heller, Peter, "Diverging Trends in the Shares of Nominal and Real Government Expenditure in GDP." *National Tax Journal* 34(1):61–74, 1981.

Heller, Peter S. and Tait, Alan A., *Government Employment and Pay.* Washington, D.C.: International Monetary Fund, Occasional Paper 24, 1983.

Hill, T. P., "Do It Yourself and GDP." *The Review of Income and Wealth* 25(1):31–40, 1979.

Katsenelinboigen, A., "Coloured Markets in the Soviet Union." *Soviet Studies* 29:1, 62–85, 1977.

King, A. S., "Ideas, Institutions and the Policies of Government." *British Journal of Political Science* 3(3–4):291–313; 409–423, 1973.

Kramer, Ralph M., *Voluntary Agencies in the Welfare State.* Berkeley: University of California Press, 1981.

Lane, Jan-Erik, ed., *State and Market.* Beverly Hills, Calif. and London: Sage Publications, 1985.

Little, I. M. D., *A Critique of Welfare Economics.* London: Oxford University Press, 1950.

Musgrave, R. A., *The Theory of Public Finance.* New York: McGraw-Hill, 1959.

Musgrave, R. A. and Peacock, Alan, eds., *Classics in the Theory of Public Finance.* New York: St. Martin's Press, 1967.

Offe, Claus, *Contradictions of the Welfare State.* London: Hutchinson, 1984.

Olson, Mancur, *The Logic of Collective Action.* Cambridge, Mass.: Harvard University Press, 1965.

Organization for Economic Cooperation and Development, *National Accounts of OECD Countries.* Paris: OECD, annual.

Organization for Economic Cooperation and Development, *Social Expenditures, 1960–1990.* Paris: OECD, 1985.

Peacock, Alan, "On the Anatomy of Collective Failure," in "Festschrift für Paul Senf," *Public Finance* 33–43, 1982.

Peacock, Alan and Wiseman, Jack, *The Growth of Public Expenditure in the United Kingdom.* New York: Oxford University Press, 1961.

Pryor, Richard, *Public Expenditures in Communist and Capitalist Nations.* London: George Allen & Unwin, 1968.

Rein, Martin, "The Social Policy of the Firm." *Policy Sciences* 14(2):117–35, 1982.

Rose, Richard, "On the Priorities of Government." *European Journal of Political Research* 4(3):247–89, 1976.

Rose, Richard, "Ordinary People in Extraordinary Economic Circumstances," in

Challenge to Governance (R. Rose, ed.). London and Beverly Hills, Calif.: Sage Publications, 1980a, pp. 151–174.

Rose, Richard, "Misperceiving Public Expenditure: Feelings about 'Cuts'," in *Fiscal Stress and Public Policy* (C. H. Levine and I. Rubin, eds.). Beverly Hills, Calif. and London: Sage Publications, 1980b, pp. 203–230.

Rose, Richard, *Understanding Big Government*. London and Beverly Hills, Calif.: Sage Publications, 1984a.

Rose, Richard, *Do Parties Make a Difference?*, 2nd edition. Chatham, N.J.: Chatham House, 1984b.

Rose, Richard, "The Programme Approach to the Growth of Government." *British Journal of Political Science* 15(1):1–28, 1985a.

Rose, Richard, "The Significance of Public Employment," in *Public Employment in Western Nations* (R. Rose et al., eds.). Cambridge, England: Cambridge University Press, 1985b.

Rose, Richard, *Politics in England: Persistence and Change,* 4th edition. Boston: Little, Brown, 1985c.

Rose, Richard and Karran, Terence, "Inertia or Incrementalism? A Long-Term View of the Growth of Government," in *Comparative Resource Allocation* (A. J. Groth and L. L. Wade, eds.). Beverly Hills, Calif. and London: Sage Publications, 1984.

Sametz, A. W., "Production of Goods and Services: The Measurement of Economic Growth," in *Indicators of Social Change* (E. B. Sheldon and W. E. Moore, eds.). New York: Russell Sage Foundation, 1968, pp. 77–96.

Smith, B. L. R. and Rosenbaum, Nelson M., "The Fiscal Capacity of the Voluntary Sector." Washington, D.C.: The Brookings Institution, typescript, 1981.

Sniderman, Paul and Brody, Richard, "Coping: the Ethic of Self-Reliance." *American Journal of Political Science* 26(3):501–521, 1977.

"Social Expenditure 1960–1990: A Symposium." *Journal of Public Policy* 5:2, 133–168, 1985.

Stoetzel, Jean, *Les Valeurs du Temps Present*. Paris: Presses Universitaires de France, 1983.

Szalai, Alexander, et al., *The Use of Time*. The Hague and Paris: Mouton, 1972.

Titmuss, Richard M., *Essays on "The Welfare State."* London: George Allen & Unwin, 1958.

Titmuss, Richard M., *The Gift Relationship: From Human Blood to Social Policy*. London: George Allen & Unwin, 1970.

Thompson, Dennis L., ed., "Policy toward Public–Private Relations: A Symposium." *Policy Studies Journal* 11:3, 1983.

Weisbrod, Burton A., *The Voluntary Non-Profit Sector*. Lexington, Mass: D. C. Heath, 1977.

White, Michelle J., ed., *Non-Profit Firms in a Three-Sector Economy*. Washington, D.C.: Urban Insitute Press, 1981.

Wilensky, Harold, *The Welfare State and Equality*. Berkeley: University of California Press, 1975.

Wolf, Charles, "A Theory of Non-Market Failure." *Journal of Law and Economics* 22:107–39, 1979.

Young, Michael and Willmott, Peter, *The Symmetrical Family*. London: Routledge & Kegan Paul, 1973.

2

Welfare and "Welfare" in America

NATHAN GLAZER

It is now twenty years since what seemed to be the final push to the completion of the American welfare state was launched. In 1964 and 1965 major action took place along three fronts. First, the largest hole in the American system of welfare provisions was in some measure filled with the passage of laws setting up a system of Medicare (contributory health insurance for the aged) and Medicaid (noncontributory health care provision for the poor). Second, the United States began in some respects to move ahead of Western Europe by launching a complex group of programs designed to wipe out poverty under the auspices of the Office of Economic Opportunity (OEO). The large number of people who, so to speak, "fell between the cracks" of even the best-developed welfare systems were to be provided with activistic programs of education, work training, political organization, and community action. Third, a major Civil Rights Act and Voting Rights Act outlawed discrimination in employment and education on grounds of race, and ensured the ability of blacks and other minority groups to register and vote. The passage of effective national civil rights legislation meant that blacks and other minorities would benefit from the new social legislation without discrimination, and opened the way to other national social legislation, such as federal aid for poor children in schools.

But in social policy as in other forms of public action, there is no such thing as completion or finality: old problems, it turns out, have not been adequately addressed, and, even when they have been, new problems have risen almost immediately upon their ashes.

No sooner had the final push to the completion of the American welfare state been launched than problems arose that delayed, raised doubts, and finally turned back the movement to reach a fully developed welfare state. The United States, having begun only in the 1930s to create a national system of protection against unemployment, old age, death, and disablement (ill health remained the one great issue that the reforms of the 1930s did not settle), never did catch up, and now appears to be in full retreat. Why is the American welfare state a somewhat abortive example, compared to the fully developed systems of other economically advanced states? What explains what remains a somewhat exceptional history?

The problem is an old one. Perhaps it is kin to another old question: Why is there no socialism in America? The answer is not a simple one. The difficulties that the enthusiasms and programs of 1964 and later ran into have been chronicled by many. One favored explanation for some years was the Vietnam War, and indeed it in some measure affected developments: apparently, intentions to have the poverty program grow were arrested by the needs of the war. However, the billion or two or three additional that might have been spent on poverty programs if there had been no war shrinks to insignificance compared to the expansion by tens of billions in the entitlement programs that were unchecked by the war. This is clearly a very partial and minor explanation. The Vietnam War did nothing to impede the rapid expansion of Social Security (insurance for old age, disablement, death), of Medicaid and Medicare, of welfare (payments for the residual poor, bearing the offical name of Aid to Families with Dependent Children, AFDC), all of which expanded at a more rapid rate than anyone expected during the war in the late 1960s and 1970s. The Vietnam War had no effect in moderating the expansion of civil rights enforcement machinery, an expansion that remained unbroken until the Reagan administration. The rapid growth of entitlement programs—as Social Security, Medicare, Medicaid, and welfare are called—was unbroken under Presidents Johnson, Nixon, and Ford, and the rate of growth was affected only moderately, after the Vietnam War had come to an end, under President Carter.

What we have to explain is a growing disillusionment with the hope that a more fully developed welfare state would bring improvement to the conditions of life not only of poor Americans and black Americans, but indeed of all Americans. In developing the story of this disillusionment, we have to distinguish between welfare as most of the world understands it, and welfare in the American context. In most countries, social welfare expenditures are overwhelmingly for education, health, unemployment insurance, and old age. The latter three are substantially insurance and contributory programs (with exceptions, such as the British National Health Service); the first is tax supported. All four major programs are seen to provide for the entire population. But the welfare state also deals with other kinds of residual distress, those that major national tax-supported or insurance-based programs cannot deal with, through the ministrations of social workers, child care specialists, and the like. In the well-designed welfare state, it is always the hope that the first type of program will take care of the vast majority of problems, and the number needing programs of the second type will be small and decline, as good education and health care makes almost every person a participant in the labor market and self-supporting.

The two kinds of programs are sharply distinguished in the American mind—perhaps because of its individualist orientation, its pioneer and immigrant origins, and the converse, the limited degree to which Americans feel part of a national community encompassing all other Americans, regardless of race, religion, or national origin.

The exceptional periods that have to be explained are those in which this mood was overcome by a national effort to deal with the problems of all Americans. Without detailing the history of the American welfare state, one can record that the first great period in its construction was the New Deal period. Even without a strong Socialist party, the United States between 1934 and 1938 had some of the elements generally associated with it, such as a growing and self-confident labor movement. The depression had cast vast sections of the population into distress, and the new national programs of the Social Security Act—old age pensions and unemployment insurance—were seen as programs for all, rather than an unfortunate minority. It was a remarkably short time before older values and political orientations reasserted themselves, and it was not until the Great Society period—once again, a brief period from 1963 to 1968— before the next great push was effective. Part of its achievement was in welfare for all through Medicaid, health insurance for all the aged, but the most distinctive element was an effort to expand those residual programs addressed to the poor who could not take advantage of the contributory programs, and to devise new ones under the general heading of the War on Poverty. By 1968, however, the moment had passed again—and the Republicans were back in power nationally.

There is a strong American bias in favor of programs for what are conceived to be independent individuals, against the programs for the dependent. That bias has grown. Welfare I—the contributory programs for all and education—still expands, and is almost sacrosanct. Welfare II—the residual programs for those not helped by the first type of program—is in increasing disrepute. Attacks on Welfare II by the first Reagan administration were in part beaten off, but efforts by those committed to it are devoted to defense, rather than expansion and improvement. The same pattern, or worse, for Welfare II prevails in the second Reagan administration.

Perhaps the radical decline in the fortunes of Welfare II can be attributed to overpromising in the 1960s, when the War on Poverty was launched. The promise was not only to help the poor but that the poor would disappear, and that would help everybody by eliminating one of the chief environmental hazards of American life. The issue thus was not only whether the poor were affected positively by these programs. More significant politically was whether these programs were affecting the ambience of life of the great majority of Americans for the better. They too expected to be improved by the improvement of the poor: there would be less juvenile delinquency, less crime, lower taxes, fewer slums, and less illegitimacy.

None of these hoped-for ends has been achieved. Indeed, on most measures, things only got worse through the 1970s as expenditures for social policy ballooned. It had been promised that the poor would be raised, that the socially delinquent would be enticed away from their destructive behavior and become independent and untroublesome fellow citizens, and that crime, the ever-present accompaniment of urban life in the United States, would decline. The elimination of discrimination and the provision of political rights would guarantee that blacks would join the racial and ethnic mix of the United States on an equal footing, and would be as little trouble as the Irish, Italians, Jews, Poles, Chinese, and all other groups. When Lyndon Johnson launched the War on Poverty the enthusiastic support in almost all quarters was not only based on an altruistic commitment to raising the poorest fellow citizens and improving the lives of the worst-off among us. It was expected to have substantial benefits for the others, too—not only the psychological benefits of removing poverty in the richest nation of the world, but also the practical benefits of improving conditions in the poorest parts of our cities and reducing the incidence of crime and costs of expensive remedial programs through a massive effort at primary prevention.

One of the most interesting and insightful evocations of the enthusiasms that accompanied the great burst of new programs in the 1960s period is from Charles R. Morris, who was a young "poverty fighter" at the time:

When the decision was taken to eliminate poverty, Johnson's top advisors—mostly holdover Kennedy technocrats, including a number of recruits from McNamara's Pentagon—set about the task with the brisk, no-nonsense, sleeves-rolled-up, let's-get-it-over-with, grim good humor that fit the cherished legend of their fallen hero. Lights burned late in brainstorming sessions all over Washington. In other times, the scale and complexity of the problem might have been daunting, but the new poverty warriors had the confidence of professional problem solvers . . . .

The programs were supposed to produce results quickly. Shriver's main criterion for including proposals in the final package was that they had to promise visible progress before the 1966 midterm congressional elections. He courted conservative congressmen assiduously with detailed estimates of the cash savings that would accrue to the nation from reduced welfare, reduced crime, increased tax payments, . . . if only the programs were enacted. . . . Shriver also went on a campaign to induce states to raise welfare payments out of the savings from the poverty programs, since welfare rolls would be expected to drop rapidly. . . .

Such a massive conspiracy of self-delusion is altogether astonishing. There was virtually no evidence to support any of the claims that were being made. . . . The slightest scraps of data and the broadest sociological associations—as that between education and income, for instance—were used to underpin huge, wobbly towers of interventionist hypothesis (Morris, 1984: 90–92).

Whether these programs were successful or not, and why, is now the subject of a major debate. There is hardly any doubt that from the point of view of politically effective public opinion, the expansion of American social policy in the later 1960s and 1970s was not a success: the last president who tried to expand the net of American social policy went down to defeat, and his successor, who has tried determinedly to eliminate many of the programs of the preceding 15 years, and to cut others, has been returned with an overwhelming majority to a second term. The judgment of public opinion may well be wrong. There are those who argue that these programs were effective, and that they would have been more effective if more money had been spent (Rodgers, 1982; Schwarz, 1983; Harrington, 1984; but on the other side, see Murray, 1984). We will not enter into that debate. But some things that definitely failed to fulfill the hopes described by Charles R. Morris in the quotation above are beyond dispute: the numbers on welfare (AFDC, the Americans residual programs for female-headed families with children and without a male provider) exploded in the later 1960s and early 1970s, until the states, which paid a substantial part of welfare costs—whether liberal Nelson Rockefeller's New York or conservative Ronald Reagan's California—imposed sharp administrative restraints. Crime increased and became more dangerous. The slums remained, and as far as simple observation could tell, became worse. The lower class black population was more afflicted by social problems of drugs, crime, illegitimacy, education failure, and economic incapacity than ever before, despite the growth of a more prosperous black working and middle class.

These nagging problems became evident during the 1970s, even as the American welfare state was further developed under the surprising auspices of Richard Nixon. Whether this was because Daniel P. Moynihan truly convinced him that he should play the role of Disraeli, a Tory nationalist raising the conditions of the poor, or because a Democratic Congress still insisted on expansion, or because elite public opinion was not yet disillusioned with the possibilities of social engineering, the fact is that neither Nixon's nor Ford's administration indicated any retreat. Analysts of federal and other expenditure have concluded that the retreat began under Carter, and accelerated under Reagan (Glazer, 1984a; Nathan, 1983: 45–48; Palmer and Sawhill, 1982, 1984).

Disillusionment did come, though. The American welfare state came under attack long before it reached the levels of the European welfare states, whether measured in percentage of gross national product (GNP) taken in taxes for social purposes; in percentage of population in poverty; by extensiveness of protection by public programs against unemployment or ill health or loss of wages in sickness, or of child care services; or by degree of subsidization for housing. Indeed, possibly in only one respect, pensions for the aged, is the American welfare state comparable to the advanced European states. Without ever having reached European levels, the American welfare state has been in retreat since 1981.

To give a simple summary of the changes that have taken place in the
four years since 1981 is not easy. American social policy operates through
hundreds of discrete programs, but there are only a few large ones, and
the course of change is clear. There have been substantial efforts to arrest
and reverse the growth of programs directed primarily to the poor:
AFDC, Food Stamps, and Medicaid. These attacks have been in modest
measure successful, though not as successful as they would have been if
the Congress had not resisted. There have been less substantial efforts to
arrest and reverse the growth of the largest redistributive programs,
Social Security, unemployment insurance, and Medicaid, programs that
in large measure go to the middle class. Here there has been some modest
reduction in the rate of previous growth. President Reagan has succeeded
in arresting the growth of social expenditures or even introducing cuts in
benefit levels, yet his policies, despite the political *Sturm und Drang* that
surrounds them, are in some measure a continuation of previous trends
(Figure 2.1; Table 2.1).

One should neither exaggerate nor understate the changes introduced
by the Reagan administration. They clearly indicate that innovation in
social policy, if there is any, for some time to come will consist principally of cost cutting. It takes a number of directions: reductions in the
ceilings that define eligibility for AFDC, Food Stamps, and Medicare;

Figure 2.1. Basic monthly benefits for median four-person AFDC unit and single
SSI unit. Data points represent available information. Trend lines were drawn by
interpolation. First full year of operation for the SSI program was 1974. (Repro-
duced from John L. Palmer and Isabel V. Sawhill, eds., *The Reagan Record.* Cambridge: Ballinger Publishing Co., 1984, Figure 6.3, p. 194.)

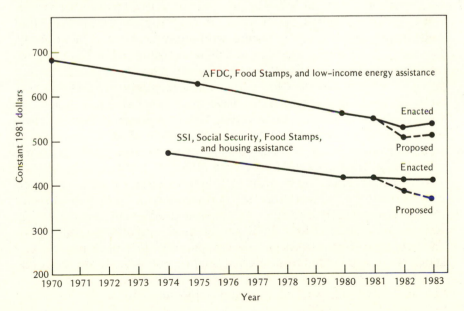

Table 2.1. Average Annual Real Growth Rates in Federal Social Program Outlays

	Average annual growth rate (%)			
	Kennedy–Johnson FY 1961–69	Nixon–Ford FY 1969–77	Carter FY 1977–81	Reagan FY 1981–85[a]
Payments to individuals				
Social insurance and other	6.7	9.2	4.0	2.5
Low-income assistance	8.7	12.0	4.7	0.1
Other grants	37.6	9.9	0.7	−7.4
Total	7.9	9.7	3.9	1.5

Source: From Palmer and Sawhill, *The Reagan Record* (Cambridge: Ballinger, 1984; Table 2A, p. 350).

[a]Calculated on the basis of Congressional Budget Office estimates of 1984 outlays and projections of 1985 outlays based on 1984 policies.

returning programs to the states; reducing the federal directive role and allowing more diversity among the states, hoping indeed for cost-cutting initiatives from the states (or, if they choose further program development, the states will have to pay for it); depending on, hoping for, or expecting that some of the holes opened up by the federal withdrawal will be taken up by private, voluntary, non-profit-making organizations, or even profit-making organizations.

What has been abandoned is any effort to "complete" the welfare state—for example, taking up the unfilled large gap in health cost insurance or trying to integrate, as Nixon's Family Assistance Plan and Carter's Program for Better Jobs and Income did, AFDC with other means-tested programs aimed at the poor. If the problem of the American welfare state is that it is fragmented, with too many sources of authority, too many individual programs, and that it does not reflect a national commitment and a national philosophy (as many critics assert), it is going to remain that way for a long time. Even if a new Democratic administration had replaced the Reagan administration in 1984, we would not have seen as much innovation as Carter attempted. There would not have been a new welfare reform proposal, or a major expansion of health insurance. At best, benefit levels for some of the programs addressed to the poor would have been raised.

What explains the "backwardness," if backwardness it is, of the American welfare state? "Backwardness" is placed in quotes because it seems there is now generaly agreement that no one model exists for the welfare state. In the 1960s, as the OECD and other organizations wrote reports and as scholars began to analyze the comparative development of welfare states, there seemed to be an international competition; those states that collected more in taxes and distributed more in benefits seemed to be "ahead." After all, we had no philosophy, no political position, that argued that there should be *less* collected in taxes and distributed in benefits. While there were always some free-market liberals who looked on these developments skeptically, there were few compared to the 1980s.

That does not seem to be a sensible position anymore. That Sweden or the Netherlands or Denmark collect more in taxes and spend more in benefits than some other West European countries no longer suggests they are a beacon to be followed, a model to be duplicated. Their circumstances depend on a specific history, a specific concatenation of forces. That Switzerland or Japan bring up the rear no longer serves, except for ideologues, to indicate *their* backwardness. Different mechanisms exist there than in Sweden or the Netherlands or Denmark to deal with distress; and their success is indicated by the absence of a large permanent poverty population—no massive slums, no underclass threatening the life and property of ordinary citizens.

The United States, however, is different not only because it spends less on welfare and has a less complete system of protection than most welfare states, but also as compared to countries with well-developed welfare systems, it has a larger poor and problem-making population. How one demonstrates this is not easy. International comparisons of "how many in poverty" run into the problem of not only how one defines poverty in a single nation but how one defines it across many nations. International comparisons indicate that there is indeed more poverty in the United States than in most other major developed welfare states and that there may be a somewhat more unequal distribution of income, but the facts that suggest a more severe problem in the United States are not measures of distribution. They are measures such as the amount of crime, of youth unemployment among minorities, of broken families, of illegitimate children, and the condition of the neighborhoods in the great cities in which poor minority families live.

Few people in the United States would be worried if the only indication of American exceptionalism was that the bottom 20 percent of the income distribution had only 5 percent of the income, or that 15 percent of the population fell below an officially defined poverty standard. That would concern those committed to equality as such, but that is not the position of the great majority of the American population (Glazer, 1983b). The issues that concern the people of the United States are the social conditions plausibly linked to poverty, even if poverty is not the only cause. This paradoxical situation makes the United States exceptional in the degree to which social disorder coexists with an advanced economic position.

The uniqueness of the United States consists not only in the lateness and the incompleteness of its social policy system, but also in the scale of its social problems. Are the two related? It would appear so. It can be argued that if there is too great an inequality in income distribution, it is because an insufficient amount is collected in taxes and redistributed as benefits on the basis of need. If there are large numbers of poverty, it is because insufficient funds are provided them to get out of poverty. If there are slums it is because they are not cleared by government provision. If the poor live in inadequate housing, it is because they are not provided with subsidized housing. If they are unemployed or without jobs, it is because the system of education does not have enough funds, or the system of relating education to work or of retraining workers is inadequate. And if there are family breakup, juvenile delinquency, and crime, it is because of all of the above, not to mention other inadequacies.

These not unsurprising assertions and conclusions are commonly made in politics, although put so baldly they are somewhat naive and incomplete. Nevertheless, it seems reasonable that there should be such relationships. But perhaps nowhere is the challenge to the assertion of such relationships as sharp as in the United States. It is there we will find arguments, whether old conservative, reactionary, or neoconservative, or even, as they are now called, neoliberal, which look skeptically at trying to deal with our social problems through expansion of government-provided social services. The socialist vision of a planned society, making rational provision on the basis of need, eliminating from society the driving force of profit, may be somewhat battered in much of the Western world, but it persists. The United States once shared in such a vision and even provided classics, such as Edward Bellamy's *Looking Backward,* that embodied it. As we know, socialism as a political force of any kind disappeared in the United States fifty years ago. While the Democratic party at one time evolved in a direction not very different from the Socialist parties of Europe, and its policies could not have been sharply distinguished from theirs, there was a striking difference. In Europe these policies had been developed as part of a larger vision; they were the surviving fragments (or more than fragments) from a fallen utopia, and that utopia, perhaps to be realized someday, always existed as a support to the system of social policy. In the United States, the same proposals (even though socialists or ex-socialists participated in shaping them) had to be presented on purely pragmatic grounds. They were not surviving fragments of a great utopian vision: those who proposed them had to deny they shared any part of that vision. They were simply sensible ways of dealing with problems. There must be a difference when a social policy descends from the heavens in which its complete form can be glimpsed, and when it arises from immediate needs with no necessary hint that a larger picture is to be completed. This is the ideological dimension of the problem of incompleteness in American social policy. The ideal of a planned and rational society eliminating social problems has not had the same presence or appeal in the United States.

In addition to the absence of socialist ideology, we find the weakness in the United States of the key social institution that supported this vision in Europe, a socialist-inspired labor movement. The American labor movement is not and never has been socialist, despite having socialists within it. It was characteristic that its shaping leader, Samuel

Gompers, opposed national health insurance as an unnecessary paternalistic reform that would create a system of state supervision of the people's health. In an acrimonious debate at the 1916 congressional hearings on a national commission, Gompers assailed "[a] Socialist's belief that government had to be called in to ensure workers' welfare and gave a ringing defense of the success of trade unions in raising workers' standards of living" (Starr, 1982: 249).

This position did change: the labor movement did in time become one of the strongest supporters of Social Security, national health insurance, and other parts of a national system of social policy, and remains so. But the unions are also a much weaker and smaller part of the working class than in most other developed nations, and a declining share, 30.8 percent of nonagricultural employment in 1970 and 25.2 percent in 1980.

Social policy expansion is buttressed by neither a socialist ideology nor a strong labor movement. In general, the link between a system of social policy and social problems, reasonable as it may appear, is nowhere challenged as sharply as in the United States. It is challenged on broad ideological grounds, the grounds that have put socialism to flight in the United States. It is challenged by more detailed analysis. Each of the points that might serve to support a more complete system of social policy is attacked. If there was more redistribution, it is asserted that there would be less investment, lower productivity, less competitiveness, more unemployment, and more misery. If we provided more assistance to the poor, then we would encourage the poor to reduce work effort, and if this assistance, as in AFDC, was provided because the working husband and father had left his wife and children, we would encourage more of this family breakup. If there was less generous unemployment insurance there would be less unemployment. The public housing we have provided has turned to slums in many cases, creating doubts that this expensive provision really provides better housing and environment.

The critique of American social policy has been extensive and devastating. Indeed, far from supporting the common sense that says more social policy means fewer social problems, it has argued quite the opposite: more social policy means more problems. The increase in expenditures for welfare and for activist poverty programs in the mid-1960s was accompanied by a rise in youth unemployment, withdrawal of minority men from the labor force, and the increased breakup of black families, and easier availability of welfare encouraged this (Gilder, 1978, 1981; Murray, 1984).

Admittedly, the links between some of our social problems and social policy initiatives cannot be sustained, for example, the increase in crime. And some of our efforts in social policy cannot be attacked on the ground of aggravating what they were meant to cure, such as Medicare and Medicaid, but these policies are attacked on the grounds that they have increased the inflation in medical costs and have not been efficient in improving health care. Only Social Security seems to be immune from attack: pensions do not lead to antisocial behavior in the aged. This program is alone in receiving the heartfelt support of both major parties. In the United States, as in other developed nations, the old are numerous and are increasing in number.

The debate is a curious one. Much larger tax burdens for social policy and much more extensive provision for the poor and unemployed are not as problematic in Europe as they are in the United States. Of course there is controversy over social policy in Europe. But whereas we in the United States think that a tax burden of 30 percent of GNP will have devastating consequences on investment, productivity, and economic growth, tax burdens of 50 percent higher, primarily for redistribution, seem less controversial in Europe. Wilensky (1979) has pointed out that we in the United States have tax revolts at much lower rates of taxation than is common in Europe—perhaps because a higher proportion of our taxes, such as income tax and property tax, are visible.

But there are other specific features in the American political and social environment that must be brought into an account of the character of American social policy, if we are to explain why social policy initiatives are relatively stunted and incomplete in the United States. There are a number of characteristics of American society that argue against, undermine, or prevent the universalism of social provision that has been the general ideal in welfare states. These features operated in the past to prevent the United States following in the footsteps of Bismarckian Germany or Lloyd George's England. The Great Depression reduced their effects and created a burst of national legislation and social welfare institution creation. The Civil Rights revolution had a similar effect in the 1960s and 1970s. But the antiwelfare features are resurgent today. That is why the further development of American social policy will take a course that continues to be divergent from that of European countries, and divergent from that of Japan. The weakness of universal social provision as an ideology in the United States, and the weakness of efforts to create national and uniform systems of social provision reflect five features of American society.

1. The first is American federalism, which, despite the hopes of nationalists, is still strong, ideologically and institutionally. The greater role states play in social policy under Reaganism is not just a result of the effort to save money or a distaste for social programs; it is due in equally large measure to the strong hold the principle of federalism still has on the American mind, despite its obvious weakening since the depression.

2. The failure of universalism results from ethnic and religious divisions in the United States. The earliest efforts of cities and states to respond to social problems had to take into account the heterogeneity of religion and ethnic groups; universal provision was unacceptable. The development of statewide or national policies had to deal with and accept a diversity of welfare institutions that had originally been created by a heterogeneous population.

3. A separate obstacle to universalism is the problem of the blacks, originally slaves and subsequently maintained for a hundred years in a position of social and legal inferiority. This has introduced enormous complexities into efforts to establish universalism.

4. Must we also take into account a particularly strong individualistic trend in American society, to account for the resistance to national and universal systems of social policy? I believe we must, but how do we demonstrate that? It is not easy, but consider that the United States is still (or once again) a country to which 600,000 legal immigrants come every year, many of them hoping to establish businesses or professional practices, or looking to improve themselves. Admittedly, many immigrants have come as workers without individualistic hopes or ambitions. Still, the country is shaped by the notion that people will advance themselves without state assistance; the strength of this sentiment is enormous.

5. There is still a remarkably strong sentiment that problems should be taken care of by autonomous, independent institutions, and even by profit-making businesses, rather than by the state. That one can handle social problems, such as the problem of the poor, through profit making might seem bizarre; yet this is widely believed to be a reasonable approach, and not only by Republicans.

All this combines to make the American welfare state unique. Let me introduce some specifics under each of these headings.

Federalism

The unceasing attempts of the Reagan administration to return a variety of programs and responsibilities to the states is a means of reducing the costs of social services. Typically, it involves a trade-off of increased power to the states and less federal funding for the programs. It is also a way of reducing the federal government's role in a host of programs in line with the administration's distaste for a strong federal role in social policy. But it also testifies to the strong role that federalism retains within the American polity. Even if the states were reduced in large measure to claimants for federal funds during the 1960s, their structures existed, strongly grounded in the Constitution, and in the political institutions that maintained complete constitutional governments in each state. More power to the states has been seen for many decades as a part of conservative ideology, consistent with a less activist role for government generally. But federalism is no synonym for conservatism. Today, with most of the states headed by Democratic governors, the attack on the central government's policies tends to come from the Left, not the Right, as it did when a liberal national government was seen as the protector of the rights of trade unions, blue-collar workers, and blacks. There are and always have been progressive states as well as conservative ones. Many states would like to go beyond what a conservative central government considers desirable—and some do, just as many in the past have resisted

doing as much as a liberal government required, as in the 1950s and
1960s, when the federal government imposed liberal standards in welfare
programs on resistant southern states (Steiner, 1966).

If the role of the states today is to serve as an alternative to the federal
administration of social programs because of the ideology of a conservative government, their role in the past was to help determine the form
of the American welfare state—and in doing so to prevent it from being
as national, as uniform, as rational, as universal, as many of the reformers
of the 1930s hoped. It was taken for granted in the first few decades of
the twentieth century that the states were the place for reform. One of the
first major successful efforts to deal with the casualties of industrial societies were workers' compensation laws, which spread through the states
in the earlier part of this century. Progressive states such as New York,
under governors such as Al Smith and Franklin Delano Roosevelt, and
Wisconsin, with its strong progressive tradition, pioneered various forms
of social policy.

When the depression struck in the 1930s, it was a president from New
York, with a secretary of labor and other major advisors from New York,
combined with experts from Wisconsin, who created a cautiously drafted
system of social insurance, one that took cognizance of the fact that neither Congress nor, very likely, the Supreme Court would allow for a fully
national system. Old age insurance was the only part of the proposed system of Social Security that was to be entirely national and uniform.
Unemployment insurance was to be in the hands of the states, though an
ingenious use of the taxing power of the national government forced all
of them to adopt it. What was to become known as "welfare"—the noncontributory aid to the dependent aged, blind, and disabled, and aid to
families with dependent children—all remained under the states, with
contributions from the national government (Skocpol and Ikenberry,
1983; Ikenberry and Skocpol, forthcoming). This is more or less the structure of the system today. The reforms of the 1960s and 1970s added three
major programs, two of which (Medicare and Food Stamps) were
national and uniform, and one of which (Medicaid) was again diverse
and administered by the states with Federal aid.

Some regret the substantial role that states were given in American
social welfare policy in the 1930s. But even in regretting it, they are aware
of the great difficulties a fully national system would have had in getting
through Congress in the 1930s. The fear of a strong government is not
only a characteristic oddity of our present national mood, but also a
recurrent major theme in American history. Thus, the power of the states,
as represented in Congress, shaped what could and could not be done by
the federal government in introducing the major programs of the Social
Security Act in the 1930s.

By now, there is something almost anachronistic in the complaints
against the failure to establish national program standards aside from old
age insurance. It is true that national standards for unemployment insur-

ance and for welfare might have mitigated some problems—for example, the fact that some states became more attractive to migrants because of generous welfare benefits. It may also be asked whether a substantial state role is necessary after the reduction in the difference of standards of living among regions in recent decades, and the elimination of the distinctive pattern of southern race domination that for so long was the principal reason for demands for state autonomy. Yet it seems there is less demand for national uniformity today than ever before. If New York insists on paying high welfare benefits—possibly contributing to its own problems, both financial and social—there is no one, outside of the taxpayers of New York, interested in telling New York that it should not. If Texas insists on paying low welfare benefits, as it does, it is recognized by now that this is a problem for Texas, and Texas is sufficiently prosperous and democratic to be able to change its policies if it wishes, and does not require the interference of the federal government.

The Reagan reforms meant more power to the states, and less federal money. Many states were forced to raise taxes. Paradoxically, the recent improvement in the national economy now provides them with surpluses: they now have more programs for which they are responsible, and more money to deal with these programs and to consider innovation. Their response has been variable, reflecting their politics (Nathan and Doolittle, 1984; Petersen, 1984). We see a resurgence of energy in state government. Some may consider that an unfortunate obstacle to national uniformity. My impression is that fewer and fewer do. The state role is accepted not only out of pious respect for a 200-year-old Constitution, but because the states do reflect the inevitable diversity of a very large country, and do have the institutional and political capacity to deal with a wide variety of social problems. But even if in the mind of objective observers or analysts all this could be better managed from Washington, American political reality has never permitted it; and the Reagan changes mark a sharp shift along the spectrum from national to state power that is a permanent reality of American life.

Ethnic and Religious Diversity, and Voluntarism in Social Services

Social services in the United States in their origins reflect communities. Sometimes these communities were homogeneous (as in early New England). The local community reflected the values and desires of a small population, and thus could provide for the poor, the ill, and the orphaned without conflict. Very early in the development of the United States this homogeneity was broken. New York and Philadelphia, almost from their origins, were religiously and ethnically diverse, and primitive social services developed for distinct groups or communities within them, a pattern that became larger and more fixed with immigration in the nineteenth century. Thus, we have the Hebrew Orphan Asylum or Catholic Charities, Mount Sinai or Lutheran or Presbyterian Hospital.

This is one key strand in the American pattern of social services. It does not affect insurance for the aged, or unemployment insurance, AFDC, or welfare. It does affect the provision of old age homes, of children's services (for care, fostering, adoption), of work training programs, and of the entire gamut of social services that are the pride of advanced welfare states. In the United States these functions may be carried out by public bodies, branches of local and state government; as likely, they are conducted by private, "voluntary" agencies created by ethnic and religious and neighborhood groups. Initially entirely supported by the groups that created them, in time they could lay claim to public funds for support, which were state and local in the nineteenth and first half of the twentieth centuries, but which in recent decades have been increasingly federal, distributed to the states, and eventually to the host of voluntary agencies carrying out what is considered a public function. They also carry out other functions, serving for group survival, or the enhancement of group prestige, or simple institutional maintenance. The complexities of the interplay of the "private," voluntary world and the public world of social services have been studied by Neil Gilbert, and some indication of how they interact gives a sense of the scale of voluntarism in the United States:

> ... [T]he distinction between financing of services through the public and private sectors of social welfare has faded close to the vanishing point. This transformation came about through the use of "purchase of service" arrangements, whereby public agencies contract with the private sector to provide social welfare services.... Between 1962 and 1973 there was an enormous expansion in the use of public funds to purchase services delivered by private agencies.... [A] study in the trend in government payments to Jewish-sponsored agencies reveals a twenty-fold increase in these payments from $27 million to $561 million.... [I]n the brief span of one decade government payments as a proportion of the total income received by Jewish-sponsored agencies rose from 11% to 51% (Gilbert, 1983: 7).

The significance of this system of private, nonprofit agencies, in part governmentally funded, is twofold. It prevents uniformity on a nationwide (or in many cases, citywide or sattewide) basis, and it also provides a means of disengagement for an administration that wishes to reduce the government's role in providing social services.

Since the voluntary agencies exist, government can say that there are agencies to take care of the homeless or hungry. Indeed these agencies, which had gotten somewhat sluggish under government funding, do in fact remain vigorous, with their boards of directors, their supporters, their fund-raising mechanisms. Even while complaining, they are ready to expand the scope of their fund raising and services in response to the pressures created by government cutbacks.

The Republican administration is roundly charged with cynically making use of the voluntary sector to justify its own reductions in funding and withdrawal from public services. But just as in the case of federalism, it would be a serious mistake to see the Reagan administration's glorification of the voluntary sector as simply a conservative means of saving money. Efforts at uniform national social services have again and again come into conflict with the reality of ethnic, racial, and local diversity. Efforts have been more successful when they tried to accommodate this diversity—as in the case of the popular preschool Headstart programs, run by local neighborhood and church groups, very often black—than when they tried to ride roughshod over them as in the case of the effort to create a national system of child care in the early 1970s. Liberals and radicals, as well as conservative ethnics and Catholics, try to protect these local services from the imposition of standards by a central money provider that may conflict with local tastes and values (Glazer, 1983a).

The most thorough analysis of the impact of the Reagan administration on the voluntary sector comes to negative conclusions. Lester Salamon argues that federal cutbacks to these agencies seriously harmed them, while the concurrent tax cuts reduce the incentive of private givers to contribute to nonprofit, tax-exempt organizations. Nevertheless, there has been an increase in income of the average agency from corporations, foundations, religious funders, direct individual giving, and, most substantially, from imposition of fees and charges. A report on giving for 1983 showed an 8.3 percent increase in giving over 1982 to 300,000 nonprofit organizaitons of many different kinds. While the reduction in tax incentives led to a reduction in large gifts (the average gift of millionaires was 32 percent less), this seems to have been made up by the fact that there were more millionaires (Salamon, 1982; *New York Times,* May 2, 1984).

The voluntary nonprofit sector does play a substantial role in American social services. It very often argues against national and uniform services, and its existence serves as an argument against public expansion of these services.

Race

The United States is not unique in having a division between the major national insurance programs (Social Security, unemployment insurance, Medicare) and the residual programs based on need (AFDC, Food Stamps, Medicaid). But the United States is unique in possessing so large a population of working age that is supported, along with their children, by residual programs, because it is not eligible for assistance by insurance programs. This population, stabilized at about 11 million since restrictions imposed on its growth by the states in the early 1970s, is about one-half black, and such groups as Puerto Ricans are also disproportionately represented.

While any system of social policy has difficult cases, in the United States the difficult cases form a mass cutoff from the insurance programs in which benefits are provided as of right. Although noncontributory "welfare" is also a right, as courts have clearly ruled, it is a right that to the great mass of Americans is charity. The effort to surround it with the same sense of legitimacy, the same dignity, as Social Security or unemployment insurance or Medicare fails. The question that inevitably comes up is whether it fails because it is in large measure a program for blacks and some other minorities. The issue is not racial discrimination in administration of programs. National programs do not permit discrimination; state programs, such as welfare, also do not discriminate, and under the generally sharp supervision of the federal government arising from its substantial contribution, states that tried to treat blacks differently were disciplined. Discrimination is a matter of the past. But the fact is that there are two different systems, and one operates in large measure as a system for blacks and some other depressed minorities.

The great hope of American social policy reforms from the early 1960s to the late 1970s was in some way to reduce the large group of families dependent on welfare, and to incorporate them into a national system under uniform rules and uniform treatment. The initial approach to a problem already troubling in the early Kennedy years was to provide more assistance to states to undertake intensive social work programs with people on welfare. This was rapidly superseded by the poverty program and subsequent programs in which various approaches were taken to welfare: increasing the numbers on welfare through community action, under the claim that it was a right (which on the whole was enforced in the courts, in cases making access to welfare easier, removal harder, and treatment better); trying to make the welfare mother and the fathers of her children economically productive; or—quite another matter—trying to track down absconding fathers and make them economically responsible for their children.

The most amibitious effort to "reform" welfare, by incorporating it into a national system in which its demeaning and isolating features would be reduced, were the plans proposed by President Nixon (the Family Assistance Plan) and by President Carter (the Program for Better Jobs and Income), which were variants of the negative income tax that had once been proposed by Milton Freidman. The notion of the negative income tax was that just as those who earned income paid taxes *to* government, so those who did not earn sufficient income would receive benefits *from* government. Both the Nixon and the Carter proposals failed (Glazer, 1984b), and both efforts to create a larger degree of national uniformity failed because of the role of race.

Race came into play in a number of respects. First, the proposed reform, by reducing state control of welfare in favor of a national system, would have had a strong impact on wage rates in the South, where wage rates are lower, particularly for blacks. One reason wage rates are low is that welfare benefits in southern states are so skimpy. One reason they are so skimpy is that they go largely to blacks. Thus, the women with children who can withdraw from the labor market in the North do not find it easy to do so in the South. Domestic labor and other forms of labor are still comparatively cheap and plentiful. This was always a problem in getting southern members of Congress to accept a national system.

Second was the fear, perhaps stronger in the North than in the South, that the reduction in the stigma of welfare by incorporating it into a national system would not reduce the behavior that makes welfare necessary (i.e., withdrawal from the labor force, male irresponsibility toward their children, creation of broken families, and the increase in illegitimacy) but would simply make it more acceptable. This seemed to be the finding of the "income maintenance" experiments designed to test the effects of a reformed welfare system involving something close to a negative income tax (Glazer, 1984b). The racial angle is that these behaviors—withdrawal from the labor force, female-headed families, illegitimacy—are far more marked among the black population. If a national and uniform system would only accentuate these effects, as the experiments showed, there seemed to be no reason left for the reform.

National systems, treating everyone alike, based on insurance and dignity, do not work in the United States as they do in Europe—or would in Japan—because America has large differences, related to race and ethnicity, in how people behave. Discrimination is not major today: laws against discrimination, and a prevalent public opinnon that accepts fairness of treatment, prevent significant discriminatory behavior. Nevertheless, the group differences in behavior exist, presumably because of the enormous impact of a heritage of severe discrimination. Group differences are barriers to universalism. In one respect the United States bears comparison to developing countries, where the protection of labor tends to involve only a small elite of government workers and workers in large firms, whereas the great mass of the population, without access to regular jobs, is outside the system of social policy. In the United States the numbers are reversed. About 85 percent of the population has protection through insurance against unemployment, old age, disability and illness, and only a small minority is dependent on public charity, but the two categories exist. Undoubtedly, one reason they exist is that our largest minority was held as slaves, and held down by discrimination for a hundred years after emancipation.

When there are large differences in a population, differences of race and ethnicity related to differences of income, productivity, culture, and values, the introduction of a national, uniform system is difficult. Differential behavior leads to greatly disproportionate claims on the system; indeed the system may well encourage differential behavior, because it may offer more than available work does to the less qualified.

It is easier to create a nationally uniform system where there is an expectation that behavior throughout the society will be similar, values will be similar, responses will be similar. Once such a uniform system is in place, it will not be abandoned if strains are introduced into it by differential behavior related to differences of race and ethnicity. Thus, European countries now accommodate large numbers of foreign workers and their families, who may make larger claims on the system of social provision than natives. But a commitment once having been made to the uniform system, it will not change. When a nation is ethnically homogeneous, it is easier to see social benefits as designed for "us"—all of us— rather than for "them," a minority.

Individualism

Yet it may not be the sheer objective fact of ethnic and racial diversity that determines whether people see social benefits as designed for all, and therefore desirable, or designed for others, and therefore to be restricted. There may be another factor that the word individualism suggests. There are substantial differences among nations in the degree to which they *desire* egalitarianism, or blame the poor for their troubles (Table 2.2). Why (see column 5) do so many more of the British attribute the causes of poverty to "laziness and lack of willpower" of the poor? Why do so many fewer (column 4) feel it is important to reduce inequalities? Rudolf Klein describes Britain as "a relatively inegalitarian society, with little support for egalitarian policies—and unique in that the British people tend to blame the poor for their own poverty. . . ." That sounds like the United States. His tentative explanation is that "support for 'altruistic' policies is a function of economic prosperity. . . ." (Klein, 1981: 169– 170).

I suspect that comparable public opinion evidence would show the United States is in the same position, but it could not be explained by lack of economic prosperity. Is there an element of Anglo-American "individualism" here? This term is unsettlingly vague, and yet I think it can be argued that Americans are more likely to expect to make it on their own, and are scornful of those who do not. It is, after all, a society of free immigrants and their descendants (except for Indians and blacks), who came expecting to work hard and get ahead—and until recently expected no or very little assistance from government in doing so. It is a country of markedly greater and easier mobility than other comparably highly developed states. One might think that home ownership, characterizing a majority of Americans, might anchor people to geographical locations as housing subsidies do in Britain, but this does not seem to be the case. In the United States it is easier to open a business and to close it when it fails, or easier to sell a house, and more common to move in search of jobs. One of the chief and most successful charges of Reagan against the federal government was that it regulated business too much, and he has made a determined effort to reduce regulation. As in the case of so many Reagan proposals, one can see this as simply class interest; businesspeople do vote Republican. But there are not enough businesspeople in the electorate to make it so attractive as all that. Rather, Americans generally appear to be hostile to the idea of regulation, even when regulation is designed to reduce monopoly profits or protect consumers and workers.

Table 2.2. Relation of Appreciative Systems of Different Populations to Social and Economic Conditions[a]

	Average annual growth in private consumption expenditure[1] (%) 1965–76	Gini-coefficient of incomes inequality[2]	Incomes maintenance expenditure[3] (% GDP)	"Egalitarians"[4] (% of population)	Blaming the poor[5] (% of population)	View society as "unfair"[6] (% of population)	Below poverty line[7] (% of population)	"Postmaterialists"[8] (% in population)
Germany	3.3	0.386 (7.1)	12.4	30	23	10	3	9
France	4.0	0.417 (10.9)	12.4	49	16	26	16	10
Netherlands	3.6	0.264 (6.6)	14.1	36	12	13	n.a.	15
United Kingdom	1.6	0.327 (6.1)	7.7	18	43	17	7.5	5

Source: From Rudolf Klein (1981: 170).

[a]Numbers 1–8 refer to sources of data for each column:

1. OECD, *National Accounts*, 1976. The figures refer to per capita private final consumption expenditure.
2. Table 11, M. Sawyer, "Income Distribution in OECD Countries." *OECD Economic Outlook*, Paris, July 1976. The figures refer to posttax incomes, adjusted for family size. (The figures in brackets refer to the ratio of the unadjusted posttax income of the top 20 percent to that of the bottom 20 percent of the income distribution.)
3. Table 1, *Public Expenditure on Income Maintenance Programmes*, OECD, July 1976. The figures refer to the early 1970s. GDP, Grass domestic product.
4. Appendix Table 1, *Euro-Barometre* No. 5, July 1976. The figures refer to the proportion of people who consider it "very important to try to reduce the number of both very rich and very poor people."
5. Table 29, *The Perception of Poverty in Europe*, Commission of the European Community, 1977. The figures refer to the proportion of people who attribute the causes of poverty to the "laziness and lack of willpower" of the poor.
6. Table 18, *Ibid.*
7. Table 29, *Public Expenditure on Income Maintenance Programmes*, op. cit. n.a., Not available.
8. Table 9, *Euro-Barometre* No. 7, July 1977.

American blue-collar workers are considered among the most conservative in the world. They own their own homes, go hunting or fishing on their vacations, have small hunting camps in the woods—at least that is, the image. Those who know the unionized workers of the great mass production industries of the heartland of the United States, now in decline, insist it is so. Blue-collar workers are likely to be suspicious of a socially enlightened leadership pressing for extensions of social benefits, because they are also homeowners and taxpayers and make a close calculation of whether it will result in a net benefit or cost. They are likely to vote Republican in disconcertingly high percentages, albeit this conservatism may be due to Catholicism and European peasant background, rather than to "individualism."

Americans will take government benefits as much as the next person does. But they like to see government benefits assisting their own hard efforts, rather than simply maintaining others in failure. So they see Social Security and other popular programs as "insurance," which is only true in part, and deductions for home mortgage payments and local taxes as assisting the individualistic, upwardly mobile homeowner.

There is no operational test for individualism: I speak of a mood, a feeling, a tendency, which many observers suggest characterize the United States, and there are enough facts to support the possibility that it is really so. I believe individualism plays a role in making the ideal of a uniform and universal welfare state less attractive in the United States than it is in many other countries.

Voluntarism and Profit-Making Agencies in Social Policy

It would be normal for voluntary agencies to resist public agencies taking over their roles. On the whole, public agencies also are happy not to have to undertake what are often delicate tasks affecting religious and racial and ethnic sensitivities (e.g., foster care for children and child adoption), preferring simply to provide money so the voluntary agencies carry on.

The United States, like other capitalist countries, has major enterprises that make profits from doing the kind of thing government does, for example, insurance companies selling pensions and insuring life, and against ill health. The private sector has always been a major obstacle to national, uniform social policies, because it saw these as competition. Can one say that American insurance companies were more potent in their resistance to health insurance than those in other countries? Very likely: simply because political movements started later, and American insurance companies were already on the scene ready to fight national programs, and perhaps they were more aggressive and expansive.

In almost every area the American social system seems to throw up more resistance from profit-making enterprise than other countries do. It may perhaps be explained by the fact that government was always more sharply limited here (no supreme executive, no supreme parliament, and

only recently a supreme judiciary), surrounded by suspicion, such that
our greatest work of political philosophy, *The Federalist,* had to be
penned as a cautious defense of central government. The private sector,
voluntary or profit-making, always has had more prestige in the United
States. Whether or not it has prestige, it certainly has strength, and plays
a much larger role in social policy than in any other country. Examples
are rife:

> Proprietary [that is, profit-making] agencies are prominently represented in
> many social service programs including homemaker/chore, day care, transpor-
> tation, meals-on-wheels, and employment training. The most conspicuous area
> is that of nursing home care. Between 1960 and 1970 the number of nursing
> home facilities increased by 140% and the number of beds trebled. Close to 80%
> of these facilities are operated for profit; public funds, mainly from the Medi-
> caid Act of 1965, account for $2 out of every $3 in nursing home revenue. This
> area of service is typically referred to as the nursing home 'industry;' the child-
> care 'industry' looms just over the horizon. . . .
>
> *Tender Loving Greed,* the title of a study of abuses in the nursing home
> industry, is an evocative expression of the antipathy toward having the func-
> tions of family care assumed by agencies committed to economic gain. How-
> ever, it must be said that this study found the quality of care at nonprofit homes
> was not necessarily better than that offered by proprietary homes (Gilbert,
> 1983; 10–11).

Recently, we have had an astonishing rise in the number of proprietary
(i.e., for profit) hospitals, which many look upon as a means of relief from
the rapidly growing costs of health care. Paul Starr concludes his fasci-
nating account of the distinctive structure of American medicine with the
prediction that this sector, which organizes chains of hospitals just as the
child care industry does, will become dominant in American medicine,
and that the powerful, independent American physicians, who have
made the principle of the exchange of medical services for fees their Ten
Commandments, will be increasingly forced to submit to the control of
medical corporations. The most surprising branches of social policy, it
turns out, can be made to turn a profit, as when major corporations
entered the field of training poorly educated and unskilled youth for jobs
under the poverty program. Even profit-making jails have developed. Of
course, the income for all these forms of profit making in the fields of
custody of prisoners, health, nursing care, child care, work training,
comes almost entirely from government.

Why then does not government do the work itself? In the United
States, we seem to be convinced that when government does it, it
becomes more expensive and less effective. Even Richard Titmuss's
impressive attack on commercialism in American blood services has
stimulated a counterattack in the United States (Titmuss, 1971; Sapolsky
and Finkelstein, 1977). Profitmaking may have a bad name in much of
the world and may be surrounded with restrictions. Despite the strong

suspicion against big business in the United States, it still retains a surprisingly strong hold and is expected to provide solutions to a host of problems that in other countries government undertakes directly.

American social policy is different. Other countries struggle with inexorable increases in pensions for the aged and in medical costs; the United States does, too. But in other areas of social welfare, the United States is far more dependent on a great variety of private, voluntary, ethnically and religiously sponsored, nonprofit and profit agencies to maintain the public welfare—even if in a somewhat private and individualistic way. Nonpublic resources in American welfare are greater than is found in any other major nation. American health, welfare, and education statistics regularly indicate the role that private expenditures play in social policy, and it is considerable. Thus in 1982, private expenditures for health exceeded public ($186, to $137 billion). In elementary and secondary education, $14.5 billion of a total $124 billion was private, and in higher education, $40 billion of $77 billion was nongovernmental. In 1978 even in income maintenance there was a private total of $31 billion against a public expenditure of $178 billion (*Statistical Abstract, 1981:* 319, 1984:109,138).

The present mood of the United States, one that will likely last through the 1980s, does not favor a fully developed national system of social policy; that mood seems to be based on more than economic exigency. It reflects rather a considered judgment by many Americans that, despite the cost in social disorder that prevails in their society, they prefer it that way.

REFERENCES

Gilbert, Neil, *Capitalism and the Welfare State: Dilemmas of Social Benevolence.* New Haven, Conn.: Yale University Press, 1983.

Gilder, Geroge, *Visible Man.* New York: Basic Books, 1978.

Gilder, George, *Wealth and Poverty.* New York: Basic Books, 1981.

Glazer, "Towards a Self-Service Society?" *The Public Interest,* Winter, No. 70, pp. 66–91, 1983a.

Glazer, Nathan, "Why Isn't There More Equality?" *This World,* Fall, No. 6, pp. 5–16, 1983b.

Glazer, Nathan, "The Social Policy of the Reagan Administration: A Review." *The Public Interest,* Spring, No. 75, pp. 76–98, 1984a. Also, "The Social Policy of the Reagan Administration," in *The Social Contract Revisited* (D. Lee Bawden, ed.). Washington, D.C.: Urban Institute Press, pp. 221–240, 1984.

Glazer, Nathan, "Reforming the American Welfare Family: 1969–1981." *The Tocqueville Review,* Spring–Summer, 6(1):149–168, 1984b.

Harrington, Michael, *The New American Poverty.* New York: Holt, Rinehart & Winston, 1984.

Ikenberry, John and Skocpol, Theda, "From Patronage Democracy to Social Security: The Shaping of Public Social Provision in the United States," in *Stagnation and Renewal* (Gösta Esping-Andersen, Lee Rainwater, and Martin Rein, eds.). Armonk, N.Y.: M. E. Sharpe, forthcoming.

Klein, Rudolf, "Values, Power and Policies," in *The Welfare State in Crisis.* Paris: Organisation for Economic Co-operation and Development, 1981.

Morris, Charles R., *A Time of Passion: America, 1960–1980.* New York: Harper & Row, 1984.

Murray, Charles, *Losing Ground: American Social Policy, 1950–1981.* New York: Basic Books, 1984.

Nathan, Richard, "Retrenchment Comes to Washington." *Society* 20(2), 1983.

Nathan, Richard P. and Doolittle, Fred C., *Overview: Effects of the Reagan Domestic Program on States and Localities.* Princeton, N.J.: Urban and Regional Research Center, The Woodrow Wilson School, Princeton University, June 7, 1984, manuscript.

New York Times, May 2, 1984, "'83 Charity Gifts Put at a Peak $65 Billion."

Palmer, John L. and Sawhill, Isabel V., eds., *The Reagan Experiment.* Washington, D.C.: Urban Institute Press, 1982.

Palmer, John L and Sawhill, Isabel V., eds., *The Reagan Record.* Cambridge: Ballinger Publishing Co., 1984.

Petersen, George E., "Federalism and the States: An Experiment in Decentralization," in *The Reagan Record* (J. L. Palmer and I. V. Sawhill, eds.). Cambridge: Ballinger Publishing Co., 1984.

Rodgers, Harrell R., Jr., *The Cost of Human Neglect: America's Welfare Failure.* Armonk, N. Y.: M. E. Sharpe, 1982.

Salamon, Lester M., "Nonprofit Organizations: The Lost Opportunity," in *The Reagan Experiment* (J. L. Palmer and I. V. Sawhill, eds.). Washington, D.C.: Urban Institute Press, 1982. pp. 261–285.

Sapolsky, Harvey M. and Finkelstein, Stan N., "Blood Policy Revisited—A New Look at 'The Gift Relationship'." *The Public Interest,* Winter, No. 46, pp. 15–27, 1977.

Schwartz, John E., *America's Hideen Success: A Reassessment of Twenty Years of Public Policy.* New York: W. W. Norton, 1983.

Skocpol, Theda and Ikenberry, John, "The Political Formation of the American Welfare States in Historical and Comparative Perspective." *Comparative Social Research* 6, 1983.

Starr, Paul, *The Social Transformation of American Medicine.* New York: Basic Books, 1982.

Statistical Abstract of the United States, 1981. Washington, D. C.: U. S. Department of Commerce, Bureau of the Census.

Statistical Abstract of the United States, 1984. Washington, D.C.: U.S. Department of Commerce, Bureau of the Census.

Steiner, Gilbert, *Social Insecurity.* Chicago: Rand McNally, 1966.

Titmuss, Richard, *The Gift Relationship: From Human Blood to Social Policy.* New York: Pantheon, 1971.

Wilensky, Harold, "Taxing, Spending, and Backlash: An American Peculiarity?" *Taxing and Spending,* July, pp. 6–11, 1979.

3

The Development
of the Welfare Mix in Japan

NAOMI MARUO

During the 1950s and 1960s Japan's economy grew in real terms at an annual rate of about 10 percent, and Japan joined the ranks of the advanced industrial nations in terms of per capita gross national product (GNP). Nevertheless, social security, working conditions, and living standards remained at a relatively low level. In the 1970s, these and other areas of social welfare made tremendous progress. For example, government spending on social security as a proportion of national income nearly trebled from the 1960s to 1982.

The Japanese standard of living has continued to improve remarkably from the mid-1960s to the 1980s. Indicators of per capita income, safety, health, and education show that Japan is now one of the world's most advanced nations. The average life expectancy of the Japanese is among the highest in the world, while Japan's infant mortality rate is, along with Sweden's, the lowest in the world. In Japan, too, the incidence of murder and other violent crimes and robbery, and most likely the on-the-job accident mortality rate as well, are the lowest of any nation for which such statistics are available. The percentage of students enrolled in institutions of higher learning is the second highest in the world after the United States.

Moreover, although the growth rate has slowed, the Japanese economy is still growing at an average annual rate of around 4 percent, about twice the rate of other OECD nations. The unemployment rate is only just over 2.5 percent, and the annual rate of increase in consumer prices was around 2 percent from 1982.

It would seem that Japan's future is bright, whether measured in terms of its economy or of the welfare of its people. The Japanese economy, however, must clear several hurdles if it is to keep on growing. The first is the question of energy and resources, which hardly needs elaboration. Japan's economy relies on petroleum for over 60 percent of its energy consumption, and relies on imports for 99.8 percent of the petroleum it needs. It is therefore built on a very vulnerable foundation.

The second challenge is the rapid ageing of the population. Japan's population as a whole is ageing at a rate faster that that of any Western country, as the result of a sharp decline in the birth rate coupled with an increasingly long life expectancy.

Third, Japan's economic growth and competitive strength in international markets owe a great deal to the nation's stable and highly integrated labor–management relations. The characteristically Japanese labor–management system may, however, eventually fall apart, paving the way for the onset of the so-called British disease, and a slowing down in economic growth.

In addition, there are certain fields where Japan is still obviously behind as a highly industrialized nation. The relatively low standard of housing, very limited public park space in large cities, an inadequate sewerage system, and long working hours are important examples.

Whether the Japanese economy can maintain steady growth in the years to come and thus sustain a society with a high material standard of living and of social welfare will depend, then, on whether or not the nation can successfully clear these hurdles.

THE UNIQUE DEVELOPMENT OF JAPAN

Just as the industrialization of Japan began later than in European countries, so did its development of social policy. It was not until the Meiji Restoration that social policy was introduced at a national level, although there had already been several local authorities with their own social policy.

The first social policy introduced by the central government was the Poor Salvation Act in 1874, six years after the Meiji Restoration; it authorized social policies of local authorities. The most important actions since then are listed in Table 3.1. Virtually no welfare legislation was enacted before World War I, and very little between the wars. Contemporary Japanese welfare state programs principally reflect legislation since 1946. Thus, the welfare state came later to Japan than to Europe.

The development toward a welfare state in Japan may be divided into three stages. In the first stage the character and main motives of social policy were similar to those of the nineteenth-century laws in Europe. One of the dominant social policy theories in Japan insisted that the main motive of enacting social policy in a capitalist society was the requirement of the capitalist class as a whole to maintain and reproduce a sufficient quantity and quality of labor force. In the case of the health insurance and national pension schemes for the working class just before and during World War II, it was similarly alleged that the main motive of enactment was to maintain and to reproduce the health and physical strength of a military force.

Table 3.1. An Outline History of the Development of Social Security and Social Services in Japan

Year	Event
1874	Poor Salvation Act
1921	First health insurance for employees enacted, coming into force in 1925
1929	Poor Protection Act, coming into force in 1932; care of poor people became obligation of local authorities
1938	Ministry of Health and Welfare established
	Health insurance for self-employed enacted; pensions for aged, disabled, and surviving families introduced
1944	Employees' Pension (Kosei Nenkin) Insurance enacted
1946	National Assistance Law enacted
	Juvenile Welfare Act
1947	New constitution established; peoples' right to enjoy health and decent minimum life specified in constitution
	Unemployment insurance enacted for the first time in Japan
	Industrial Injury Insurance for employees enacted
1948	Welfare of the Handicapped Law enacted
	Council for Social Security established
1951	Social Welfare Services Law enacted
1952	Law for the Sick and War Wounded enacted
1953	Health Insurance for Day Laborers enacted
1954	Employees' Pension Insurance (Kosei Nenkin) Act reformed
1958	New Health Insurance Act approved, covering all Japanese
1959	Employees' Pension Insurance reformed
1961	Social Welfare Pension (Fukushi Nenkin) for those not covered by Employees' Pension Insurance introduced, so that all Japanese covered in principle by one or another of the public pension systems; Social Welfare Act for the Aged enacted
1969	Medical care of aged people, 65 years old and over, made free of charge in Tokyo
1971	Child Allowance Law enacted
1973	National Health Insurance reformed; medical care became free nationwide for all aged 70 years and over, except the affluent
1975	Unemployment Allowance Act developed into Employment Insurance Act
1983	Health insurance for the aged introduced: small patient charge reintroduced
1984	Employees' National Health Insurance reformed; patients must pay 10% of medical cost within an upper limit of Y35,000 per month

The second stage of progress toward a welfare state in Japan began after World War II. According to the democratization policy of the U.S. occupation forces, landowners who were not themselves directly engaged in agriculture were forced to relinquish their farms, except for only 1 hectare, to tenant farmers. Fields and forests were not redistributed. Traditional class distinctions were nearly completely abolished. Large monopolistic companies and shareholding companies *(Zaibatsu)* such as Mitsui, Mitsubishi, and Sumitomo were divided into many independent companies and financial institutions. A severe antimonopoly law was enacted at the same time. Trade unions were organized, and various kinds of joint consultation systems between employers and employees were then set up in most of the large private companies.

The introduction of social policy reforms was also promoted in this new democratic atmosphere. The unique features of the welfare state and industrial relations in Japan may thus be explained by this unprecedented postwar experience, when democratic and egalitarian reforms were suddenly introduced into a semimodernized country where paternalistic features still remained strong in families, firms, and local communities. The dualistic character of the welfare state and industrial relations in Japan stems from this unique experience. The Meiji Restoration in 1868, too, was a sudden implantation of European systems into a semifeudalistic society; the dualistic character of modern Japan may therefore be traced back to the Meiji Restoration.

It is true that some paternalistic or community-oriented practices have survived in Japanese families, companies, and social life. Yet Japan is also more egalitarian in certain respects than most European countries, and, generally speaking, class distinctions and class consciousness are less obvious than in Europe. More than 80 percent of the Japanese people think that they belong to the middle class. In companies, white-collar and blue-collar workers usually belong to the same union. There is less distinction between white-collar and manual workers, and between employer and employees. According to an inquiry conducted by the Employers' Federation of Japan, about 16 percent of the members of boards of directors of large companies are former trade union leaders.

There are contrasting views about the Japanese society: some emphasize that it is still a half-modernized paternalistic country, while others stress that it is an egalitarian society.

The reason there are such contrasting views about the character of the welfare state and industrial relations in Japan may be explained by the dual character of Japanese society. Figure 3.1 shows differences in patterns of social change between European countries and Japan. The characteristic form of all societies, prior to modernization, was that of an undemocratic semifeudalistic community *(Gemeinschaft)*. European societies have tended to alter both these primary characteristics, changing from a Gemeinschaft community to a highly voluntaristic society based on free association *(Gesellschaft)*, while concurrently establishing a democratic political system. The result in a country such as Sweden can be characterized as a democratic and highly rationalized society. By contrast, Japan has undergone democratization, but it still maintains many

Figure 3.1. Alternative patterns of social development in Europe and Japan.

	Undemocratic	Democratic
Community *(Gemeinschaft)*	**I** Semifeudalistic society	**III** Democratic society with strong community (Japan)
Association *(Gesellschaft)*	**II** Rational autocracy	**IV** Democratic and highly rationalized society (Sweden)

of the characteristics of a traditional Gemeinschaft society, for social relations have not yet been so rationalized.

The third stage in the progression toward a welfare state in Japan began in 1973, which was named *Fukushi Gannen* (the first year of the welfare age). Expenditure on social security expanded remarkably under the new cabinet headed by Prime Minister Tanaka. The claims of social security expenditure upon national income increased sharply. Part of the increase can be explained by the sudden decline of the rate of economic growth in real terms as a result of the first oil crisis. But political factors have also played an important role.

Japan's social security system is complex and not easily understood by Japanese or by foreigners. However, we can conclude that both pension and health insurance in Japan are comprehensive, in the sense that all Japanese people are covered. That coverage is unequal, though, because of the dualistic structure of the public and private sectors, and the separation of big business, small business, and the self-employed.

JAPAN'S DISTINCTIVE WELFARE MIX

The provision of welfare in modern Japanese society, drawing upon non-state as well as state resources, remains distinctive by comparison with European countries in such fields as family care, education, and labor–management relations.

In Japan, much care for the elderly is still concentrated within the family, because about two-thirds of elderly people live within an extended family of two or three generations (Table 3.2). An official survey found that most elderly couples were living with a son or daughter, as well as their spouse, and only 5.7 percent of the elderly were living alone.

Table 3.2. Aged People Living with Family, East and West

Family member lived with[a]	Country (%)				
	Japan	Thailand	United States	Britain	France
Wife or husband	65.4	51.1	47.0	49.1	55.8
Married son	41.0	25.3	0.9	0.5	3.5
Married daughter	9.2	37.8	2.5	1.9	5.6
Son's or daughter's spouse	34.0	49.2	1.6	0.7	3.5
Unmarried son or daughter	18.7	33.0	9.0	5.1	10.6
Grandchild	41.0	62.6	3.8	1.1	5.8
No person	5.7	4.7	41.3	41.6	30.0

Source: Prime Minister's Office (1981).

[a]Since more than one answer is possible, columns total more than 100 percent. Aged person is anyone 60 years or older.

Although this pattern is common in other Asian countries, such as Thailand, it is normally thought to characterize a premodern society. Industrialization and its concomitants are expected to encourage the growth of a single-generation nuclear family; in Japan this is not so.

More than 40 percent of older people in the United States and Britain live alone; in France, where rural peasant values still linger, the proportion is 30 percent. These figures are five to seven times higher than in Japan (Table 3.2). Fewer than one of thirty-three older Americans or Britons live with a son or daughter, compared to more than half in Japan. In terms of material possessions a Japanese home may be modern, but the pattern of family life, with two or three generations living together, is not modern as that term is understood in Europe or America.

The elderly live with their adult children because they want to, and their children accept it. The practice does not reflect poverty, but distinctive values. In Japan, 55 percent of the elderly want to live with their family, and in Korea the figure is similar. By contrast, in the United States 94 percent do *not* express a wish to live with their family, and in Britain and Canada that proportion is also above 90 percent (Table 3.3). In Europe, the proportion wanting to live with their family in old age is very low too by comparison with Japan.

Home help and allied personal social services for the aged are also quite distinctive in Japan. An investigation conducted by the Social and Economic Congress of Japan[1] shows large differences in the home help services of local communities in Japan as compared to Britain and Sweden, albeit the number of local commmunities investigated is limited (Table 3.4).

In Japan, as in Britain and Sweden, substantial reliance is placed upon part-time home helpers, who almost equal full-time staff in number. The difference arises in the much greater proportion of home helpers in relation to the elderly population in Sweden and Britain. In Malmö, Sweden, there is nearly 1 home helper for every 25 elderly persons; in London

Table 3.3. Aged People Wanting to Live with Their Family: Cross-Cultural Differences

Country	Desiring to live with family (%)
Korea	58
Japan	55
France	20
W. Germany	13
Britain	9
United States	6
Canada	5

Source: Ministry of Health and Welfare (1983).

Table 3.4. Differing Characteristics of Personal Social Services in Cities in Japan, Britain, and Sweden

Characteristic	Japan				Britain (London)		Sweden
	Musashino (Tokyo)	Machida (Tokyo)	Kamakura (Kanagawa)	Fujisawa (Kanagawa)	Richmond	Wandsworth	Malmö
Total population	132,663	299,084	173,392	308,314	163,000	219,700	233,803
Elderly people, 65 years and older (as % of population)	8.9	5.6	10.1	7.0	17.2	17.6	18.6
Family size (average)	2.43	3.17	3.07	3.10	2.45	2.47	2.03
Home helpers for aged people[a]	42	6	58	55	200	538	2,100
Part-time home helpers	35[b]	0	50[b]	45[b]	193	512	1,892
Home helpers (as % of elderly)	0.4	0.04	0.3	0.3	0.7	1.4	4.8
Recipients[c] of home help services (as % of elderly)	0.6	0.3	0.2	0.2	5.4	10.3	27.6
Home helpers per 10,000 population	3.16	0.20	3.34	1.78	12.26	24.48	89.81
Total costs home help services, 1980 ($\times$ Y1,000)	45,206	n.a.[e]	46,166	n.a.	281,070 (£624,600)	890,392 (£1,973,540)	6,255,000 (Kr.139,000,000)
Total costs per home helper ($\times$ Y1,000)	1,076	n.a.	810	n.a.	1,405[d]	1,655[d]	2,979[d]
Total cost per inhabitant (yen)	340	n.a.	266	n.a.	1,724	4,052	26,753
Average wage, full-time home helpers per month (yen)	228,600	155,800	182,439	n.a.	154,454	n.a.	247,320
Homes for aged people	1	5	4	4	22	17	15

Source: The statistical figures shown in the table are obtained by inquiry of the local government officials in charge of personal social services for elderly people.

[a]Home helpers employed by the local government.

[b]Semivoluntary home helpers.

[c]Aged people only.

[d]Pounds and kronor are converted at 1980 exchange rate.

[e]n.a., Not applicable.

boroughs studied, the figure was about 1 for every 100 elderly persons, and in the Japanese cities, about 1 for every 300 elderly persons. In consequence, more than one-quarter of Swedish elderly people appear to be receiving personal social services from their local government, and 1 in 10 to 1 in 20 in London. By contrast, in Japan, only one in several hundred elderly persons receives home help from a local authority, for the coverage of Japanese programs is very low. While Japanese local authorities pay a substantial wage to full-time social workers that they do employ, by comparison with European cities aggregate spending is far lower, because the number of personal social service workers employed in Japan is much lower (Table 3.4).

The absence of public provision of welfare services for the elderly Japanese does not mean that they receive no care. Traditional Japanese values lead most adult children to care for their elderly parents within the same household. The persistence of community values is also reflected in the institution of district welfare commissioners. The minister of health and welfare appoints about 160,000 commissioners to work on a voluntary basis to mobilize semivoluntary home helpers to provide a variety of personal social services for the elderly within their local community. The elderly in Japan now rely on the state for pensions and for most health care, but they still look to informal community and family arrangements for much personal care.

Japan is similar to the United States in the high proportion of young people who go to college after secondary school. The two countries both differ from the more selective European pattern of higher education. In Japan, 94 percent of those who finish junior high school continue to senior high school, and more than 35 percent of the population aged 19 or 20 is studying in some kind of college or university. This is a far higher proportion than in Europe, and approaches the American level.

The funding of education in Japan comes from both public and private sources. Education accounts for 10 percent of the central government budget and 23 percent of the local government budget. In addition to a small number of private shcools, there are many informal schools called *Gakushu Juku,* which provide supplementary tuition to help youths pass examinations for entry to better secondary schools and universities. Middle-class families particularly are anxious to pay extra to Juku in efforts to secure a better education for their children. Of university students, 76 percent are at private universities and colleges; a minority are in state universities. At work, companies are prepared to provide in-house vocational training for their labor force, and a pattern of lifetime employment in large firms encourages them to make long-term capital investments in the skills and knowledge of their work force.

The Japanese tend to see their system of labor–management relations as distinctive from that of Europe, in that it involves far more cooperation between managers and workers than in a conflict-oriented European model. A survey of opinion leaders conducted by the Social and Eco-

Table 3.5. Perceived Uniqueness of Japanese Labor–Management Relations

Parameter	Score (maximum score = 5.0)
1. Labor union within a company	4.78
2. Lifetime employment	4.53
3. Trade union consciousness of dependency on the company	4.39
4. Company–family consciousness	4.27
5. Harmony within a group	4.00
6. Active employee education within a company	3.98
7. Informal and daily communication between employers and labor union leaders	3.95
8. Employees' pride in their company	3.95
9. Nemawashi (implicit consensus before formal decision)	3.93
10. Strong desire for promotion	3.89

Source: Survey reported in Maruo (1977).

nomic Congress of Japan illustrates this. Of the five characteristics of labor–management relations rated above average, four emphasized the solidarity between the employee or his union and the company, and the fifth, lifetime employment, as an expression of the obligation that the sense of community places on the employer (Table 3.5).

Japanese think they most resemble other countries in a strong desire for promotion; hence this ranks last in the catalogue of distinguishing features of the industrial relations system. In Japan solidaristic values are also consistent with a desire for individual advancement.

When opinions are sought about the need to maintain or reform characteristics of industrial work, there is a sharp distinction between half a dozen attributes generally regarded as worth sustaining, and an equal number that ought to be reformed (Table 3.6). The integration of workers and management at the factory level is considered well worth keeping. A desire for advancement in skill and positon is valued more than lifetime employment.

Many of the work practices regarded as requiring reform are those that involve discrimination among employees, and thus conflict with solidaristic community values. The differences are of two types: those within the firm (e.g., between permanent and temporary employees, or more senior and less senior workers regardless of performance) and those between firms (e.g., between big employers, and small firms that often cannot offer so many benefits and opportunities for advancement).

THE PRESSURES FOR GROWTH IN THE STATE'S ROLE

Rapid growth of welfare expenditure in the postwar era is a common phenomenon in the highly industrialized countries, and Japan is no excep-

Table 3.6. Evaluation of Perceived Uniqueness of Japanese Labor–Management Relations

	Should be maintained (%)	Should be reformed (%)
1. Active workers' education in companies	90.1	7.0
2. Employees' strong desire for promotion	83.4	12.8
3. Workers' union organized at company level	78.4	20.0
4. Possibility of former union leaders to be promoted to top management	75.3	20.0
5. Workers' union composed of both white-collar and blue-collar workers	70.1	21.2
6. Lifetime employment	59.4	37.4
7. Company's practice of employing new school leavers only, in principle, and differential treatment for those who are employed later on	32.5	64.4
8. Differential treatment between permanent employees and temporary employees	20.6	76.2
9. Large differential in welfare benefits, facilities, etc.	11.4	85.0
10. Various differentials between employees of big business and those of small and medium enterprises	6.8	89.7
11. Seniority wage system: lack of generally recognized standard of wages by job and workers' ability to perform their jobs	6.0	91.3
12. Neglect of female workers' ability	2.5	94.9

Source: Survey reported in Maruo (1977).

tion. The share of social security expenditure as a percentage of national income increased from 4.9 percent in 1960 and 11.9 percent in 1978 to 14.5 percent in 1984, and as a share of the GNP from 3.5 percent to 11.6 percent. Since the growth rate of Japan's GNP and national income[2] in the same period was the highest of industrialized nations, the growth in the value of social security expenditure in Japan was therefore exceptionally high. Between 1960 and 1981, the national income of Japan increased more than fifteen times, so that by 1981 social security benefits in nominal terms were forty-two times the 1960 figure. Even after deflating by the consumer price index, the increase in social security expenditure is 970 percent in real terms in slightly more than two decades.

Political, economic, and social factors can each influence the level of social expenditure. For example, a new welfare law will commit the government to spend more money; this occurred with pensions in 1973. An increase in the proportion of elderly people in the population will increase the number of pensions that must be paid, and an increase in the national income will provide more money to spend for health care for the elderly. Multiple regression analysis is an appropriate method for testing which of a variety of influences are most important in determining the increase in social expenditure. Many regressions were tried to explain social expenditure's share of national income in the period of rapid growth from 1957 to 1981, and separate analyses were made for four different categories of social expenditure; personal social services, health insurance, state pensions, and social security in total (see Appendix to this chapter). The principal conclusions are outlined below.

1. *Total social security expenditure* is principally determined by the proportion of the total population accounted for by the aged. The increase in the proportion of elderly people in the population means that the government is committed to pay more pensions. Over the past quarter of a century the Japanese government has also made a commitment to pay higher pensions to elderly people, further increasing the weight of demographic pressure upon total social expenditure. The percentage of people unemployed is the only other noteworthy influence on social expenditure, but its weight is limited because unemployment is low in Japan.

2. *State pension benefits* were subjected to a separate regression analysis. It was evident that the proportion of the elderly in the population, while important, is not the only influence on pension expenditure. A political decision to increase pension expenditure in 1973, measured by a dummy variable, is also significant (see also Castles, 1982). An additional influence is the pressure of increasing numbers of new entrants to the labor force, making it harder for the elderly to continue working and thus making them claim a pension at an earlier age than has been customary in Japan.

3. *Health insurance costs* increase along with the increasing proportion of the elderly in the population; the cost of medical care for a person aged 65 or over is 3.4 times that of the population as a whole (Social and Economic Congress, 1983). In addition, an increase in the number of medical doctors available also increases health expenditure, as doctors' income is derived principally from public programs. Changes in the proportion of medical costs borne directly by patients decrease public spending on health, but not enough to offset the combined influence of factors pushing up health expenditure.

4. *Personal social services expenditures* involve a range of activities in which public employees meet the needs of elderly people, single-parent families, and other disadvantaged citizens. In Japan, the political decision in 1973 to increase personal social services is one major cause of increased spending. Other influences are the increased numbers of people who need help, principally the elderly and the unemployed.

Altogether, the regression analyses in the Appendix emphasize three points. The first is that some influences on welfare expenditure in Japan are common to all industrial societies. In every country with a state pension system, an increase in the proportion of the elderly will increase spending on pensions. Where there is a national health service, an increase in the number of elderly or of doctors will increase spending on health care. A second and related point is that these demographic pressures exert a predictable influence. The great increase in the elderly as a proportion of Japan's population means that spending on pensions, health insurance, personal social services, and total social security expenditure is likely to increase, all else being equal, because all are significantly determined by the proportion of the elderly in the population.

Third, the influence of political factors, also registered in the regression analyses, emphasizes that the future of welfare expenditure in Japan is not predetermined. In 1973 the government used its authority to increase entitlements to social benefits; in the 1980s, however, government is proposing to reduce entitlements in order to limit pressure for increased public expenditure at a time when the economy is growing more slowly. For example, the cost of health insurance would rise by almost one-third from 1982 to the year 2000 (from 6.2 percent to 8 percent of national income), on the basis of generous pre-oil crisis standards. Hence, the Nakasone government increased in 1984 the contribution that the individual must make in the employees health insurance system. Whereas previously an insured employee only had to pay the first Y800 (about $3) for an initial medical examination and Y400 per day during hospitalization, now a recipient of health care will have to pay 10 percent of the cost, up to a limit of Y51,000 (about $200) per month. This change will not only reduce the state's contribution to health expenditure; but also narrow the gap between the state insurance scheme for employees and that for the self-employed, in which the patient is expected to pay 30 percent of the medical cost up to the limit of Y51,000 a month.

The pressures for political action on pensions are even greater, because of the continuing increase in the proportion of people aged 65 or over in the population. In 1950, the elderly constituted 4.9 percent of the Japanese population, and in 1975, after pensions were expanded greatly, 7.9 percent. As of 1985, the elderly comprised 10 percent of the population. This was less than in Sweden or Britain, but the Ministry of Health and Welfare forecasts an increase to 11.6 percent in 1990, to 15.6 percent in the year 2000, and to 21.8 percent by the year 2020. The proportion of the elderly is increasing even faster in relation to the population of working age. Whereas any likely political choice will still involve a considerable increase in public spending on pensions in the next few decades, the alternative choice of doing nothing is—as Noguchi shows in Chapter 8— the most expensive of them all.

THE FUTURE PROSPECT FOR JAPAN: STILL WELFARE WITH A DIFFERENCE

The production of welfare in Japan is distinctive in two senses. The state's role in the political economy differs from that of most Western nations, and the society's contribution to total welfare production is more important. Both of these differences are likely to persist in the foreseeable future; thus Japan is a modern industrial society with a high level of welfare that is provided in a different way than in European countries.

At first sight, the role of the Japanese state in the national economy appears puzzling. On the one hand, it is often said by Western writers that in Japan the government interferes actively in business, and the relationship between government and business interests is closer than in Europe. On the other hand, quantitative indicators such as the share of the national product devoted to government expenditure or social security expenditure show that government is less important in Japan than in other highly industrialized countries.

These two aspects of the role of government seem contradictory initially, but if we classify the type of government intervention from two points of view—public expenditure and administrative control—then the paradox is resolved. In the European version of the mixed-economy welfare state, government is expected to be frequently and directly involved in the regulation of the economy through planning and wage–price mechanisms, as well as levying a large portion of the GNP in taxes to finance welfare state expenditure. The opposite of this—a system in which the government is not involved in the economy and keeps taxes low in absolute terms—does not exist among industrial societies today. Japan is distinct because it levies a relatively low (though growing) portion of the national product in taxation, but it is relatively high in the degree of influence of government on the economy through controls and regulations. It thus differs from both the pure welfare state model, as advocated by European social democrats, and the pure market model, as advocated by Anglo-American economic liberals.

Because of the differences in the Japanese system, Japan has been less concerned with the problems typically faced by welfare states in contemporary industrial societies (cf. Rose and Peters, 1978). The typical European welfare state has a substantially higher level of taxation, and its spending commitment for welfare services is also much higher than in Japan. Thus, it needs a richer economy to fund high public expenditure, and the growth of public expenditure requires a high growth rate. European economies have had slower growth rates than Japan, but they have a greater fiscal need for growth.

Japan has not been seriously afflicted by these difficulties to date because, first, unlike the great majority of industrial societies, Japan's public sector is smaller than that of any industrial European society, as well as the United States. Moreover, the market continues to play a major role as a producer of welfare, funding pensions and retirement benefits through corporate employers, health care through partial payment by patients, and education through a large private university system and schools providing additional tuition for younger pupils.

Second, families in Japan produce more welfare than families in European countries or the United States. This observation is especially significant because in Japan, as in most societies, an increase in the proportion of elderly in the population will bring about the most critical welfare needs in the foreseeable future. In Japan more care is given to the elderly within the home than in Europe. Private savings and savings through company pensions are relatively high, and the market also supplements the state.

Furthermore, the strain of communal solidarity or paternalistic regard for the welfare of others remains strong in Japanese society, within the household, in communities, and in the work place. For this reason, Japanese society has suffered less from social anomie than most industrialized countries, as reflected in Japan's low crime and divorce rates. An incidental consequence of this is the relative absence of demand for public action that arises in societies where social disorganization leads to the creation of an underclass of multiply deprived people.

Third, the redistribution policies of the military occupation government immediately after World War II and the very rapid rates of subsequent growth have greatly broadened the distribution of wealth within Japanese society. An increasingly affluent society—and a continuation of Japan's relatively high growth rate for the next decade would, by a process of compounding, make it wealthier than most industrial societies—gives more and more families the income to make provision for their needs in the market, by hard work and savings. In turn, this reinforces an already strong Japanese work and savings ethic.

Finally, the continuing predominance of the Liberal Democratic party (LDP) government means that there is a party in office that has the power to take major decisions, once agreement is reached within its complex processes of consultation. Just as the expansion of the welfare state in the early 1970s (as shown by regression equations) reflected a new group norm for greater public action, so in the 1980s the LDP is able to establish a new group norm in favor of putting the brakes on public expenditure. The Nakasone government in 1983 and 1984 showed that it *is* possible to make marginal changes in entitlements to health benefits, and it is promoting the idea that this too should be done for pensions.

Although the absolute contributions of the state, the market, and the family are likely to alter with increasing economic growth, making the state more important, the relative distinctiveness of Japan is likely to remain. While Japan's economy becomes more and more integrated with and pervasive in the world economy, the provision for welfare within Japanese society is likely to remain unique among other industrialized nations.

NOTES

1. The author was the chairman of the research committee.
2. In Japan measures of public expenditure are conventionally related to the national income, rather than to the Gross Domestic Product, as is usual in Europe and America.

Since Japanese national income is about four-fifths of GNP, this makes Japanese welfare expenditure appear higher than it would by European calculations. To obtain Japanese figures comparable with those of Europe and America, multiply the ratio of public welfare expenditure to national income by 0.8.

REFERENCES

Castles, Francis G., ed., *The Impact of Parties: Politics and Policies in Democratic Capitalist States.* London and Beverly Hills, Calif. Sage Publications, 1982.

Maruo, Naomi (with Hiroshi Kato), eds. *What is Participation?* (Keiei Sanka Towa Nanika). 1971. Tokyo: Japan Productivity Center.

Maruo, Naomi, ed., *Industrial Relations in Transition* (Henbousuru, Roshi Kankei). Tokyo: Social and Economic Congress of Japan, 1977.

Maruo, Naomi, "Econometric Analysis of the Relationship between Labour–Management Relations and Productivity: Do Labour–Management Relations Matter? *The Journal of Economics,* May 1983.

Ministry of Health and Welfare. *White Paper on Health and Welfare* (Koseihakusho). Tokyo, 1983.

Prime Minister's Office, *Way of Life and Opinion of the Aged: An International Comparison.* Tokyo, 1981.

Rose, Richard and Peters, Guy, *Can Government Go Bankrupt?* New York: Basic Books, 1978.

Appendix 1. Regression Analyses of Social Expenditure in Japan

1. $\dfrac{\text{Social security expenditure}}{\text{National income}} = -8.0862 + \underset{(7.83)}{1.4654} \dfrac{\text{No.}}{N} + \underset{(6.43)}{3.3920U}$

    $r = .9781;\ \text{D.W.} = 1.1125$

2. $\dfrac{\text{State pension benefits}}{\text{National income}} = -0.00384 + \underset{(5.92)}{0.8047} \dfrac{\text{No.}}{N} + \underset{(7.51)}{0.03011U} + \underset{(4.22)}{0.6330} \dfrac{N_e}{N}$

    $\qquad\qquad\qquad\qquad\quad + \underset{(3.02)}{0.1297D} - \underset{(-2.56)}{0.0618Y}$

    $r = .9864;\ \text{D.W.} = 2.3689$

3. $\dfrac{\text{Health insurance}}{\text{National income}} = -1.4017 + \underset{(5.61)}{0.05623N_m} - \underset{(-6.73)}{0.1049\text{rm}} + \underset{(2.25)}{0.2405n}$

    $r = .9804;\ \text{D.W.} = 1.2145$

4. $\dfrac{\text{Personal social services expenditure}}{\text{National income}} = -0.9609 + \underset{(7.49)}{0.1468} \dfrac{\text{No.}}{N} + \underset{(4.62)}{0.2008U} + \underset{(6.74)}{0.2912D}$

    $r = .9923;\ \text{D.W.} = 1.5182$

where Y : Rate of economic growth in real terms
   N : Total population
   No. : Number of people aged 65 years and over
   U : Rate of unemployment
   e : $\dfrac{\text{Number of employees}}{\text{Total working force}}$
   N_m : Number of medical doctors per 100,000 population
   rm : $\dfrac{\text{Costs paid directly by patients}}{\text{Total medical costs}}$
   n : Rate of change of $\dfrac{\text{No.}}{N}$
   N_e : Number of total working force
   D : Dummy variable. Before 1973 = 0; 1973 and after = 1.0.
   D.W. : Durbin–Watson ratio

Note: Figures in parentheses are t statistics. For full details see Maruo (1983).

4

The Dynamics of the Welfare Mix in Britain

RICHARD ROSE

Is then the lesson to be learned that the proper policy for governments should be one of systematic abstention . . . before the increasing horrors of the later 1980s? No. We need a recipe for the contemporary situation, on which our salvation depends.
—Lady Wootton, *New Society,* 10 February 1983

If one wants salvation, one should go to a bishop and not to a politician.
—Prime Minister Harold Macmillan

The distinction between the state and society is rarely made in Britain, and when an attempt is made, it usually involves importing a continental European mode of thinking. The English way is to blur the distinction between affairs of state and social affairs. Whereas in *étatiste* societies, the state is an active agent giving direction to social affairs, in Britain the feeling that "something ought to be done" about a problem leaves vague the institutions expected to act. Because British government has never been conceived as an authoritarian state standing apart from society, it is not a threat to citizens. Government does not keep all social activities under close surveillance, nor are citizens offered welfare benefits to remain subordinate, as in the Kaiser's Reich.

Britain combines two distinctive traditions: liberalism that places a high value on individual freedom and responsibility—albeit not carried to the extreme of contemporary American reactions against the public provision of welfare—and trust in government that has much more in common with solidaristic Scandinavian societies than with the United States. In the nineteenth century both traditions flourished, leading to the

Written as part of a program of research on the Growth of Government sponsored by British Economic and Social Research Council grant HR 7849/1. Assistance in compiling data was very usefully provided by Richard Parry, Department of Social Administration, University of Edinburgh.

organization of political parties and the trade union movement for mass collective action, and the extension of the right to vote to all individuals.

The collective provision of welfare by government, by other social agencies, or by the two working together goes back for centuries in England. The proponents of making a permanent, public commitment to universal standards of welfare assumed that, just as production in a mixed economy would come from both public and private sectors, welfare would come from a mix of sources. The 1942 Beveridge Report on social insurance declared:

> Social security must be achieved by co-operation between the state and the individual. The state should offer security for service and contribution. The state in organizing security should not stifle incentive, opportunity or responsibility; in establishing a national minimum it should leave room and encouragement for voluntary action by each individual to provide more than that minimum for himself and his family (quoted and reaffirmed by Beveridge, 1948: 7).

Public opinion studies show that the majority of people continue to endorse having welfare from a mixture of sources. Taylor-Gooby and Papadakis (1985: 82) conclude that "the political rhetoric of state versus market does not do justice to the opinions of the majority of citizens. They want the status quo or more welfare from whatever source."

In Britain the public provision of welfare has been continuing for more than a century. Moreover, Britain emerged from World War II with its political regime and wartime commitments to social welfare intact, rather than in suspense because of military occupation or a change of regime. Most writers describe this process as the creation of a welfare state; growth of state provision of welfare is assumed to have crowded out provision of welfare by the market or by the family. The fiscalization of welfare (or Margaret Thatcher's rhetorical ideal, the defiscalization of welfare) is seen as the sole issue of welfare. The hypothesis that the oldest welfare programs should grow most (Wilensky, 1975: 9) implies that welfare should more nearly approach state monopoly in Britain than in Scandinavia, where development of major welfare services occurred substantially later than in Britain, or than in the United States, where prosperity has been greater and the idea of public provision of welfare has been weaker.

Britain today is an appropriate society for testing the extent to which total welfare in society is becoming a state monopoly because of the fiscalization of welfare, or retains a pluralistic welfare mix involving the market and the household as well as the state. A society where the Industrial Revolution began two centuries ago has had ample time to monetize welfare production. A society in which free elections and a reform-minded civil service was created in the nineteenth century (cf. Heclo, 1974) has had ample time for political pressures to create a state-dominated system of welfare. Insofar as welfare production in Britain remains pluralistic, this is important evidence that an increase in the state provision of welfare need not drive out the market and the household.

EXAMINING THE EVIDENCE OF THE WELFARE MIX

Given two centuries of industrialization and a century of welfare provision by the state, Britain is very appropriate for testing generalizations about the dynamics of welfare advanced in Chapter 1. To what extent has the monetization of welfare driven out the provision of welfare by the household? To what extent has the development of state programs fiscalized welfare, crowding out provision by the market? Are Britons today solely dependent on public welfare services, as socialist analysts often assume, and conservative analysts fear? Or has a combination of disparate elements of society, politics, and economics (Rose, 1965) sustained a pluralistic welfare mix?

To understand the provision of welfare in Britain today, it is important to review a variety of welfare goods and services important to every family at some stage in its life cycle: income, food, housing, personal social services, health care, education, and transportation (see Chapter 1). To concentrate attention solely on the national health service and social security just because they are major innovations of public policy in the twentieth century, is to assume what remains to be proven, namely, that state action is the primary or exclusive source of welfare in British society.

In order to test whether the state's role has been changing, it is necessary to review data about welfare production for a substantial period of time. It takes more than a generation for the consequences of public welfare provision to become evident in society. Suitable data are normally available for the period since the 1945–51 Labour government. Data from the interwar years sometimes differs in form, because public policies and institutions were different then. Where possible, data from the pre-1914 era are marshaled. When programs are reviewed over the long term, it is possible to see the cumulative effects of inertia (cf. Rose and Karran, 1984). The great historical changes from the mid-nineteenth to the mid-twentieth century do not necessarily mean a linear continuation of growth since 1951. For example, what can follow the creation of a comprehensive national health service?

Money Income

In a money economy, everyone has an immediate and continuing need for a cash income. Today, no British family can live without substantial weekly expenditure for necessities. The need for a money income is primary, but the sources of income are multiple: *transfers within the household* (e.g., from parents to children or from husband to housewife), *paid employment* (income earners in the conventionally defined work force), and *income transfers from the state to those not in employment* (e.g., pensioners and the unemployed).

Britain was an urban industrial society by the mid-nineteenth century. More than half of all incomes came from the market, and the other half came from transfers within the household; hardly any came from government (Table 4.1). The household transfer of income was usually from a father with a paying job to a wife and children. Public employment and income maintenance programs developed slowly. As of 1911, 5.5 percent of Britons received an income from the state, compared to 55 percent receiving an income from within-family transfers. The proportion working in the private sector appeared to fall only because of the increase in the number of children at home, due to improved public health, and more years of compulsory education. The number of incomes provided by the market increased by more than half. By 1938 the state's role as a source of income had increased, but it was small compared to that of within-family transfers, or the market.

In the post–World War II era, the welfare state has matured, making the sources of incomes completely pluralistic. Today the state is the chief source of income, through income maintenance payments and public employment for 38.5 percent of the population. Income from within-family transfers is second in importance. The market—first in the mid-nineteenth century and second in 1951—is today third in importance; it provides incomes for 29.9 percent of the British population. If the total population is divided into two groups, those whose income is derived from paid work and those receiving money from income transfers within the family or from the state, then those in paid employment are little more than two-fifths of the population.

Table 4.1. Changing Sources of Individual Income in Britain, 1951–1981

Provision by:	Year (%)					Changes (%)
	1851	1911	1938	1951	1981	
Market (private employment)						
Nonagriculture	39.2	37.1	37.1	32.0	28.8	−10.4
Agriculture	9.9	3.7	2.0	2.5	1.1	−8.8
Total market	49.1	40.8	39.1	34.5	29.9	−19.2
State						
Public employment	1.2	3.0	4.7	12.5	13.7	+12.5
Income maintenance	0	2.5	8.9	12.5	24.8	+24.8
Total state	1.2	5.5	13.6	25.0	38.5	+37.3
Household transfers	49.7	54.8	47.3	40.5	31.6	−18.1
Total population (× 1000)	20,815	42,081	47,494	50,225	55,776	+34,961

Sources: Calculations by the author from employment figures since 1851 and income maintenance since 1951, as reported by Parry (1985: Tables 2.1, 2.2, 2.12). Income maintenance data for 1911 and 1938 calculated from Parker (1972: Table 12).

From the perspective of the state, public provision of incomes has grown enormously, principally through pensions and public employment. Whereas income maintenance grants were paid to 12.5 percent of the population in 1951, by 1981 this group had doubled in size. Public employment, a second means of providing income through the state, has increased sixfold since 1851, and trebled since 1938.

While the provision of income through public employment and income maintenance grants has grown faster than private sector employment throughout the OECD world (Rose, 1985b: Tables 1.17–18), this has not made the state the monopoly or dominant source of income. Incomes today come from a mix of three sources: the state, the household, and the market. Since there are many two- or three-income households, a mix often occurs within the family as well.

Food

Whatever the level of economic development, food is a necessity. Such is the prosperity of OECD nations today that the consumption of food is usually ignored or mentioned only briefly in conventional reviews of social conditions and social indicators. Halsey's (1972) major survey of conditions in twentieth-century Britain makes no mention of food, and the British government's *Social Trends* (1985: 92ff) treats food as only one among many objects of household expenditure. Yet nothing is more fundamental to survival than food.

From the perspective of centuries, the great transformation in food production was monetization: the shift from subsistence agriculture, in which agricultural laborers and tenants raised nearly everything that they ate, to the purchase of food by urban dwellers in the marketplace. The 1887 Allotments Act made plots of less than an acre of land available to urban dwellers; however, the relatively small number of allotments are cultivated as much for flowers as for food. After prewar economic difficulties and wartime rationing that extended to 1954, the household as of 1963 produced only 3 percent of all food. In 1981, 98 percent of food was bought in the market (Table 4.2).

Even though an adequate diet is logically a precondition of good health, the fiscalization of food has not occurred. States that spend generously for health care do not provide food as a merit good free of charge. Food remains a commodity bought and sold in the marketplace. After decades of increased affluence, nearly everyone can buy the food they need; the Gallup poll (1984) report found that 96 percent say that they have enough for proper meals for everyone in the family each day. The provision of food is virtually a monopoly of the market. Even though the money used to purchase food may come from the state, decisions about what to buy are made by the consumer rather than by bureaucratic regulations.

Meals are a joint product of the market and the household. Although food is bought in the market, meals are normally prepared in the home (Table 4.2). The meals that people eat are not normally produced by paid

Table 4.2. Provision of Food and Meals in Britain, 1963–81

	1963 Value		1981 Value		
	Pounds	Percent	Pounds	Percent	Change (%)
Food					
Purchased	4.90	97	22.95	98	+1
Home-grown	0.14	3	0.48	2	−1
Meals					
Purchased	0.68	12	4.25	15	+3
Prepared at home[a]	5.04	86	23.43	82	−4
Institutional meals[b]	0.14	2	0.87	3	+1

Sources: Family Expenditure Survey (annual); Ministry of Agriculture, (1966: Table 3; 1983; Table 2); *Annual Abstract of Statistics* (annual).

[a]Labor value estimated as equal to the total cost of food prepared.

[b]For those in hospitals, military service, and prisons, 1.3 percent of the population in 1963 and 1.7 percent in 1981.

labor, as would be the case if all meals were purchased in restaurants or in state institutions giving away meals as a social service. In a past era, when domestic servants were plentiful, this cost was sometimes registered by the employment of a cook and butler in the home. Today, more than four-fifths of meals are produced at home by unpaid household labor.

Since the beginning of the twentieth century, the eating habits of the British people have undergone substantial change, increasing total welfare by providing a better balanced diet and preventing malnutrition. Changes have occurred with virtually no direct intervention by the state. They have reflected rising real incomes and major changes in the technology of food processing, in the marketing of food, and in the household.

The household accounts for more than four-fifths of the labor involved in the preparation of meals. Given that the cost of a restaurant meal is more than double that of a meal prepared at home, estimating the value of the household preparation of meals as matching the value of the food consumed, as is done here, is a conservative estimate of the value of the labor. The additional charge for a restaurant meal can reflect the convenience element, or a restaurant meal can be a form of leisure consumption rather than nutrition per se.

The provision of food in Britain is a virtual monopoly of the market, and the preparation of meals is dominated by the household. The state's contribution to this welfare necessity is trivial. Moreover, the particular mix of household and market provision appears stable for many decades.

Housing

A place to live is a necessity for every family, whatever the design or the quality of the house. Industrialization in the nineteenth century faced Britain with an enormous task of rehousing millions of people in new industrial urban centers, because of a shift of people from rural to urban areas. A population explosion created a need to house millions more.

In the twentieth century, housing is provided in three different ways. First, there is market provision by landlords renting property; the tenant pays an inclusive weekly rent, just like paying weekly food bills. Second, a house can be occupied by its owner; owner occupation results in the market-cum-household provision of housing. The household buys the home in the market, but an owner-occupier can maintain it by non-monetized do-it-yourself labor. In Britain a significant third alternative is tenancy of a house or flat owned by the local council. Council housing is market provision inasmuch as the tenant pays a rent, but it is state provision inasmuch as public subsidies result in a submarket rent, and a local government authority owns and maintains the property.

The stock of housing in Britain has more than doubled since 1914, reflecting both population increase and changes in the composition of families. Economic growth has resulted in a great improvement in the standard of mass housing; housing built since 1918, and especially since 1945, has a much higher level of amenities. The millions of substandard nineteenth-century houses, lacking an indoor toilet or fixed bath, have been razed in the postwar era, usually being replaced by council houses built to a higher standard of amenity.

The construction of more than 11 million houses in this century has been paralleled by a reduction in the pure market allocation of housing by landlords (Table 4.3). Before World War I, 90 percent of the population rented housing in the market. Owner occupancy has grown from 10 percent in 1914 to 59 percent today. The private sector rental of housing now accounts for only one-eighth of the population and is often transitional, serving workers moving from job to job, students, or immigrants.

Owner-occupied housing is best regarded as market-cum-household; the owner pays a market price to purchase the house, but much of the annual cost of house maintenance can be met by nonmonetized labor substituting or supplementing market services. Nearly three-fifths of fam-

Table 4.3. Provision of Housing, 1914–81

	1914	1938	1960	1971	1981	Change
			(% all housing).			
Strictly market (private rental)	90	58	31	19	13	−77
Market-cum-household (owner occupation)	10	32	44	53	59	+49
Market-cum-state (council houses)	0.3	10	25	29	28	+28
Total houses (million)	7.9	11.4	14.6	17.2	19.0	+11.1

Sources: For England and Wales, Department of Environment, (1977: Table I.23; 1983: Table 9.3). Scotland is omitted because of a separate structure of housing that is heavily weighted toward council housing. Including Scotland, housing in Britain as a whole in 1981 is 57 percent market-cum-household, 31 percent market-cum-state, and 12 percent pure market.

ilies in Britain are now housed on a market-cum-household basis. In the 1980s the proportion of families in this type of housing is likely to expand further, as Conservative government policy favors owner occupation and the sale of council houses to tenants, and discourages the construction of much more council housing.

Council housing is best regarded as market-cum-state, since a part of the cost of council housing is met by public funds. The provision of council housing on a market-cum-state basis expanded gradually between the wars, and reached a peak after 1945, as slum clearance programs were undertaken on a massive scale by local authorities, and Labour governments encouraged council housing. Many Labour councils kept council house rents well below market levels as an act of party policy, believing housing should be cheap. However, the Labour party has never proposed that housing should be a free merit good, as is education. Councils have continued using nonmarket criteria even after central government switched in the 1970s to a means-tested income supplement to encourage market rents. Many councils use criteria of need to allocate council houses on social rather than market grounds. Economic pressures on local authorities, reinforced by central government legislation, have reduced but not eliminated the role of government in council house finance.

The household makes a major nonmonetized contribution to housing maintenance. The cost of housing not only reflects the amortization of capital and local property taxes, but also the cost of repairing and improving the fabric of the house. When nine-tenths of property was rented, this cost fell almost entirely on the private landlord, who financed maintenance from rents, and often minimized what was done. Today, owner occupiers have the choice between making a market payment for maintenance in the official or shadow economies, and undertaking nonmonetized do-it-yourself maintenance. Council tenants have little incentive to maintain or improve their tenancies; the work is paid for by local authorities, and in high-rise council flats it is difficult for tenants to do.

The magnitude of the household's contribution to housing maintenance can be estimated from official data. Council house maintenance cost £1.2 billion in 1981. National income accounts for that year reported a total consumer expenditure of £3.2 billion on housing maintenance. In addition, £1.7 billion was spent on the purchase of do-it-yourself supplies for household maintenance. Given the labor-intensive nature of most household repairs, it is reasonable to estimate that the use of do-it-yourself supplies requires nonmonetized labor worth about treble the cost of supplies, that is, £5.1 billion. On this basis, the household accounted for 45 percent of productive work for housing maintenance, the market for 44 percent through paid labor and the sale of supplies, and the state for the remaining 11 percent. Housing maintenance is produced by a duopoly of market and household, and this has been the pattern for at least a quarter of a century.

The total number of households has more than doubled since 1914; concurrently, there has been a substantial substitution effect as between sources. In 1914 there were 7.1 million rented residences; by 1981 the number had fallen by two-thirds to 2.4 million. The decline in private rented houses has reduced the gross increase of 15.8 million homes to a net increase of 11.1 million. A virtual monopoly by landlords has given way to pluralism. The state and the household are both important in house building, and the market and the household are both important in maintaining houses.

Personal Social Services

So deeply ingrained is the notion of the family that we do not think of family relationships as involving the production of goods and services. Yet family members continuously provide services for each other. In addition to meals, and housing maintenance, the family is the primary unit caring for children, and often caring for the elderly as well. The personal social services produced within the family are a priceless mark of affection. Yet they also constitute welfare production, for one member of a family must labor to care for another.

The significance of the household production of personal social services can be seen by considering the welfare that the state would provide in the absence of a family. If a child is orphaned or abandoned by parents, it will be taken into full-time care at public expense. If an elderly person is unable to look after himself or herself and has no one else to do so, then the state either provides domiciliary services in the home, such as meals and at home help, or moves the person to a home for the elderly, where medical and social services are provided by public employees at public expense.

In 1981, 270,000 public employees were providing social services in Britain, 3.5 percent of all public employees (Parry, 1985). Gross public expenditure on personal social services accounted for about £2.1 billion in 1983–84, almost 2 percent of total public expenditure. The state also pays cash benefits to people in need of continuing care within the family, such as the severely disabled. The invalid care allowance is a weekly cash payment to family members unable to take a paid job because of caring for a handicapped member of the family. In 1983, 450,000 people were receiving attendance and invalid care allowances from the state. Many services that the state provides or pays others to provide affect relatively small groups, such as the blind, disabled war veterans, the mentally handicapped, and persons on probation.

Of the cost of state-provided personal social services, 15 percent is covered by user charges; the principal source of income is payment for residential care for the elderly and infirm (Treasury, 1985: Table 3.11; Judge and Matthews, 1980). Historically, nonprofit agencies have also been significant in providing personal social services, for example, Dr. Barnardo's

Children's Homes, and the Royal National Institute for the Blind. But nonprofit agencies are normally monetized. The Charities Aid Foundation (1984) describes them as a £10 billion a year business, bigger than the motor trade. Their income from charitable contributions is falling; it is now one-tenth of total expenditure. The state now provides so much of the income of nonprofit agencies that the Charities Aid Foundation warns that they risk being "hijacked" by the state. Even in local associations, where inputs of unpaid volunteer labor are likely to be greatest, public funds can play a significant part (cf. Wolfenden, 1978; Obler, 1981).

To give empirical focus, attention here is concentrated on two types of services that families require at some stage in the life cycle: care for children, and care for the elderly. The empirical question is, how much care comes from within the household, from the market, and from the state?

Care for preschool children can be provided in many different ways. The state or market may provide day care for children outside the home on the grounds that it is good for children to be under professional child care; it also makes it possible for mothers to take paid employment. But public or market day care for children does not eliminate care by the household for part of each day and on weekends.

Within Britain the household is the primary source of care for infants (Table 4.4). In 1949, 91 percent of children were looked after exclusively in the home, and the level was similar in earlier decades of the century.

Table 4.4. Sources of Care for Preschool-Age Children, 1949–80

Sources of care	1949 Hours[a]	%	1959 Hours[a]	%	1970 Hours[a]	%	1980 Hours[a]	%	Change (%)
Household									
Exclusively at home[b]	3,200	91	3,670	97	3,155	71	1,816	48	−43
Partly at home	252	7	52	1	640	14	977	26	+19
Total	3,452	98.5	3,722	99	3,795	86	2,793	74	−24
Market									
Registered nurseries, child minders[c]	23	0.7	9	0.2	324	7	484	13	+12
State									
Day nurseries, schools[d]	29	0.8	43	1.1	316	7	493	13	+12

Sources: Calculated from *Health and Personal Social Service Statistics: England 1982* (London: HMSO, 1982), Table 7.6, and earlier annual reports from the same source.

[a]Hours × 1,000.

[b]Estimated as 84 hours a week care per child.

[c]Estimated as 40 hours a week.

[d]Estimated as 40 hours a week for day-care nurseries, 20 hours a week for full-time nursery education, and 20 hours a week for part-time nursery education.

Only 7 percent of children were looked after for part of the week by registered nurseries and child minders, or by state nurseries. By 1980 the proportion of infants receiving some care outside the home had risen substantially, divided almost equally between those looked after in the market, and those cared for by public agencies. Two-thirds of children remain almost exclusively the responsibility of their parents.

Children receiving organized care still spend most of the week in their own home. When hours of care are the unit of accounting, then the household provided 98 percent of all care in 1949, and 74 percent in 1980. The market is tied for second in importance, providing an estimated 13 percent of care, more than the state, because the market offers day care when working mothers want it—that is, throughout the working day and throughout the year. By contrast, public nurseries may offer care only during school hours. Donnison (1983: 2) describes this as "devised to suit teachers rather than children or their parents." The household does not have a complete monopoly on child care, but it is by far the dominant source.

The elderly differ from infants in that they can care for themselves. An elderly person living at home can obtain there nearly all the care required from the attentions of a spouse, a relative, or friends, or produce it for himself or herself. The household is virtually a monopoly provider of care for the elderly; 96 percent of the elderly live in a normal family setting with their spouse, offspring, or companions, or live alone (Table 4.5).

While personal social services are available from local authorities, these are not required by most aged persons. Home helpers are used by 8 percent, health visitors by 6 percent, and meals on wheels or old per-

Table 4.5. Primary Source of Care for the Elderly, 1901–81

| | Year (%) | | |
	1901	1951	1981
Household	95	96.5	96
With spouse	n.a.[c]	n.a.	43
Alone	n.a.	n.a.	33
With offspring	n.a.	n.a.	8
With other companion	n.a.	n.a.	12
State hospitals and homes[a]	5	2.7	2
Market[b]	n.a.	0.8	2

Source: Calculated from *Census, 1981: Persons of Pensionable Age Tables* (1983: Table 4); and household types from *General Household Survey* (1980: Table 10.2) *Census 1901 General Report* (1904: 161, 207). Elderly defined as persons of pensionable age: 65 for men, and 60 for women.

[a]Hospitals and homes for ill, disabled, and psychiatric patients; in 1901, included indoor paupers in work houses.

[b]In nonstate homes for the old and disabled (one-third of total) plus hotels, boarding houses, hostels.

[c]n.a., Not available.

sons' lunch clubs by 5 percent (*General Household Survey,* 1982: Tables 8.48–49). Given the cost of monetized care by bureaucratized welfare staff, expenditure on personal social services per elderly person can run into hundreds of pounds a year (cf. Judge and Matthews, 1980: 138). But by the same criterion, the shadow price of household-provided personal services would be thousands of pounds per person a year, and the total shadow value well over £10 billion a year. The household has a virtual monopoly on the provision of social services for the elderly; the state and the market supplement this only to a limited extent.

Health

Unlike many welfare programs, health is best when provision is absent; a person in good health will not need medical or hospital treatment from any source. Health care is normally reparative, returning to good health an individual who has become ill. Insofar as good health reflects actions that an individual takes to maintain his or her own body, then health is not a good that can be produced and exchanged like other welfare products. Insofar as returning a person to good health is a service that can be produced by doctors, by hospitals, and by care in the household, it is suitable for analysis here.

Care for ill health can be provided by the household as well as by the state and the market (Stacey, 1984). For example, a child can be born at home rather than in a maternity hospital; in 1950, 38 percent of British births occurred at home, falling to 1.1 percent by 1981. A child too ill to go to school will be cared for at home by a parent, and a spouse may care for a mate who is ill. In addition, a person can buy a variety of self-medication drugs to treat a cold, headache, or other complaints. Treatment within the home is not so professional as treatment in a doctor's office or a hospital, but it is not so expensive and is very common for minor illnesses and complaints. Moreover, household treatment is often a necessary complement to treatment by the market or state. A person who sees a doctor may be told to stay home for a few days rather than be sent to a hospital. A hospital may discharge a person after a very short stay, with the remainder of recuperation occurring at home.

In the period up to World War II, British statistics on health care give only a rough indication of the scale of market provision, and virtually no indication about household provision. Yet household provision was important at a time when the money cost of treatment was substantial, and the advantages of professional as against home treatment were less, because medicine was less developed. The introduction of a compulsory health insurance scheme by the pre-1914 Liberal government assured state-mandated health insurance for some employees; one-third of the population was covered in 1911, and two-fifths by 1931 (Table 4.6). A similar proportion of hospital beds was in public hands, including those operated by local authorities, poor law boards, and infirmaries (cf. Car-

Table 4.6. Sources of Health Care, 1911–81

	Year (% of total health expenditure)			
	1911	1931	1961	1981
State				
Compulsory insurance	32	40	—	—
National Health Service	—	—	68	56
Market[a]			7	7
	{ 68	{ 60		
Care for sick in household[b]			25	37

Sources: 1911–31: Board of Trade (1937: Table 71); figure for market and household is the remainder after subtracting the insured population.

1961–81: Calculated from *Digest of Health Statistics 1970:* (1970: Table 12.3) and *Annual Abstract of Statistics* (1984: Table 3.18) (days of sickness certified); *National Income and Expenditure 1982* (1983: Tables 4.8 and 9.4), and *National Income and Expenditure 1972* (1972: Table 49) (expenditure on health care, public and private); *Digest of Health Statistics 1970* (1970: Tables 2.9 and 4.2); *Annual Abstract of Statistics 1983:* Tables 3.29–31; and *Health and Personal Social Services Statistics: England 1982* (1982: Table 4.1) (hospital occupancy and unit costs).

[a]Consumers' expenditure on pharmaceutical products, medical equipment, and private health services, including NHS charges. Estimated for 1961.

[b]The number of certified days of nonhospitalized sickness in the labor force (191 million, 1961; 303 million, 1981) plus the same amount of sickness assumed for nonworking population. Care in the home valued at half the average weekly cost for an inpatient in a chronic sick NHS hospital ward (£12.88, in 1961; £200 in 1981).

penter, 1984: 82; Parker, Rollett, and Jones, 1972: Tables 11.19–20). Other hospitals were usually run by nonprofit associations. For this period there are adequate data about monetized health care or care in the household.

The establishment of the National Health Service in 1948 gave state coverage to 100 percent of the population, but it did not eliminate other sources of health care. A small but growing proportion of the population opts out of the National Health Service for coverage by private insurance schemes: 0.2 percent in 1950, 3.6 percent in 1970, and 6.3 percent in 1982 (See Maclachlan and Maynard, 1982: Table 3). There is also a market element in the National Health Service, as patients are asked to pay part of the cost of prescriptions, and for a variety of optical, dental, and peripheral supplies and services. In addition, many pharmaceuticals and medical supplies may be bought without prescription in a local shop.

Health care within the household remains important too. Among those in the labor force who are certified as ill, 80 percent remain at home because they are not sick enough to be hospitalized. Treatment of those with chronic health problems—the disabled, mentally ill, or very elderly—often involves care in the home, which is considered more desirable than long-term institutionalization in a hospital or other state residence. The sale of medical remedies without prescription shows a significant amount of self-diagnosis and self-treatment for minor or recurrent aches and pains.

Within the monetized sector, the creation of the National Health Service made the state much more important than the market (Table 4.6).

Advances in medical science since 1948 have increased the effectiveness of the state services, and also the cost. By contrast with the United States, in Britain the state has used its monopolistic buying power to contain the total cost of health expenditure as a proportion of the national product, albeit it has risen with increased demand.

Pluralism in health care still prevails; the household remains important. When the amount of sickness treated at home is evaluated, even after discounting for the lesser cost of simpler household treatment, household health care equaled 37 percent of the total in 1981. On first sight, this is surprising. But the rationale is sound. If every person who went to a doctor because of illness had to be sent to a hospital rather than sent home to bed, the cost of hospital treatment could easily double. Just as the family provides important personal social services for its members in good health, so too those in ill health are often looked after in the home.

Education

Of all the welfare programs of government, education is distinctive not only in being provided without charge, but also in being compulsory since 1870. It has thus had a long period of time to accumulate a monopoly position vis-à-vis the market. While informal learning in the home is in some ways significant, the increasingly technical content of education and the emphasis on the credentials of examinations and formal certificates have greatly reduced the scope for tuition by parents.

Notwithstanding the very considerable attention given to what are misleadingly called public (i. e., private fee-paying) schools, such as Eton and Harrow, the great bulk of English people have been educated at state expense throughout the twentieth century (Table 4.7). In the period up to the 1944 Education Act, education was compulsory at primary level only, and schools were of two types: those owned and funded completely by local education authorities, and those involving the church as well as the

Table 4.7. Sources of Education, 1900–82

Source	1900	1938	1950	1982
	(% schools[a])		(% pupils)	
State	34	56	93	94
Church	58	43	n.a.[b]	n.a.
Market	7	1	7	6

Sources: A. H. Halsey, J. Sheehan, and J. Vaizey (1972: Table 6.3); *Education Statistics for the United Kingdom* (1983: Table 3); and *Annual Report of the Ministry of Education 1950* (1951: 141). No basis for estimating education within the household.

[a]State schools are local authority primary schools; church schools are principally Church of England, plus some Roman Catholic primary schools.

[b]n.a., Not available.

local authority in funding and management. But secondary education was to a substantial extent paid for by parents; 38 percent of secondary schools were fee-paying in 1938.

Since World War II state education has expanded substantially and the role of the market has been further reduced. Secondary education has been made compulsory, the school-leaving age raised from 14 to 15 and then to 16, and more youths voluntarily stay on at school beyond the minimum age. Concurrently, the old division between local-authority schools and those jointly managed with churches and other voluntary bodies has been greatly reduced in significance. The market sector of education retains social prestige and has higher per capita expenditure per pupil, teaching 6 percent of pupils, but accounting for 9.7 percent of total education expenditure. Nonetheless, more than 90 percent of pupils are enrolled in state schools.

Education, defined as a formal process in which one person provides instruction to another, is hardly provided in the household today. Prior to the introduction of compulsory education, it was of substantial significance, for a child depended initially on parents for whatever was learned, often supplemented by rudimentary education and indoctrination at a variety of church-run schools. The monopoly of the state in producing education is today virtually complete. But learning is not solely a product of state efforts. A pupil's achievement within a school reflects family background. Moreover, if state instruction is to succeed, a pupil must make an effort to learn. No source of instruction—the state, paid tutors or parents—can substitute or compensate fully for individual pupil effort.

Transportation

Physical mobility is an important but often neglected feature of welfare in society. Confinement to the home would be considered a condition of deprivation and disability. In a Gallup poll (1984) survey of what British people could not afford, transportation enabling people to get around as necessary was the most frequently cited need, mentioned by 14 percent. The proportion of British people who perceive a need for transportation is thus three times the number who say they lack adequate food.

Transportation is pluralistic, mixing public, private, and household production. An individual can walk to work and to shops. The importance of walking is often overlooked, because this pedestrian activity is not monetized and familiar. Yet for many people—children going to school, a housewife doing shopping, anyone wishing to visit neighbors— walking is simplest. It is socially significant, because it reflects the proximity of personal contacts.

The most common forms of getting to work—travel by car, motorcycle, bus, or rail—combine resources from the market and the state (Table 4.8). Travel must be paid for, whether by a fare for public trans-

Table 4.8. Sources of Transportation, 1951–80

Sources	Year (% of passenger km traveled)			Change (%)	Journey to work 1980 (%)
	1951	1961	1980		
State marketed					
Bus and coach	42.0	24.0	8.0	−34.0	18
Rail	19.0	14.0	7.0	−12.0	4
Air	0.1	0.3	0.5	+0.4	n.a.[a]
Total	61	38	15	−46	22
Market-cum-household					
Private car	29	58	84	+55	53
Household					
Cycle	10	4	1	−9	4
Walking	n.a.	n.a.	n.a.	n.a.	20
Totals (in billions of km)	199	279	503	+304	24

Source: Calculated from data in Department of Transport (1982: Tables 1.1, 1.2).
[a]n.a., Not available.

port, which is subsidized but not free, or through the running costs of an automobile. The government subsidizes private motorists by public expenditure on roads, which motorists can normally use without paying a toll. It also provides 295,000 mobility allowances to help disabled people purchase appropriate mechanized transportation.

The economics of the postwar era have made it easier for an individual to have an effective choice between public and private transport. Whereas the cost of education and health care have been rising, the relative cost of a car has been falling. Rising real wages have also given more families a discretionary income that can be spent, if desired, on buying a car. There is thus a competitive market, with the state and the private sector selling transportation to people who can afford to buy some of each.

Because public transport makes charges to passengers, it is in the market. But because public transport is state owned, it is supposed to operate on a "more than the market" basis. The postwar era has seen a great shift from state-provided transport to private motorists driving themselves, a market-cum-household form of transportation. Whereas in 1951 61 percent of all passenger kilometers were by public transport, a decade later this had fallen to 38 percent, and by 1980 to 15 percent. The private motor car now provides 84 percent of all transportation (Table 4.8).

Nonmonetized transportation remains substantial; 24 percent of journeys to work are on foot or by bicycle. Moreover, the expansion of automobile ownership means that the great majority of people are no longer transported by others; public employment in the railways and buses has dropped by nearly half since 1951. Most people now make many journeys by car; the unpaid driver has replaced paid public transportation workers.

MORE WELFARE BUT MUCH THE SAME MIX

Because Britain is an old urban industrial society, virtually the whole of
the employed population was working in the market economy by the
mid-nineteenth century. The monetization of production and exchange
thus occurred more than half a century before the first rudimentary steps
were taken toward the creation of the contemporary welfare system. This
implies that growth in the gross domestic product is a precondition for
growth in welfare production: the more money there is, the easier it is to
increase the provision of monetized welfare, whether by the market or
the state.

Monetization by Economic Growth

By every conventional money measure, the national economy of Britain
has increased very substantially in the twentieth century. In pounds valued at 1983 purchasing power, the gross domestic product per capita has
risen nearly fourfold: it was £1154 in 1911, increasing by one-third to
1938, by another two-fifths to 1951, and reaching £4602 in 1983. The
increase in per capita wealth has brought higher living standards to virtually everyone in society. The goods and services that employed people
can buy—or can have provided by the state from greatly increased tax
revenue—are far greater than 50 or 100 years ago. The increase in the
national product not only increases national income in aggregate, but also
finances greater welfare from the state or the market.

By almost every conventional measure, welfare levels have risen
greatly in twentieth-century Britain. The amenities of housing have
improved, and so too has the amount of space available. Food need no
longer be confined to seasonal staples; food processing technology as well
as higher income have greatly increased the variety of foods available in
the market. Health has improved greatly, as evidenced by lower infant
mortality rates and greater longevity as well as by higher public expenditure. Far more education is provided everyone through the gradual raising of the minimum school-leaving age from 11 to 16, and there is much
easier access to further education. Technology and rising income have
transformed transportation. Personal social services are the only major
welfare product that cannot confidently be said to have increased greatly
with economic growth.

The great growth in the British economy has not been part of a conscious state strategy to fund an increase in state welfare. For the first four
decades of the twentieth century, neoclassical economic thinking dominated British government, which Keynes criticized on the ground that
government policy actually reduced the rate at which the economy could
grow. World War II maximized production for the war effort, resulting
in full employment and the rapid development of state welfare services
as part of total mobilization to achieve military victory (cf. Titmuss,

1950). In the postwar era, the British economy has been a mixed economy. The government's role has been directed toward reducing the ups and downs of cyclical economic trends, concentrating on such targets as unemployment, inflation, and the balance of payments in trade with the rest of the world. Market forces have grown in importance since the 1960s as international competition has increased, and Britain's position in the world economy has been eroded compared to its comparative advantages immediately postwar. The postwar British economy has experienced a substantial increase in real per capita national income. The fact that growth has not been as rapid as that of European and extra-European competitors—or as successive Conservative and Labour governments would wish—should not detract from the record of absolute progress (cf. Gwyn and Rose, 1980).

After allowing for growth in aggregate welfare, two crucial questions remain about the dynamics of welfare: (1) Has the twentieth-century growth in state activity led to the progressive fiscalization of welfare, crowding out the market and the household? (2) Is the provision of welfare in contemporary Britain a state monopoly, or is it pluralistic?

Fiscalization

A great increase in the money spent to produce welfare services is not ipso facto proof of fiscalization. As the constant-value national product per capita has increased from £1529 in 1938 to £2150 in 1951 and £4602 in 1983, then the amount of money spent on welfare ought to increase. The fiscalization theory hypothesizes that the state's relative share of welfare expenditure ought to increase with income. But this will happen only if state expenditure on welfare grows faster than spending through the market or activities in the household, crowding out these alternative sources of welfare production.

When the long period of time from before World War I to the 1980s is examined, then the state's role has increased relative to the market and the household. The state now provides a far larger share of incomes to the employed and the unemployed. Compulsory sickness insurance and subsequently, the National Health Service, have increased the state's significance in health care, and made the market's role limited. The expansion of free secondary education has similarly marginalized private education or church-related semistate education. Council housing now accounts for a significant proportion of total housing, whereas it did not exist before World War I. In transportation, the nationalization of railways and airlines as well as many bus services has increased the state's role. Only in the provision of food has there been no increase in state provision, and in personal social services the state's share has increased only a little.

It is almost tautological to say that the creation of a repertoire of state welfare programs has led to an increase in the state's contribution to the welfare mix. In fields in which state activity has grown, it has done so at the expense of the market (housing or health), the church (education), and household (transportation), or the market and the household (incomes). But it has not normally established a monopoly role for itself.

The more interesting question is whether or not the establishment of large-scale welfare programs has altered the state's role from being part of a mix to being a monopoly supplier. The crowding-out hypothesis is best tested by references to changes in the welfare mix since 1951, by which time the "cradle-to-grave" welfare state envisioned in wartime planning had been put into effect.

In Britain since the mid-1950s, the state's contribution has scarcely changed as a proportion of total welfare production in society. It has increased slightly in income, albeit principally through a growth in the number of pensioners and other recipients of income maintenance grants; public employment was already high in 1951. The state's contribution has decreased substantially in transportation, as motor cars have assumed far greater importance than nationalized railways or buses. In education, the state's established monopoly has not been eroded, nor has its hegemonic position as the principal producer of health services.

By definition, fiscalization occurs when the state begins to make a contribution to the welfare mix. A necessary consequence of the rise in the state's significance is a decline in the relative contribution made by the market or the household. But a change in the mix is not evidence of "crowding out," leading to state monopolization of welfare production. Nor is it evidence of the demise or the absolute decline of the market or the household.

The relative shares of household, market, and state have remained relatively constant since 1951. In a fully developed system of welfare provision, the welfare mix is likely to remain relatively constant because of limits on the fiscal capacity of the state, the persistence of an active market sector encouraged by buoyant personal disposable income, and the persistence of families with free time to devote to household activities.

Pluralism

The welfare mix can be pluralistic in either of two very different ways. Each major domain of welfare could have a monopoly supplier, because of a comparative economic advantage of one source, or a conscious political decision to make a particular service a merit good and thus a state monopoly. Insofar as this occurred, then collectively welfare services would involve a plurality of producers, but for any one service there would be a monopoly.

Pluralism becomes complementary or competitive within a given domain insofar as a welfare service can be produced by the market and the household as well as the state, or by at least two of these three sources. In such circumstances families can choose between alternative sources of supply or make complementary use of services, depending on their income level, phase in the life cycle, or other considerations. When a multiplicity of welfare producers can substitute for each other, then pluralism is complementary.

The provision of welfare in Britain today normally involves complementary pluralism (Table 4.9). Three domains of welfare—income, housing, and transportation—are completely pluralistic, involving substantial provision by the state, the market, and the household. The state is relatively more significant in the provision of income, inasmuch as it both pays people for working and makes income maintenance grants to the elderly and unemployed. The state is not the most important source of housing or transportation, but its role is very substantial; public and private transportation are often complementary, and roadbuilding is complementary to private motoring. In housing, the state funds the construction of council houses, which it then lets at submarket rents. But it also influences the private housing market through legislation on rent controls, land use planning regulation, tax allowances for interest payments on mortgages, and macroeconomic policy generally. The household's role is also substantial in all three areas.

There are for food and health two principal sources of welfare: the state and the household. Their roles are complementary in that the household provides the seemingly small but cumulatively very significant health care services that are deemed beneath or outside the notice of professionalized and bureaucratized hospitals and medical staff. Food is produced

Table 4.9. Plurality of Contributors to the Welfare Mix in Contemporary Britain

	Source (% of total welfare produced)		
	State	Market	Household
Three principal sources			
Income	38	30	32
Transportation	22	55	24
Housing			
Supply	28[a]	13	59[a]
Maintenance	11	44	45
Two principal sources			
Food[b]	2	56	41
Health care	56	7	37
Monopoly provision			
Personal social services			
Children	7	8	85
Elderly	2	2	96
Education	94	6	0

Sources: Tables 4.1–8.
[a]Conjoint state-cum-market, and market-cum-household.
[b]Average for production of food and preparation of meals.

and sold in the market, but the meals made from this food are usually produced in the household.

Monopoly provision characterizes two areas of welfare, but the monopoly supplier is different in each. Education is today provided almost exclusively by state institutions, but personal social services are provided almost entirely by the family. The virtual monopoly of each source reflects comparative advantages. State education has a price advantage over private education, being a merit good supplied free of charge. State and market agencies provide personal social services, but most people prefer to rely on the family to provide affectionate care for children and the elderly, as against the impersonalization and cost of care through public bureaucracies or the market.

The explanations of the welfare mix in Britain are general, rather than being distinctive to English history. Income is provided by a mixture of state, market, and household sources everywhere in the OECD world (cf. Rose, 1985a), as are transportation and housing. State assistance to housing is found in many countries. The mix for other programs also is not unique to Britain: neither is nonmonetized do-it-yourself household maintenance.

The most distinctive feature of welfare provision in Britain is the limited economic base for further expansion. Because Britain has one of the slowest growth rates of any OECD economy, the scope for increased provision by the state or the market is very limited. Ironically, the world's oldest urban, industrial society becomes more dependent on preindustrial nonmonetized household production of goods and services to expand welfare, insofar as the mixed economy cannot expand as fast as demand for goods and services may grow.

WELFARE IN THE FAMILY: THE TOTAL PICTURE

In Britain the state provision of welfare is viewed as a means to the end of the betterment of social conditions; it is not perceived as a means to produce better soldiers or more loyal subjects, or of producing a more disciplined work force. While social scientists may define social conditions in statistical aggregates and distributions between aggregates such as classes, most British people view welfare in terms of consumption within their own family.

In 89 percent of British families today the state makes an important contribution to welfare, providing a major benefit (Table 4.10). In some cases a benefit is shared by the whole household, for example, a council house tenancy or a pension. In other cases a single individual is the beneficiary, as with hospital treatment or education, but all members of the household share in the satisfaction given by the benefit. The most commonly used public benefit is not a merit good, supplied free of charge, but public transportation, a necessity for the 38 percent of families still without an automobile. The fact that transport is a necessity does not lead

Table 4.10. Percentage Distribution to Households of State Welfare Benefits, 1984[a]

Benefit description	Receive	Do not receive
Dependent; public transport; no car	38	62
Pension	36	64
Regular treatment, doctor	35	65
Education	34	66
Housing	30	70
Hospital care in past year	29	71
Unemployment benefit	23	77
Personal social services	5	95

Source: Calculated by the author from Gallup poll (1984) survey ($N = 1988$). Food omitted from survey, as negligible public provision.

[a]Only 11% of households surveyed received no benefits.

government to provide it free. Pensions are second in importance; the number of people with a pensioner in the household is higher than the proportion of pensioners in society, since those with a pension often live with those who do not receive a pension. With unemployment high, nearly one-fifth of families have a member drawing an unemployment benefit, albeit there is usually at least one wage earner in the family as well.

The average household receives more than two welfare benefits—for example, a council house tenancy and subsidized public transport, or a pension and treatment by the National Health Service. Those not in receipt of any benefit (11 percent of the population) are the exception, such as a young single person with good health, a car, and living in privately rented accommodation. The impact of any one particular welfare state service is limited; the proportion not using a particular service ranges from 62 percent independent of public transport to 95 percent not using state-provided personal social services.

The market provides welfare services for virtually every family too. Even when state institutions organize services, a charge for use may be made; this is the case with housing and public transportation. Everyone relies on the market for food, and most people in paid employment think of themselves as earning their income by what they produce, whether in the market sector or as public employees. Education and health care are the only major welfare services that most British people do not expect to pay for in the market, albeit they can see many advantages in doing so if it is affordable (Taylor-Gooby and Papadakis, 1985).

Most people spend most of the week in the household rather than in paid employment or consuming publicly provided welfare services. Time–budget studies show that after allowance for paid employment, sleeping, and essential personal care (eating, bathing, etc.), the average person has sixty-one hours a week of discretionary time. A portion of that time is spent in the market enjoying leisure products that can be purchased (e.g., going to a cinema or a pub). A portion is spent in pastimes that cost no money and are not productive (e.g., talking with friends or going for a walk). An adult on average spends about twenty-three hours a week in productive household activities in the domestic economy, doing such things as making meals for the family, doing laundry, undertaking minor household repairs, or servicing the family car (cf. Gershuny, 1981: Table 1; Rose, 1985a: Table 5). Changes in sex roles within the family have hardly affected the amount of time spent in aggregate in productive household activities, most of which provide welfare in a narrower or broader sense. Whereas little more than half of the adult population is in paid employment, every adult produces a substantial amount of welfare in the household.

The relative importance of the household as a source of welfare is indicated by comparing the twenty-three hours spent in productive tasks within the household with the smaller portion of time that an employed worker must spend to pay income and social security taxes; ten to twelve hours a week. When allowance is made for the fact that about half the taxes paid are not spent on welfare services but on other public programs such as defense or debt interest payments, the amount of work effort devoted to "producing" state welfare is further reduced.

The consumption of welfare in the home is affected by the life cycle. Elderly people need a pension, young people need an education, and middle-aged people want a secure job. Many state welfare services would appear to be designed particularly to benefit one age group within society, especially the young (e.g., education) or the elderly (e.g., health care and pensions). Insofar as services are only of use at one phase of the life cycle, they will not be consumed by everyone simultaneously. That explains why a majority of people do not make use of any one state welfare service examined in Table 4.10. But people not making use of one welfare service, such as pensions, are likely to be at a phase in the life cycle making use of another, such as education. Independence from any one state welfare service is a temporary phase in the life cycle. Benefits not consumed at one phase of the life cycle may nonetheless be appreciated by a process of anticipatory socialization.

Many welfare benefits affect several generations within a family or extended family. This is most evident with parents of young children. There are a variety of ways in which generations can live together within the same household. Even when families do not live in the same house, they may be concerned with the welfare of their parents or children. Middle-aged couples will be concerned with the health and income of parents in retirement, and older people with the life of their children, and with grandchildren too. Multiple cross-generational ties reflect interdependence between generations. Intergenerational interdependencies are so strong that the effect of the life cycle on the use of welfare services is limited; it is a matter of degree, not kind. This is shown when the consumption of welfare services is examined in three different age groups: young, middle-aged, and pensioners.

Of the major state welfare services, housing and public transportation tend to be distributed evenly across generations, and so too is hospital treatment for family members. Elderly people make more use of doctors than others, but only by a margin of 16 percent. Pensions constitute the one program that has the great age bias, but 22 percent of nonpensioners also live in a household with a pensioner. Unemployment is second in age bias, because 31 percent of those under age 30 live in a family where someone is unemployed, as against 19 percent of middle-aged people and 5 percent of those in retirement. Education too shows a skewed distribution, as older people are less likely to have anyone in their immediate household in school, albeit grandchildren in their extended household will often be pupils.

Many values central to the family are also independent of the life cycle. When Britons are asked about the importance of different concerns relevant to their welfare, the young and middle-aged, as well as the elderly, put health first (Table 4.11). Second in importance for the young and middle-aged is getting along with other members of the family; young people are concerned about getting along with their parents, and parents and older people with their children and grandchildren. Getting along with the opposite sex or a newly married spouse is a major concern of young people, and of middle-aged people too. Elderly people are more prepared to be alone, but a majority also want to talk with others each day. Two of these primary welfare concerns (getting along within the family and with other people) cannot be produced by the market or by bureaucratized state activities. The state health service can provide health care for those who lack health, but most British people want good health, not treatment for ill health.

When people are asked to evaluate their role in the market, here too there is a concern with social relations for their own sake, as well as with material advantages. An interesting job is regarded as more important than a well-paid job by most people of working age. Among Britons in

Table 4.11. Social Welfare Priorities in the Life Cycle

	Age group (% saying very important)		
	Young	Middle aged	Retired
Health	92	95	91
Getting along with others[a]	71	88	60
Getting along with parents/children	70	88	79
Job security	78	75	n.a.
Interesting job/things to do	71	73	74
Money	71	52	71
Spare-time activities	46	45	n.a.

Source: Gallup poll (1984). Young defined as age 18–29; middle-aged, men age 30–65, women age 30–60; retired, men age 65 plus, women age 60 plus.

[a]For young, opposite sex; for middle-aged, spouse; for retired, people to talk to each day.

retirement, more people believe it very important to have things to do to make life interesting than to be secure about money. Among those of working age, job security is also viewed as more important than money. This is the case even though only 25 percent of young people, 33 percent of the middle-aged, and 19 percent of the retired say that they are very satisfied with their income. The conventional economist's evaluation of welfare by income, and of income solely in terms of its money value, gives a partial and misleading picture of the priorities of welfare in British society. Most British people do consider money important—but it is less important than health, family relationships, and good social relationships with others.

From the perspective of the family, total welfare is a very real concern, but it is not reducible to that which can be bought in the market, and even less to that which can be given without charge by the state. Welfare is jointly the resultant of interdependent producers. It is appropriate to speak of the household, the market, and the state as separate institutions, for each has unique characteristics and capabilities for providing welfare. However, it is misleading to think of the welfare consumed by the family without also thinking of interdependencies among activities that can be separated analytically but cannot be separated by ordinary people in everyday life.

Welfare is mixed, since each major welfare need is usually met by two or three different sources. Furthermore, no one of the three sources (i. e., state, market, household) is consistently dominant as the producer of welfare. The persistence of the welfare mix rejects the one-dimensional extremes of the Fabian socialist proponents of the universalist and monopolistic state provision of welfare, and of market-oriented supporters of Margaret Thatcher, who wish to promote the market through privatization. The choices such groups pose are flawed by an all-or-nothing approach that assumes there can only be one source of welfare in society, albeit disagreeing about what that source should be. Neither provides an accurate empirical description of the actual mix of welfare sources in Britain today. Judging by the stability of the mix since 1951, the foreseeable future is likely to see Britons depend on a plurality of sources—the state, the market, *and* the household—for total welfare in the family.

REFERENCES

Annual Abstract of Statistics. London: Her Majesty's Stationery Office (HMSO), annual.

Annual Report of the Ministry of Education 1950. London: HMSO Cmd. 8244, 1951.

Beveridge, Lord. *Voluntary Action.* London: George Allen & Unwin, 1948.

Carpenter, Glyn, "National Health Insurance, 1911–1948." *Public Administration* 62(1):71–89, 1984.

Census 1901 General Report. London: HMSO Cd. 2174, 1904.

Census, 1981: Persons of Pensionable Age Tables. London: HMSO, 1983.

Charities Aid Foundation, *Charity Aid Statistics 1983-84.* Tonbridge, England: Charities Aid Foundation, 1984.

Department of Environment, *Housing Policy Technical Volume.* London: HMSO, 1977.

Department of Environment, *Housing and Construction Statistics, 1972-1982.* London: HMSO, 1983.

Department of Transport, *Transport Statistics: Great Britain 1981.* London: HMSO, 1982.

Digest of Health Statistics. London: HMSO, annual.

Donnison, D. V., *Urban Policy—A New Approach.* London: Fabian Society Tract No. 487, 1983.

Education Statistics for the United Kingdom, London: HMSO, 1983.

Family Expenditure Survey. London: HMSO, annual.

Gallup poll, *Britain's Families at Work* (a survey of 2064 analyzed by the author), 1984. For a brief overview, see *Gallup Political Index* No. 285, 1984, pp. 22–35.

General Household Survey. London: Social Survey Division, OPCS, HMSO, 1984.

Gershuny, J. I., "Changement des Modèles de Loisir, Royaume Uni, 1961–1974/5."*Temps Libres* 4:115–134, 1981.

Gwyn, William B. and Rose, Richard, eds., *Britain—Progress and Decline.* London: Macmillan, 1980.

Halsey, A. H., ed., *Trends in British Society since 1900.* London: Macmillan, 1972.

Halsey, A. H., Sheehan, J., and Vaizey, J., "Education," in *Trends in British Society* (A. H. Halsey, ed.), 1972, pp. 148–191.

Health and Personal Social Service Statistics: England 1982. London: HMSO, 1982.

Heclo, Hugh, *Modern Social Politics in Britain and Sweden.* New Haven, Conn.: Yale University Press, 1974.

Judge, Ken and Matthews, James, *Charging for Social Care.* London: Allen & Unwin National Institute Social Services Library No. 38, 1980.

Maclachlan, G. and Maynard, A., eds., *The Public/Private Mix for Health.* London: Nuffield Provincial Hospitals Trust, 1982.

Ministry of Agriculture, *Domestic Food Consumption and Expenditure, 1964.* London: HMSO, 1966.

Ministry of Agriculture, *Household Food Consumption and Expenditure, 1981.* London: HMSO, 1983.

National Income and Expenditure. London: HMSO, annual.

Obler, Jeffrey, "Private Giving in the Welfare State." *British Journal of Political Science* 11(1): 17–48, 1981.

Parker, Julia, "Welfare," in *Trends in British Society* (A. H. Halsey, ed.) 1972, pp. 372–406.

Parker, Julia, Rollett, C., and Jones, K., "Health," in *Trends in British Society* (A. H. Halsey, ed.), 1972, pp. 321–372.

Parry Richard, "Britain: Stable Aggregates, Changing Composition," in *Public Employment in Western Nations,* R. Rose, ed. Cambridge, England: Cambridge University Press, 1985, 54–96.

Rose, Richard, "England: A Traditionally Modern Political Culture," in *Political Culture and Political Development* (L. W. Pye and S. Verba, eds.) Princeton University Press, 1965, pp. 83–129.

Rose, Richard, "Getting by in Three Economies: The Resources of the Official, Unofficial and Domestic Economies," in *State and Market* (J. E. Lane, ed.). London and Beverly Hills, Calif.: Sage Publications, 1985a, pp. 103–141.

Rose, Richard, "The Significance of Public Employment," in *Public Employment in Western Nations* (R. Rose, ed.). Cambridge, England: Cambridge University Press, 1985b.

Rose, Richard and Karran, Terence, "Inertia or Incrementalism? A Long-Term View of the Growth of Government," in *Comparative Resource Allocation* (A. J. Groth and L. L. Wade, eds.). Beverly Hills, Calif.: Sage Publications, 1984, pp. 43–71.

Social Trends. London: Central Statistical Office HMSO, Number 15, annual, 1985.

Stacey, Margaret, "Who are the Health Workers? Patients and Other Unpaid Workers in Health Care." *Economic and Industrial Democracy* 5:2, 1984.

Taylor-Gooby, Peter and Papadakis, Elim, "Who Wants the Welfare State?" *New Society* (London), 19 July, no. 1177, 1985.

Titmuss, Richard M., *Problems of Social Policy.* London: Longmans & HMSO, 1950.

Treasury, *The Government's Expenditure Plans, 1985–86 to 1987–88.* London: HMSO, Cmnd. 9428-II, 1985.

Wilensky, Harold, *The Welfare State and Equality.* Berkeley: University of California Press, 1975.

Wolfenden Committee, *The Future of Voluntary Organisations.* London: Croom Helm, 1978.

5

The Civic Conception
of the Welfare State in Scandinavia

ERIK ALLARDT

In Scandinavian countries the welfare state has been seen as natural and normal; the state intervenes in order to guarantee a modicum of welfare and social security for all. A positive attitude to state intervention did not suddenly emerge during the twentieth century. Rather, it developed through the centuries under political conditions in which the state came to be conceived of largely as a benefactor of the common people.

Welfare theoreticians distinguish between two different, alternative approaches to the public commitment to social welfare (Wilensky and Lebaux, 1965: 130; Titmuss, 1974; Esping-Andersen and Korpi, 1984: 17). The terminology varies slightly, but one may speak about the residual and the comprehensive models of social welfare. The *residual* model refers to that residual group in society that is unable to help itself; it strongly emphasizes that the major part of the population can and ought to provide for its own welfare. According to this model, public sector benefits should be allocated on a means test basis.

The *comprehensive* model of social welfare, on the other hand, contains a strong value commitment to universalist welfare provisions; the welfare of the individual is considered the responsibility of society. There is a belief that social welfare should be guaranteed by political means rather than by the market mechanism. Means tests are rejected because they are viewed as negative acts of discrimination against the receivers of welfare provisions. Redistributive policies are crucial as a means of obtaining comprehensive welfare in a society.

The Scandinavian welfare systems approximate the comprehensive model. The Danish expert on social policy, Bent Rold Andersen, emphasizes comprehensiveness but adds that the Scandinavian welfare state cannot be grasped entirely on the basis of formal criteria or statistical data.

Nordic social welfare does not consist of social security and social service alone. Certainly, the folk high-school movement, the unusual extension of farmers' and consumers' cooperatives, the high rate at which wage-earners organize, the unity of the trade unions, and other factors, may have done more than social legislation to eliminate poverty and promote equality. Moreover, the geographic and demographic conditions in the Nordic countries favor decentralized agricultural and industrial structures, and these pull in the same direction. Yet is it beyond dispute that the Nordic countries are regarded as welfare states primarily because of their comprehensive system of cash benefits and their extensive public systems for the delivery of free services in the areas of health, education, and welfare. Not the totality, it is nevertheless the core of Nordic welfare (Andersen, 1984: 113).

The fit between the Scandinavian welfare state and the comprehensive model is not perfect, but the drive toward comprehensiveness has been a dominant tendency in the Scandinavian countries, and they are closer to the comprehensive model than other capitalist democracies. Yet, there are also more or less clear deviations on three main counts. First, there are clear differences among the Scandinavian countries. Although welfare expenditures in Sweden and Denmark are the highest in the world, the proportion of the labor force employed by general government does not place all the Scandinavian countries in a special position. Second, there are exceptions to the comprehensive model in some fields of social policy. Although there is a clear tendency to make social benefits independent of previous contributions, there are earnings-related pensions in all the Scandinavian countries. Third, although the Scandinavian welfare systems have deep historical roots, the rapid growth of social expenditures has occurred during the period after World War II. This has been a period in which the strength of the Social Democratic parties have been strong.

Nevertheless, it is reasonable to speak of the Scandinavian model. The uniqueness of the Scandinavian countries consists not of the size of the nonmarket sector but rather of the way in which services and benefits are organized, the rules of entitlements, and the absence of a connection between financing benefits and the entitlement to receive benefits.

The Scandinavian welfare system aims to be comprehensive on three counts. First, the welfare provisions are not targeted to special problem groups but are supposed to cover the entire population. Typical examples are national health insurance for all citizens and for all types of illnesses, and the old age pension, a flat-rate, noncontributory payment to all citizens after a given age. Second, the welfare programs are institutionalized by legislation in such a fashion that it is a statutory right of the citizen to have a modicum of publicly provided social welfare and social security. The claim on welfare services is largely independent of market criteria. In the main, the old liberal belief in the responsibility of the individual has been replaced by collective responsibility to help everyone maintain a normal standard of living. Third, the welfare provisions are supposed to cover a very wide range of life situations, including family concerns, leisure time activities, and political participation.

The drive toward comprehensiveness in the welfare system of the Scandinavian countries stands out clearly when compared to other welfare systems. In some countries, notably the United States, Australia, and New Zealand, social welfare tends to be organized in means-tested social assistance schemes. In times of hardships and difficulty the great majority is supposed to rely on privately contracted insurance programs. These countries adhere strongly to the residual model.

In continental countries in Europe, the social insurance programs are institutionalized in such a fashion that the coverage is much greater than in the above-mentioned English-speaking countries. Still, benefits usually depend on previous contributions, and in particular, on previous employment. Those outside the main groups in the labor market tend to be left outside the systems of insurance and social benefits.

In the Scandinavian countries there are insurance programs covering all citizens, and the tendency is to make social benefits independent of previous contributions. There are differences among the Scandinavian countries. In Esping-Andersen's and Korpi's comparative analysis (1984), Sweden comes closest to the comprehensive model. In a comparative perspective, the Scandinavian welfare model is clearly of the comprehensive type.

THE HISTORICAL ROOTS OF THE SCANDINAVIAN WELFARE MODEL

Statistical data about programs and laws of social policy describe central institutional welfare provisions, but an understanding of the totality of the welfare system requires an awareness of historical traditions and values prevailing in a society in order to grasp the social character of the Scandinavian welfare model.

Studies of individual well-being in the Scandinavian countries include a measure of political resources. This is true for both national, governmentally sponsored studies of the level of living (Johansson, 1971: 187) and for comparative, academic analyses of the general level of well-being (Allardt, 1981). The amount of a person's political resources has been measured by his or her participation in different kinds of political activities. The idea behind the measure is to ascertain to what extent individual citizens can influence or feel they can influence the world around them. There is nothing unique in measuring political participation and in considering political activity as a precondition for democracy. What is remarkable, however, is the persistence with which political resources are considered crucial and integral for the individual level of living and well-being.

The tendency to emphasize political participation as an integral part of individual well-being is rooted in the historical past. Even if the Scandinavian countries were not free of feudalism as much as envisaged in popular historical presentations, it is nevertheless correct to emphasize the

role of the land-owning peasantry in the development of the Scandinavian societies. Particularly in Sweden, there were on several occasions
alliances between the king and the peasantry against the nobles. More
important is the fact that the nobility in the Scandinavian countries was
never strong or large enough to eliminate the peasantry as a political
force. The Swedish Parliament, in which Finland also had representatives, was already founded in the fourteenth century, but the parliamentary tradition was finally institutionalized during the sixteenth and seventeenth centuries. The freeholding peasantry formed one of its four
estates.

The peasants also shared the burden of the defense of the state. During
the Middle Ages there had existed a fairly legitimate system of conscription, and a universal system of conscription was created at the end of the
seventeenth century. The system prevailing in Sweden and also in Finland until 1809 was a forerunner of the later democratic military draft.
Its base in Sweden and Finland was the peasantry.

There were considerable intercountry and intracountry variations in
the position of the peasantry during the sixteenth and seventeenth centuries. The most striking differences existed between Denmark and southern Sweden on the one hand, and most of Norway and Sweden on the
other. Denmark during these centuries was on the brink of becoming similar to the clearly feudal eastern European societies (Wallerstein, 1980:
223). Yet, in the eighteenth century the differences between the countries
with regard to the position of the peasantry and land-holding practices
began to diminish as a result of increased peasant proprietorship and
enclosure movements (Alestalo and Kuhnle, 1984). In a comparative
study of agrarian structure and peasant politics in Scandinavia, Øjvind
(Østerud) (1978: 69) has shown how during the eighteenth and nineteenth
centuries there occurred a clear privatization of agriculture. The transfer
of land to peasant proprietorship was based on state intervention, and it
happened before the actual modernization of agriculture and farming
methods. The land reforms were a prerequisite for technical innovations
in farm management. The land reforms also created social differentiation
between the land-holding and the landless population, as well as considerable regional differences.

The land reforms established a positive tie between the rural population and the state at the time preceding industrialization and the great
migration to the cities. This transformation of land-holding and tenure
systems is certainly one of the most important factors for an understanding of the fact that the state in the Scandinavian countries has not traditionally been conceived as an oppressive monolith, as in many continental countries. The state has in many respects carried an image of a
benefactor of the common people.

Equally important, the strength of the land-holding peasantry kept the
political Right from ever developing into a strong political force. The
British scholar Francis Castles (1978: 138) has explained the compara-

tively strong position of the social democratic parties in the Scandinavian countries by the traditional weakness of the political Right. This weakness in turn was an outcome of cultural and economic conflicts between urban elites and rural peasant producers. Peasants voted liberal or radical in defense of their interests and way of life.

The development of the Scandinavian welfare state was facilitated by a fairly widespread positive attitude to state interventionism. For centuries large groups of the common people did not feel themselves as being outside the political system. The difference between public and private, so crucial in many debates in the Anglo-American countries, was of minor importance in the Scandinavian countries. For example, until recently it has been considered legitimate for the state to collect and publish records of individual citizens. It is probably no accident that Sweden and Finland have the oldest population statistics in the world. Public participation has not been in contrast to the private and individual world. On the contrary, public participation has been a sign of individual activity and well-being.

Despite the historical roots of the Scandinavian welfare state, the comprehensiveness of the welfare state is very much a post-1945 phenomenon. The Scandinavian welfare system was built mainly during the two first decades after World War II.

The dominant tendencies, as well as some of the foremost exceptions, are very clearly reflected in the field of pension insurance, when Scandinavian countries began to apply policies that were clearly different from the practice in other countries, especially with regard to their comprehensiveness. The policy elsewhere was to add new groups to existing insurance schemes, whereas the aim in the Scandinavian countries was to construct entirely new programs independent of previous contributions and covering all citizens. Welfare entitlements as a rule cover all citizens, including housewives and people outside the labor market. On this count the tendency to comprehensiveness has been stronger than in almost all other countries.

It all started with the old age pension program initially introduced in Sweden, and subsequently adopted elsewhere in Scandinavia. This reflects a fairly common feature: Sweden has usually been the first to introduce new programs and social policy innovations, whereupon other countries have followed suit. In 1946 Sweden introduced a universal noncontributory pension for all citizens at age 67. All citizens received the same basic pension without any eligibility requirements. The other countries adopted similar pension schemes in the mid-1950s. In the wake of the pensions reform, many other social insurance programs such as those covering accidents and sickness were expanded. Their main features were that they were compulsory and comprehensive, covering all citizens.

By the mid-1950s new developments also occurred in the pensions. These developments are very crucial, both because they reflect general tendencies in the social policy of the Scandinavian countries and because they reveal some of the exceptions to comprehensiveness. The Swedish Social Democrats proposed a compulsory work- and earnings-related pension to complement the existing basic old age pension. The rationale for this proposal was that high-income earners usually supplemented their basic folk-pension by additional private insurance, while low-income earners were either unable or unwilling to take out private insurance. The Social Democrats considered this as threatening the commitment to solidarity and equality. The fight over the work-related pension was very fierce in Swedish politics during the latter half of the 1950s. The Social Democrats won the 1958 election, in which the new pension system was the main issue, and a new compulsory, employer-financed, and earnings-related pension scheme, usually signified by the letters ATP, was introduced by legislation in 1959. It applied to all employees and self-employed. Very important was that funding was organized in publicly controlled pension funds.

The introduction of earnings-related benefits signifies a deviation from the principle of equality. Yet, the Social Democrats considered it a necessary antidote to the tendency to use private schemes and for private insurance companies to accumulate large capital sums. It was also assumed to affect work motivation in a positive way. The Swedish government has also, by different kinds of supplements to low-income households, tried to compensate for the earnings-related nature of the ATP. It has also been argued that an earnings-related pension is the only guarantee against severe income loss.

The Swedish example had a compelling effect on the other countries. There was a general tendency to initiate the same kind of legislation in the other countries, but the subsequent developments took slightly different paths. The adoption of a similar scheme to Sweden was easiest and least controversial in Norway, where it was negotiated through collective bargaining in 1960. A bourgeois government finally legislated it in 1967, an example of the relatively consensual nature of social policy developments in Scandinavia.

Finland represents a different case. A scheme similar to Sweden's was accepted in 1962 with one very notable exception. Funding in Finland was organized in private insurance companies. It reflects the fact that Finland as a rule has a bourgeois majority in its parliament, and that the Social Democrats have never reached a dominant position as in the other Scandinavian countries.

In Denmark the Social Democrats and the labor movement have not succeeded in legislating reforms as in the other Scandinavian countries (Esping-Andersen, 1980; Esping-Andersen and Korpi, 1984: 20). There was a modest ATP-type reform in 1964, but the benefits are very small. There was also a law on noncontributory social pensions from 1971, but it is paid from public tax revenues and its benefits are likewise small. Thus, private and occupational insurance schemes *not* institutionalized into a comprehensive state pension system continue to form the dominant part of old age insurance in Denmark. While the ATP schemes have been implemented only to a minor extent, in Denmark general government revenues play an exceptionally heavy part in financing social expenditure.

One obvious consequence of the tendency to institutionalize compulsory, universal insurance schemes is that the middle-class and middle-income brackets become favored in comparison with low-income groups from the working class. The middle-income groups pay the same for health care as the low-income groups, but the former are usually more knowledgeable in taking up benefits. In this sense, means-tested programs have greater redistributive effects than do comprehensive, universal schemes. Generally the principles of universality and solidarity have in the Scandinavian welfare systems outweighed the concern for short-time redistribution. It has been assumed that programs stressing solidarity will in the long run have redistributive effects. In addition, the Social Democrats have assumed that redistribution is most effectively accomplished by progressive taxation.

DIFFERENCES AMONG THE SCANDINAVIAN COUNTRIES

The differences between the welfare systems in the Scandinavian countries stand out clearly when the developments of pension insurance are compared. As a general characterization, by about 1960 Denmark, Norway, and Sweden had laid a firm foundation for the modern comprehensive welfare state. Finland was a latecomer, but in many respects it caught up with the others during the 1960s.

Sweden has usually spearheaded the development and comes closest to the comprehensive model of welfare. The developments in Norway have been similar to those of Sweden, although the preference for state as against market mechanisms is less strong and obvious in Norway than in Sweden. This is perhaps most clearly seen in the field of labor market policy. By contrast to Sweden, in Norway industrial and credit policies rather than labor market policies have constituted the main means of maintaining full employment.

Denmark and Finland each in its own way deviates more from the Swedish model. Finland is a latecomer as a welfare state when compared to the other Scandinavian countries, but the time lag with respect to most major reforms has been less than ten years. Today the welfare programs in Finland adhere to the principle of the universality of coverage. Yet in such sectors as sickness and unemployment benefits, the level is lower than in the other countries.

The differences between Finland and other countries are to some extent explained by the lower GNP per capita, but there are leading Finnish politicians and industrialists who tend to maintain that the aim never has been to raise public social expenditure to the level of Sweden. Moreover,

Table 5.1. Public Welfare Provision in the Scandinavian Countries

Economic development, policies, services, and social expenditures	Denmark	Finland	Norway	Sweden
GNP per capita, 1979 (in U.S. $)	11,900	8,160	10,700	11,930
GNP yearly increase 1960–79 (%)	3.4	4.1	3.5	2.4
Public consumption 1979 (% GNP)	25	18	20	30
Public spending for education, 1979 (% GNP)	6.9	5.7	8.1	9.6
Health care, treatment of alcoholics, occupational guidance, retraining of workers, etc. 1978 (% GNP)	5.5	5.2	6.9	8.5
Social costs per capita, 1980 (U.S. $)	2,742	2,100	2,682	4,438
Social costs, 1980 (% GNP)	28	21	21	33
Income maintenance cash contributions, 1978 (% GNP)	13.7	12.6	11.6	18.3
Public expenditure, 1980 (% GNP)	53	39	41	63
Public support (% investments in housing)	29.4	14.6	32.6	26.9
New housing, 1978				
Public sector	2	8	4	20
Cooperative sector	16	—	17	10
Private sector	82	93	78	70
	100	100	100	100
Compensation for unemployment, (given to single, industrial worker), 1978 (% of salary)	79	44	64	77
Compensation for sickness, (given to single, industrial worker), 1978 (% of salary)	79	43	100	94
Annual children allowances (in families with three children), 1978 (U.S. $)	1,065	826	1,111	1,577

Source: Statistical Reports of the Nordic Countries (1984).

the social structure and the party system of Finland have some unique features in comparison with the other countries. There is a strong agrarian center party in Finland, and the development of welfare programs has required cooperation between the agrarian center party and the Social Democrats. The two parties have represented different interests.

> The Agrarian/Center Party has favored universal and flat-rate schemes, in the interest of the small-holding farming population. This gave them access to cash benefits which, despite their relatively low monetary value, were very important for them, given the still high degree of subsistence in Finnish agriculture. . . .
> The backwardness of Finnish housing policy is another example of the strength of the party: as a defender of the interests of the agricultural and other sectors of the rural population, it was not keen to support urban housing programs which, in addition to being an income transfer to the urban population, might also stimulate migration from rural to urban areas (Alestalo and Uusitalo, forthcoming).

In contrast, the Finnish Social Democrats and the trade unions have supported earnings-related schemes for the wage earners. Their aim has been to decrease the dependence on market criteria.

If the Finnish case in an inter-Scandinavian context can be explained partly by the traditional strength of the farm population and its political representations, the Danish case is similarly partly explained by the Danish social structure. Denmark has had a much larger traditional middle class than the other Scandinavian countries, and its economic life is dominated by middle-size and small enterprises (Wallensteen, Vesa, and Vayrynen, 1973: 97). Especially compared to Sweden, the economic structure of Denmark has been dominated by small units. Esping-Andersen and Korpi (1984: 55) characterize Denmark as the most residual and marginal in welfare policy among the Scandinavian countries. Inequalities also remain wider, especially in respect of housing and pensions. While social security for old age remains strongly related to noninstitutionalized forms of private insurance, on the other hand, Denmark tends to pay many lavish cash benefits from general tax revenue sources.

A comparison between Denmark and Sweden is illuminating. Sweden has gone farthest in a realization of the comprehensive model, but Swedes have usually displayed a great concern for the economic productivity of public spending. The Swedish labor movement, comprising both the Social Democrats and labor unions, set out in the early 1950s to institute a social policy that aimed at combining full employment, stable prices, economic growth, and a more equitable distribution of workers' wages. Thus, the labor market policy was directed toward retraining workers. The program also brought about a rapid increase in the average Swedish worker's standard of living and gave Sweden an edge in international markets. The development in Sweden presupposed and strengthened a fairly strong form of corporatist cooperation among the state, employers' organizations, and labor unions (Allardt, 1984a: 187). By contrast, welfare expenditures in Denmark have largely been in the form of services and lavish cash benefits with little or no bearing on economic growth.

Despite the inter-Scandinavian differences, there has been a widespread conviction that there is a right to a modicum of welfare, and that the basic social welfare of the citizens should not be based on market criteria. Welfare programs are based on a positive, trusting attitude toward the state as a guarantor of social welfare.

FINANCING PUBLIC SOCIAL EXPENDITURE

Despite some signs of attitudinal change and of weakening support for the idea of the welfare state in the 1980s, no actual cuts in spending for welfare programs have occurred in Scandinavia. Total expenditure by the state for pensions and other income maintenance payments and health programs has increased greatly as a proportion of a growing national product from 1950 to 1983. World recession struck in 1975, but increases continued, going up by one-third in Sweden (Table 5.2).

Table 5.2. Social Expenditure in Scandinavia, 1950–83[a]

Year	Denmark	Finland	Norway	Sweden
1950	8.0	7.3	6.3	8.5
1960	9.8	8.3	9.8	10.9
1970	17.9	13.6	14.7	17.9
1975	25.8	18.5	19.4	26.1
1980	20.1	21.6	21.7	32.6
1981	30.1	21.6	21.7	34.4
1983	30.7	23.5	22.2	35.7

Source: Statistical Reports of the Nordic Countries (1984).
[a]As percentage of GNP at market prices.

Public spending for income transfer and health programs are higher in Sweden (35.7 percent of GNP) than in other Scandinavian countries. The greatest increase in social costs occurred surprisingly late, between 1960 and 1970 and between 1970 and 1975. To a certain extent this is a statistical artifact for the early 1970s, since the increase in GNP was exceptionally small in 1974 and 1975.

The figures in Table 5.2 relate to public social costs required by law or instituted by income policy agreements reached by collective bargaining and binding for almost all employers and employees. There are also private insurance schemes not covered above, life insurance, voluntary health care provided by employers, and occupational training. Yet in Scandinavian countries, large-scale welfare and social security schemes have been required by law or instituted by such institutional mechanisms as broad income policy agreements.

Welfare policy in Scandinavia has been based on fairly clear redistributive and solidaristic principles. The prevailing methods of financing social security and social expenditure does not tie social benefits to individual contributions. The role of private, occupationally negotiated schemes with narrow coverage is generally small in income maintenance, health care, and most social services. Private hospital care is rare, as is private education during the compulsory school years.

The contributions by the employers, by insured individuals, and by general government revenue, vary considerably within Scandinavia (Table 5.3). In Denmark, 88 percent of welfare expenditure in 1981 was financed by general government revenue, whereas elsewhere about half comes from this source. Nearly 50 percent of the public social costs in Finland and Sweden were financed by the employers in 1981, whereas in Denmark only 10 percent of the social costs were financed by payments extracted from the employers. There has generally in the Scandinavian countries been a tendency to avoid connecting benefits to individual contributions. There are, however, differences among the countries. In Norway 20 percent of the public social costs were financed by individual contributions, while the corresponding figure for Sweden was only 1 percent.

Table 5.3. Percentage of Financial Responsibility for Public Social Expenditure in Scandinavian Countries, 1954–81

Source of financing	Denmark				Finland				Norway				Sweden			
	1954	1964	1975	1981	1954	1964	1975	1981	1954	1964	1975	1981	1954	1964	1975	1981
General government revenue	85	82	88	88	71	60	39	48	66	53	30	40	87	62	65	51
Employer contributions	3	3	10	10	23	33	52	46	11	22	47	40	3	21	24	48
Wage earner contributions	12	15	2	2	6	8	10	6	24	25	23	20	10	17	11	1
Total	100	100	100	100	100	101	101	100	101	100	100	100	100	100	100	100

Sources: Statistical Reports of the Nordic Countries (1969, 1984).

There are also quite remarkable time fluctuations in the burden of financing social expenditure. The share of the employers has doubled or trebled in all four countries, whereas the contributions of the individual wage earners have decreased. Most remarkable is the development in Sweden, where the financial responsibility of the employers has increased from 3 percent in 1954 to 48 percent in 1981. Simultaneously the contributions of the Swedish wage earners were reduced to almost nil. When there are increasing difficulties in financing welfare programs, it is politically more feasible to put the burden immediately upon the employers, a small fraction of the electorate, rather than upon employees, a majority of the electorate. In economic theory, the burden is eventually passed on to individual consumers, but in political practice, the immediate result is that the costs of benefits are *not* linked to insurance-type contributions by individuals, or to fees paid to secure services.

THE LEVEL OF WELFARE

The amount of welfare in a society cannot be directly equated with the activities of the welfare state or of the welfare programs. This is true whether we define welfare by the amount of need satisfaction in a population or by the individuals' possession of these resources by which they can master their own lives. Even when the welfare state aims at comprehensiveness, only a part of the welfare is produced by the state. Comprehensiveness simply means that the rights to a normal living standard are *independent of market criteria,* and that everybody is insured against income loss and hardships. In all societies only a part of total welfare, in the sense of need satisfaction or the possession of necessary resources, is produced by the state.

As Rose emphasizes in Chapter 1, total welfare in a society is the sum of distinctive contributions by the state, the market, and the household. Shiratori's chapter (Chapter 9) stresses that welfare in Japanese society contains three main elements: public assistance programs and public services, reliance upon activities within families, and welfare facilities and services of the local community and such private organizations as business enterprises. Nonstate sources ot total welfare also exist in the Scandinavian societies; some are common to many societies, and a few reflect Scandinavian ways of life.

There are no systematic Scandinavian data about the contributions of different producers of welfare. On the other hand, there is an abundance of noncomparative information about different contributors to the total welfare. A Finnish study has made a very systematic attempt to estimate the value of all unpaid work done in private households. For instance, the value of all unpaid cooking work done in Finland in 1980 was estimated at around 7 percent of the GNP (Suviranta and Mynttinen, 1981:

23). It is apparent that private households are very basic producers of welfare in almost all societies.

There are good data about the total level of welfare prevailing in the Scandinavian societies, regardless of the source of welfare production, from a multitide of level-of-living and quality-of-life surveys. The first comparative welfare survey of Denmark, Finland, Norway, and Sweden was conducted by the Research Group for Comparative Sociology at the University of Helsinki in the 1970s (Allardt, 1981). This comparative study systematically conceptualized and employed indicators denoting the end results, not the agents of welfare production. Thus, what was measured was the actual health of the national populations, not the health services.

In classifying the indicators in the Comparative Scandinavian Welfare Study, total welfare was defined as containing two main elements: the *material level of living,* defined as including income, housing conditions, employment, working conditions, health and level of education; and the *quality of life,* a more composite concept referring people's actual relations to, rather than their attitude toward, (1) other people, in face-to-face relations; (2) society, and (3) nature. The three indicators for the quality of life are, in greater detail:

1. *Other people:* Attachment to the local community; attachment to family and kin; attachment to organizations; active friendship relations. The assumption is that most people are in great need of attachments to other people or solidaristic relations. Some relations may have negative effects or in certain situations be felt as burdens.
2. *Society:* An active personal life is assumed in the Scandinavian countries as an important part of total welfare. Positive involvement is assumed to denote personal growth, while a negative relation stands for alienation. Indicators of social relations include the extent to which a person can participate in decisions and activities influencing his or her life (political resources), interesting things to do (doing), freedom from fear in the neighborhood (safety), the degree to which a person is needed in various contexts (indispensability).
3. *Nature:* The indicators should tap to what extent a person lives in a neighborhood reasonably free from pollution, noise, danger from explosions and so on, but they should also measure to what extent people have the opportunity to enjoy nature either through activities or contemplative experiences.

A picture of the level of welfare in the Scandinavian societies is given in Table 5.4. The order between the countries is to a certain degree the same as when the economic base and the public social expenditures were compared in Table 5.2, but the tendency is not consistent. Sweden, as the

Table 5.4. Level of Living and Quality of Life in Scandinavian Countries

Indicators	Denmark	Finland	Norway	Sweden
Material level of living				
Private consumption (% GNP)	56	55	49	53
Cars per 100 inhabitants	267	267	311	348
Telephones per 1000 inhabitants	641	496	452	792
Crowded dwellings (more than one person per bedroom, %)	3	33	6	4
Persons aged 20-64 living in dwellings with bathroom or shower (%)	90	67	93	97
Unemployed (% labor force)	7	5	2	2
Mean longevity (age)				
Men	71.3	68.5	72.3	72.5
Women	77.4	77.1	78.7	78.7
Infant mortality per 1000 births	7.9	7.6	7.5	6.9
College-level education (% total population aged 20–64)	14	15	13	17
Quality of life: Face-to-face relations				
Persons aged 20–63 living alone (%)	17	18	11	20
People living in marriages or common-law marriages (number per 100 living alone aged 20–64)	467	386	735	364
Suicides per 100,000 inhabitants	24.1	25.4	10.7	19.3
Quality of life: Relations to society				
Members, of political parties (% aged 20–64)	8	15	17	15
Members of trade unions (% aged 20–64)	77	76	61	84
Newspaper circulation per 1000 inhabitants	366	505	462	528
Access to TV (%)	93.6	93.0	—	96.3
Leisure time activities during last year (% aged 20–64)				
Read weekly magazine	—	96	84	83
Read books	—	80	78	77
Attended a sport event	—	40	38	41
Wrote a private letter, participated in a play, music or dancing	—	10	8–10	15
Attended movie, theater, concert, or art exhibition	—	70	41	37
Quality of life: Relations to nature				
Persons owning summer or leisure time house (% aged 20–64)	12	24	25	21
Persons with access to small boat (% aged 20–64)	8	4	—	17

Source: The Nordic Council (1983). Data for about 1980.

richest country, has the highest level of welfare but the order among the other three countries varies from item to item. National idiosyncrasies play a certain role, and some differences are best explained by cultural traditions.

The Swedes clearly have the highest material standard. The order among the other countries varies, but Finland is on a lower level than the others when it comes to health and housing. With reference to mean longevity, the difference of 8.6 years between Finnish men and women is noteworthy. The Finns have a lower housing standard than the Danes, Norwegians, and Swedes, but some part of the differences might be due to different cultural traditions. The absence of bathrooms and showers in Finnish households is to some extent explained by the importance of the Finnish sauna. Particularly in the countryside, a sauna is often built before beginning construction of the house.

Looking at the indicators of social relations, it is notable that the Norwegians maintain closer social relations than other Scandinavians. The comparatively low suicide rate in Norway has been subject to many interpretations; most emphasize that a feeling of community is particularly strong in the Norwegian society. Analyses have also emphasized the existence of a combination of egalitarian and consensual traditions in Norwegian society (Eckstein, 1966; Lafferty, 1981).

In political activities, newspaper reading, and other cultural habits, the Swedes are consistently most active, but the differences among the countries are small. National traditions and idiosyncrasies create differences.

The patterns of welfare consumption do not fully conform to the pattern of public welfare production in Scandinavia. Even if it has not been possible to perform a systematic comparison between welfare production and the level of total welfare, the data at least support the assumption that welfare in the society cannot be produced solely by the state. The level of welfare also depends on national ways of life, and on traditions embedded in the culture.

CHANGING ATTITUDES TOWARD THE WELFARE STATE

A positive attitude to the state, the relative weakness of the political Right, and a tradition of political participation by peasantry can explain both Scandinavian Social Democracy and the welfare state (Castles, 1978: 138f). The Social Democrats were also the architects of the Scandinavian welfare state, and for a long time the realization of the welfare state was specifically a goal of the Social Democratic movement.

An apt summary of the political goals of the Social Democrats in Denmark and Sweden has been made by Gosta Esping-Andersen (1980: 262).

Since the 1930s, the major goal of the Social Democrats has been the establishment of a modern, comprehensive welfare state in which the state takes over responsibiluty for the adequacy of any individual's or household's standard of living and social and economic security. In both countries, the model has been similar: first, the construction of an effective security net, which prohibits anyone from falling into abject poverty; second, a system of immediate aid to people who for some reason find themselves in sudden need; third, a system of income transfer to obtain more equality in the rewards structure; and, finally, a system of promoting an equalization of chances in the opportunity structure.

Esping-Andersen goes on to say that in both countries, the social democratic parties feel that by and large they have succeeded in attaining most of their original welfare goals. In the process, the welfare goals have also ceased to be that party's near-monopoly. All major political parties in the Scandinavian countries today support largely the social democratic prewar conception of the welfare state. A Norwegian study (Kuhnle and Solheim, 1981) contents that "all parties seem committed to the present format of the welfare state in Norway."

Yet, the quality and nature of the support is hardly the same as it has been. Survey studies indicate that people in the Scandinavian countries still strongly support welfare and social security programs, and that social policies rank high on voters' priority lists. According to Norwegian election studies, those who have wanted a reduction of the expenditure for social security have usually amounted to less than 10 percent of the electorate (Valen and Martinussen, 1977: 39). A so-called welfare backlash has been observed, but it has been relatively weak and has only momentarily gained some momentum. A Finnish Gallup poll in 1980 indicated that 21 percent of respondents considered the pace by which new social security programs were instituted to be too rapid, but another 21 percent considered the pace too slow, and 56 percent considered the pace to be just right. Some studies even indicate that popular support for the welfare state in Denmark and Norway has increased significantly from the mid-1970s (Kohlberg and Pettersen, 1981; J. G. Andersen, 1982).

The electorates in the Scandinavian countries do not appear to want abandonment of the traditional welfare policy. In Denmark, the anti-tax party of Mogens Glistrup has attracted worldwide publicity, but its success was only momentary. In 1973 it received 15.9 percent of the vote, but in the 1984 election the support dwindled to 3.6 percent of the total vote. In this sense, there is no reason to speak about a crisis of the welfare state in the Scandinavian countries.

There are, however, more subtle meanings of a crisis of the welfare state. The idea of the welfare state might lose its appeal as a motivating factor, even if nobody wanted to abandon it. The proliferation of patterns of state regulation of welfare and the level of living is a crucial historical process, but one that may now have lost its momentum. The increasing importance of the state and of state regulations has meant a routinization of many demands that earlier were important goals of mass organizations based on group interests. To the extent the mass organizations have been successful, their demands have been incorporated by the state. Insofar as it is true that the idea of the welfare state and the organizations behind its rise have lost some of their motivating power, then this loss is likely to be felt among young people in particular. In fact, it implies that some of the channels and socializing agents that were crucial for the transition to adulthood in the early industrial society have ceased to be important.

The observation about the decreasing motivational power of the idea of the welfare state conforms with Wolfgang Zapf's contention (1982) that one of the problems of the welfare state lies in its very success. To put it simply, human activities aimed to produce subjective feelings of satisfaction tend to be followed by disappointment as soon as they succeed. Attitudinal surveys also indicate changes in the climate of opinions. The leading Swedish pollster and sociologist Hans Zetterberg (1983) has described the changes in terms of Max Weber's well-known distinction between a *zweckrational* and *wertrational* orientation. Typical for both politics and public policy in the welfare state has been an emphasis on practical results, or in Weber's terminology, the zweckrational. The belief has been that people in politics pursue their self-interest and rights. A very basic assumption in the Scandinavian welfare policy has been that if people are provided with a sufficient set of resources they will be able to use them for the rational pursuit of their happiness and well-being.

On the basis of extensive survey data, Zetterberg points to various signs of the increasing importance of a *wertrational* orientation. People have begun to emphasize their subjective experiences, the importance of listening to inner voices, and following principles instead of social demands and the pursuit of material well-being. There is a trend toward a committed rationality, an ethics of principle apart from the ethics of consequence, to use another of Max Weber's famous dichotomies. The new mood emphasizing the fate of the individual is combined with a distrust of the political apparatus and the state bureaucracy. On the basis of comparative data, Zetterberg shows that the reborn concerns for personal growth, committed rationality, and inner experiences not only are stronger among young people than among adults, but they also tend to be stronger in Sweden than in many other nations. Attitudinal tendencies of a similar kind have also been observed in other Scandinavian countries (Galtung, Poleszynski, and Rudeng, 1980: 155; Allardt, 1984b: 20).

Overall the comprehensive model of welfare state provision has not to any noticeable extent been challenged in the Scandinavian societies. A clear majority are opposed to any sort of drastic cuts in the welfare expenditures. Neither has there been any political attempt to change the welfare systems in any important sense. The most serious criticism is voiced by the group of young people who represent the "Greens" in some European parliaments. They do not attack the welfare state, but they strongly criticize some of the assumptions on which the present social and international order as well as the welfare state is built. The comprehensive Scandinavian welfare model today suffers more from a decline in enthusiasm than it does from direct attacks.

REFERENCES

Alestalo, Matti and Uusitalo, Hannu, "Finland: The Development of the Welfare States after World War II," in *The Development of the Western European Welfare States since World War II, Vol. I: The Scandinavian Countries* (Peter Flora, ed.). Berlin: De Gruyter (also New York: Aldine, and The Hague: Mouton), forthcoming.

Alestalo, Matti and Kuhnle, Stein,"The Scandinavian Route: Economic, Social and Political Developments in Denmark, Finland, Norway, and Sweden." *Research Group for Comparative Sociology.* University of Helsinki, *Research Reports,* No. 31, 1984.

Allardt, Erik, "Experiences from the Comparative Scandinavian Welfare Study with a Bibliography of the Project." *European Journal of Political Research* 9:101–111, 1981.

Allardt, Erik, "Representative Government in a Bureaucratic Age." *Daedalus,* Winter, 113:169–197, 1984a.

Allardt, Erik, "Shifting Sources of Discontent: The New Subjectivism." *Scandinavian Journal of Development Alternatives* 3:3–24, 1984b.

Andersen, Bent Rold, "Rationality and Irrationality of the Nordic Welfare State." *Daedalus,* Winter, 113:109–139, 1984.

Andersen, Jorgen G., "Den folkelige tilslutning till sosial-politikken—krise for velfaerdsstaten?"(The popular support of social policy: a crisis for the welfare state?), in *Partier, Ideologier, Valjare* (Parties, ideologies, voters), (D. Anckar, E. Damgaard, and H. Valen, eds.). Abo: Abo Akademi, 1982, pp. 175–209.

Castles, Francis G., *The Social Democratic Image of Society. A Study of the Achievements and Origins of Scandinavian Social Democracy in Comparative Perspective.* London: Routledge & Kegan Paul, 1978.

Eckstein, Harry, *Division and Cohesion in Democracy: A Study of Norway.* Princeton, N.J.: Princeton University Press, 1966.

Esping-Andersen, Gosta, *Social Class, Social Democracy and State Policy.* Copenhagen: New Social Science Monographs, 1980.

Esping-Andersen, Gosta and Korpi, Walter, "From Poor Relief Towards Institutional Welfare States: The Development of Scandinavian Social Policy." *Institutet for Social forskning. Stockholms universitet. Meddelande* 5/1984.

Galtung, Johan, Poleszynski, Dag, and Rudeng, Erik, *Norge i 1980-Arene. Hvilke Alternativer finnes?* (Norway in the 1980s: what alternatives are there?). Oslo: Gyldendal Norsk Forlag, 1980.

Johansson, Sten, *Politiska Resurser* (Political resources). Stockholm: Allmanna forlaget, 1971.

Kohlberg, Jon Eivind and Pettersen, Per Arnt, "Om velferdsstatens politiske basis" (On the political basis of the welfare state). *Tidsskrift for Samfunnsforskning* 22:193–222, 1981.

Kuhnle, Stein and Solheim, Liv, "Party Programs and the Welfare State: Consensus and Conflict in Norway 1945–1977," paper presented at the ECPR Session of Workshops, Lancaster, England, March 29–April 5, 1981.

Lafferty, William, *Participation and Democracy in Norway: The Distant Democracy Revisited,* Oslo, University Books, 1981.

The Nordic Council, *Levnadniva och ojamlikhet i Norden. En komparativ analys av de nordiska levnadsnivaundersokningarna* (Level of Living and Inequality in the Nordic Countries. A Comparative Analysis of the Nordic Studies of the Level of Living). Goteborg: The Nordic Council, 1983.

Østerud, Øjvind, *Agrarian Structure and Peasant Politics in Scandinavia.* Oslo: University Books, 1978.

Statistical Reports of the Nordic Countries, *Social trygghet i de nordiska landerna* (Social security in the Nordic countries. Coverage, expenses and financial resources), Vol. 16, 1969; Vol. 34, 1978, and Vol. 43, 1984.

Suviranta, Annikki and Mynttinen, Arto, Housework Study, part IV: The Value of Unpaid Cooking Work. *Official Statistics of Finland. Special Social Studies SVT XXXII: 76.* Helsinki: Ministry of Social Affairs and Health, 1981.

Titmuss, Richard, *Social Policy.* London: George Allen & Unwin, 1974.

Valen, Henry and Martinussen, Willy, "Electoral Trends and Foreign Policy in Norway: 1973 Storting Election and the EEC Issue," in *Scandinavia at the Polls* (Karl H. Cerny, ed.). Washington D. C.: The American Enterprise Institute, pp. 39–72, 1977.

Wallensteen, Peter, Vesa, Unto, and Vayrynen, Raimo, "The Nordic System: Structure and Change, 1920–1970." *Tampere Peace Research Institute Research Reports,* No. 6, 1973; also in *Department of Peace and Conflict Research,* Uppsala University, Reports No. 4, 1973.

Wallerstein, Immanuel, *The Modern World System II. Mercantilism and the Consolidation of the European World Economy 1600–1750.* New York: Academic Press, 1980.

Wilensky, Harold L. and Lebaux, Charles N., *Industrial Society and Social Welfare.* New York: Free Press, 1965.

Zapf, Wolfgang, "Gegenwartsprobleme und Entwicklungstendenzen westeuropaischer Gesellschaften." *IHS-Journal* 6:121–133, 1982.

Zetterberg, Hans L., "The Victory of Reason: Max Weber revisited." *SIFO-skriftserie,* No. 2, 1983.

6

Development, Structure, and Prospects of the German Social State

WOLFGANG ZAPF

After three decades of a historically unique increase in welfare—propelled by enormous economic growth, the prevention of severe military conflicts, and the extension of social rights—in recent years the momentum has slowed. The popular theory depicts the first oil price shock of 1973 as the turning point. In theoretical discussions, the ecological, economic and social limits of growth are explored. Political debate centers on the crisis of the welfare state: its nature, extent, and the causes of the crisis. There are two big questions: What innovation possibilities do modern Western democracies have? What might their future developmental path be?[1]

In this chapter we look at the German version of the welfare state. Starting with an outline of German development in a comparative perspective, we interpret the origin of German social politics as defensive modernization, and its present order as *Sozialstaat*. The recent battle over consolidation policies brings us to a broader discussion of the basic elements of welfare production, the nature of the present crisis and innovative potentials, and the future prospects of a welfare society.

THE GERMAN CASE IN COMPARATIVE PERSPECTIVE

Germany has been called a belated nation. National unification was completed only in 1871 as the German Empire under Prussian leadership, and that solution of the nation-building problem has contributed to subsequent breakdowns that today are resulting in the division of Germany. Germany also is a latecomer in industrialization and democratization. The economic takeoff is dated at the period 1850–73, compared to 1783–1802 in Britain, 1830–60 in France, and 1843–60 in the United States (cf. Rostow, 1960: 38). A democratic constitution was not introduced until

1919, and the Weimar Republic collapsed in 1933 when it could not keep up with the totalitarian alternative of Nazism, which provoked World War II. Correspondingly, the spread of mass welfare was very late; only in the 1960s did West Germany match other European democracies.

Not only is German development belated, it is also characterized by extreme ups and downs. This is shown most clearly by the index of total industrial production, which might be called the fever curve of modern German history. It can also be demonstrated by the index of real wages in the industrial sector, which we take as the best approximation to measuring mass living standards (see Figure 6.1). Mass welfare doubled during the forty years of the imperial regime. After the business cycle crises of the imperial period, there were four severe breakdowns: World War I, the Great Inflation of 1923, the Great Depression, and the aftermath of World War II. These catastrophes have repeatedly plunged mass welfare below the 1913 level. Only the period of the Federal Republic of Germany since 1949 has resulted in high mass consumption and affluence. Although other countries too had a post-1945 boom, in West Germany the three- to fourfold increase in living standards, given historical mem-

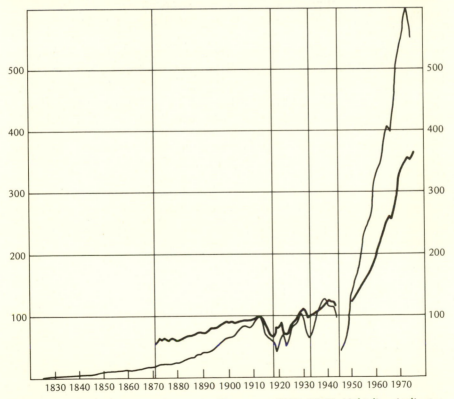

Figure 6.1. Welfare development in Germany, 1830–1975. Light line indicates volume index of total industrial production; heavy line indicates index of real weekly earnings in industry. 1913 = 100. (Adapted from Zapf, 1979: 221.)

ories and the experience of collapse in military defeat in 1945, was viewed as an economic miracle.

In order to understand the German version of the welfare state, one has to relate Germany's leading role in the introduction of public social security to that belated and erratic development. Until World War I, Germany had an impressive lead in old age, sickness, and work injuries insurance, which was introduced by Bismarck's legislation in the 1880s (see Table 6.1). These pioneering efforts have shaped the German welfare state; from the beginning it has been based on the core of obligatory public insurance systems according to the equivalence principle. Income maintenance is still today oriented to preserving market income and contribution differentials between workers while simultaneously providing security for each individual. German social politics is status preservation, with only a few elements of vertical redistribution and only a minor family component. None of the Weimar and the Federal Republic reforms have changed the system toward a common basic insurance or toward a national health service, or, for that matter, toward a comprehensive school system. Nevertheless—institutional traditions and the equivalence principle nothwithstanding—German social politics today are, in terms of coverage and benefits, in the top group of Western welfare states.[2]

Starting from the highest social expenditure ratio in 1960, the growth rate of the welfare state during the subsequent two decades was somewhat

Table 6.1. Expansion of Social Insurance Systems, 1900–70[a]

System and year	Germany	France	Britain	Sweden	Netherlands	Switzerland
Sickness						
1900	39	9	—	13	—	—
1935	52	36	79	32	(42)[b]	79
1970	67	96	100	100	74	100
Old age						
1900	53	(8)	—	—	—	—
1935	68	36	79	100	56	—
1970	81	93	83	100	100	100
Work injuries						
1900	71	10	39	—	—	16
1935	76	53	66	57	40	31
1970	95	85	94	79	73	(56)
Unemployment						
1900	—	—	—	—	—	—
1935	35	1	63	2	16	28
1970	71	61	76	55	78	17

Source: Adapted from Alber (1982: 236).
[a]Proportion of paying members given as percentage of total labor force.
[b]Data in parentheses are estimates.

slower than in some other countries, but West Germany still belongs to the top group. As far as total public expenditure and total taxes are concerned, West Germany is in the middle range of OECD countries; accordingly, the direct state financing, total transfer, and the amount of redistribution by the state are lower than in the Scandinavian welfare states. And as in the beginning, a century ago, the structure of social expenditures is dominated by old age and sickness benefits and by health care. This holds for all welfare states, but some have a stronger emphasis on family, employment, and vocational mobility. In private substitutes for public social security (e.g., private life insurance), West Germany is behind others. As to overall economic performance, West Germany was hard hit by the recent crisis, with a negative growth from 1981 to 1983, high unemployment, and a loss of jobs. On the other hand, there have been only a few strikes, regular moderate wage increases, mild inflation, and consequently no welfare loss for the employed majority.

IMPERIAL SOCIAL POLICY AS DEFENSIVE MODERNIZATION

In German social history the dissolution of the feudal and guild order is described as a burdensome process, stretching from the Napoleonic Wars (Peasants' Liberation, 1807, Freedom of Trade, 1810) until the breakdown of the German Empire and the Weimar Constitution of 1919. Whereas the reforms of 1807–10 created the preconditions of industrialization and urbanization, and whereas the foundation of the German Customs Union (*Zollverein*) in 1834 was an important factor for economic takeoff, the failure of the 1848 revolution and the authoritarian restoration meant a long-term retardation of democratization. Only the North German and German Empire trade regulations (1869, 1871) granted trade unions freedom of organization, and these liberties were soon revoked by the Anti-Socialist Law of 1878, "against efforts of the Social Democrats dangerous for the Public." The new industrial proletariat had no effective protection by trade unions and labor parties until the end of the nineteenth century. Although the unions—split into socialist, christian and liberal organizations—quickly increased their membership after 1869 and the Social Democrats won a large vote, during the imperial period the labor movement had no role in the creation of public social policies in Germany.

The nineteenth century forerunners of modern social policies were friendly society-type insurances in some crafts and in coal mining, savings banks, health insurance and benevolent funds of enterprises, and local poverty relief and charity organizations. These institutions always had the double function of social protection and social control that is characteristic of German social politics up to the present. The few local workers' funds could not form any counterstructure. A second strand of public social politics was concerned with workers' protection (e.g., the prohibition of the truck system of paying wages and the regulation of women's labor and child labor). A regulation of 1839 banned the employment of children under 9 years of age in factories and commanded a minimum of schooling for youths under 16 years of age, but there was little enforcement of these regulations. In any case, the motive for these regulations was more a concern for the health and poor educational status of military conscripts than purely social protection (cf. Henning, 1977; Lampert, 1980).

Despite these efforts, until the 1880s there was "public abstinence in social politics," insufficient protection against the loss of earnings, insufficient workers' protection, and massive inhibition of workers' interest organization—at a time when, according to the first occupational census of 1882, 34 percent of the labor force was already working in the industrial sector (compared to 43 percent in the primary and 23 percent in the tertiary sector). The subsequent rapid implementation of social security legislation therefore calls for an explanation, and perhaps the simplest and most obvious one had to do with political control and integration. The "Imperial Message" of 1881 stated "that the cure of social illness should not be wanted exclusively by ways of repression of Social Democratic transgressions but equally by the positive advancement of the well-being of the workers" (Lampert, 1980: 127).

The Law Concerning the Sickness Insurance of Workers of 1883 established an obligatory public insurance system for all manual workers and for low-paid white-collar employees, which was sustained by the existing factory health insurances jointly with new local institutions. The benefits consisted of medical service, medicine, and sickness leave pay for 13 weeks, later extended to 26 weeks. The system was financed by contributions (two-thirds from employees and one-third from employers). Representatives were also sent to the institutions' boards in those proportions.

The Work Injuries Insurance Law of 1884 was an obligatory insurance system for the same groups. It was financed by the employers only, was administered by the occupational associations, and provided medical care, pay, and pensions that extended also to survivors in case of accidents at work.

The Law Concerning Invalidity and Old Age Insurance of 1889 again was an obligatory insurance system for all manual workers (and low-paid white-collar employees), financed equally by employees and employers, offering a pension in case of invalidity and old age over 70 that amounted to 15 to 40 percent of the working income, depending on the length of contributions.

The three systems expanded rapidly (see Table 6.2). In 1895 practically all employees had work injury insurance; later on, self-employed persons were included. Invalidity and old age insurance was extended in 1899 to farmworkers; from 1911 it paid survivors' pensions, and in the same year

Table 6.2. The Early Stages of German Social Insurance Systems, 1885–1915

Year	Number of members (× 1,000)		Old age pensions (× 1,000)	Total population (× 1,000)
	Illness	Injuries		
1885	4,294	3,828[a]	—	46,856
1895	7,526	18,389	318	52,280
1905	11,184	20,243	935	60,652
1915	13,841	26,145	1,339	64,926[b]

Source: Bevölkerung und Wirtschaft (1972: 219–224).
[a] 1886.
[b] 1910.

a special institution for all white-collar employees was established. Health insurance was extended to farmworkers in 1911.

After Bismarck's resignation and the suspension of the Anti-Socialist Law, a new direction in social politics stimulated legislation in the fields of workers' protection and labor law, benefiting healthy workers and not only sick ones, unlike the insurance systems. Work on Sundays was prohibited in 1891, and child labor in 1903; the ten-hour day for women became obligatory in 1908. Wages politics could be developed on a voluntary basis. Only after the defeats during World War I, did the governors of the German Empire drop their strategy of separating the working class from trade unions and the Social Democratic party. As Lampert summarizes:

> The social politics was, at its core, patriarchal, authoritarian and repressive; it tried to withhold from the workers, their party and their trade unions always the full integration into state and society, based on equal rights; it was eventually broken only by the necessities of the World War: The guarantee of war production and the functioning of a strong economy during the war seemed only possible if the workers got, by obligatory workers' committees, participation rights on the firm level and if trade unions got full acceptance as the workers' representatives (Lampert, 1980: 136).

The rise of social politics in Germany has many undercurrents, but it can be basically interpreted as defensive modernization, that is, an effort to improve the security of the working class in order to guarantee the security of the upper classes and their regime. That interpretation is corroborated by developments in other continental European countries, in which social rights were granted as a substitute for political rights by authoritarian regimes that until 1900 had a clear lead in social security and social protection legislation. "The key for an understanding of the early developments in Western Europe is not to be found in the reform claims of the labour movement but in the legitimization strategies of national elites" (Alber, 1982: 133).

THE SOCIAL STATE IN THE FEDERAL REPUBLIC OF GERMANY

The Federal Republic has maintained to an astonishing degree the social politics tradition that dates back to the German Empire. The Weimar Republic had energetically extended workers' protection and social security, for example, by introducing in 1927 an unemployment insurance system. Next, it has strengthened policies for codetermination, labor market, and housing. Since the Nazi period, from which only a coercive family policy is noteworthy, the Federal Republic has rebuilt, enlarged, completed, and dynamized preexisting institutions. Added have been educational policies, employment policies, a new wave of housing policies, and efforts to promote a property for employees policy. There have been enormous quantitative extensions of existing systems. Whereas the total of social security expenditures was below 5 percent of GNP in imperial Germany and below 10 percent in the Weimar period, it passed the 20 percent mark in the 1960s and the 30 percent mark in the 1970s. But there has been no fundamental system change. That means that basic alternatives, developed in other countries such as Britain and Sweden, have not been adopted.

The West German version of the welfare state is the social state (*Sozialstaat*), which is legitimated, in the constitution of 1949, by formulations such as "democratic and *social* federal state" (Art. 20,1) and "republican, democratic and *social* constitutional state" (Art. 28,1). Compared to a classical liberal constitution, not only the formal but also the material freedom of citizens has to be guaranteed and developed. The state has an obligation to provide a decent standard of living and social justice, including, according to current standards, income security, employment security, and preservation of earning power. In Germany the notion of welfare state *(Wohlfahrtsstaat)* still has a rather negative connotation, as stated in a leading encyclopedia: "To be distinguished from the Social State has to be the patronizing welfare state which endangers personal initiative and responsibility" (*Brockhaus Enzyklopädie*, 1973: 637). The comprehensive British Beveridge program of care from cradle to grave or the Swedish *Volksheim* ideology are rejected. Security has priority over equality, and a broad consensus would in any event support only the principle of equality of opportunity not that of equality of results.

The basic idea of the German social state is that the state's obligation to guarantee a decent standard of living and social justice is supplemented by (1) solidarity, the obligation of associations to help their members; (2) subsidiarity, the obligation to let the small units play their part; and (3) the obligation of self-help. That might sound like an abstract philosophical discourse, but these ideas still materialize in the institutions and policies in West Germany, which are governed by group-specific compulsory insurance systems and the equivalence of contributions and benefits, as against national schemes and equal benefits. The separate old age insurance for white-collar employees introduced in 1911 is still in existence, and even the shop closing hours regulation of 1899 has survived the challenges of the affluent society. Also, the opposing political camps do not differ in endorsing the equivalence, solidarity, and subsidiarity principles.[3]

The best overview of the West German system of social security is given by the so-called social budget. It covers the total of social services from state agencies at all levels, public institutions like the insurance systems, and from employers. The social budget is classified according to functions, institutions, sources of receipts, type of receipts, and types of benefits. It is summarized in the social expenditure ratio (*Sozialleistungsquote*), which relates all social expenditures including indirect benefits (e.g., tax reductions) to the GNP (see Table 6.3). For 1983 we may note the following orders of magnitude:

Social expenditure is nearly one-third of GNP, 32.2 percent.

The major programs are as follows: old age, invalidity, and survivors' groups, 39 percent of social expenditure; health, 32 percent; family, 12 percent; employment, 9 percent; housing, 2 percent.

Social benefits are provided as follows: income transfers (e.g., pensions), 66 percent; goods and services, 20 percent; other financial benefits, 8 percent; general services, 5 percent.

The biggest social institutions are old age and invalidity insurance systems, 30 percent; health insurance, 19 percent; the civil servants' pension system, 9 percent; social aids and services including poverty relief, 9 percent, unemployment aids, 8 percent; employers' contributions, 7 percent of the social budget; indirect benefits (tax relief, housing deductions), 8 percent. Social expenditure is financed 63 percent by contributions from employees and employers and imputed contributions from state and social security institutions, and 37 percent by direct public allocations.

Sources of finance are federal, state, and local government, 40 percent; employers, 31 percent; private households, 28 percent; other, 1 percent.

Of total wages, an average of 17 percent goes toward taxes and 14 percent to social contributions, leaving a skilled worker with a take-home pay of about 70 percent of gross earnings.

However, the social budget represents only one aspect of the West German social state: the benefits in money and in kind and their financing, including the role of employers and tax reliefs. In colloquial speech and in political debate this is called the social net. A different perspective is provided by an analytical scheme of social politics proposed by Heinz Lampert, in which we might record the most striking innovations of the West German social state (Table 6.4).

In international comparison, the German social state has a number of features deserving emphasis. There is fairly well-developed protection against being fired from a job, and against wage losses due to insolvencies.

Table 6.3. The West German Social Budget, 1960–87

	1960	1965	1969	1973	1976[a]	1980	1983	Forecast 1987
Total social budget (in billions DM)	62.8	112.7	153.5	252.6	373.9	476.7	536.9	625.9
Social expenditure ratio (% GNP)	17.5	24.5	25.4	27.3	33.3	32.1	32.3	29.9
Deductions from total wages (%)								
Taxes	6.4	7.8	10.2	14.6	15.7	16.3	17.1	19.0
Social security	9.4	9.2	10.6	11.5	12.9	13.2	14.2	14.5
Take-home pay, worker with two children (%)[b]	87.3	84.0	80.2	77.1	77.4	77.8	76.1	n.a.
Net pension level[c]	63.2	59.3	65.0	63.4	70.7	71.1	73.2	n.a.
Classification of the social budget (%)								
Functions								
Family	15.0	21.7	19.7	15.5	13.4	13.6	12.4	12.4
Health	30.8	27.8	28.4	32.6	31.3	33.1	31.7	32.7
Employment	1.8	1.6	2.1	3.4	5.4	6.3	9.3	8.7
Old age, survivors	40.7	36.3	39.2	37.3	40.2	38.7	39.0	38.9
Political events[d]	7.8	5.1	3.8	2.6	2.2	1.9	1.9	1.6
Housing	1.7	4.5	3.8	2.9	2.3	2.2	1.9	1.9
Savings incentives	1.1	2.4	2.7	5.2	4.5	3.6	3.2	3.1
Special help[e]	1.6	0.6	0.5	0.6	0.7	0.7	0.6	0.6
Institutions								
Overall social security	66.2	61.5	62.4	63.9	70.5	70.6	72.8	71.6
Old age insurance	30.9	27.7	29.8	30.2	30.7	29.9	30.2	30.4
Health insurance	14.0	17.0	14.7	17.4	17.9	18.9	18.7	18.7

	C1	C2	C3	C4	C5	C6	C7	C8
Injuries insurance	2.8	2.9	2.4	2.3	2.1	2.1	2.1	2.0
Unemployment insurance	1.9	1.4	2.3	2.7	4.3	4.8	7.8	7.6
Children's benefits	1.5	2.6	1.7	1.3	3.8	3.7	2.9	2.1
Benefits for Civil Servants (pension, support)	15.1	14.4	13.8	12.9	10.3	9.7	9.4	8.8
Benefits from employers[f]	9.0	7.6	10.4	9.9	7.7	8.2	6.8	7.8
War compensations[g]	13.0	8.9	6.6	5.5	4.4	3.7	3.4	2.8
Support and incentives[h]	4.6	4.7	6.5	9.4	9.1	8.5	8.6	8.7
Indirect benefits (tax reliefs and housing deductions)[i]	9.2	17.5	14.2	11.6	8.4	9.0	8.4	9.1
Types of Benefits[j]								
Income	86		(79)		73	(66)	66	67
Goods and Services	14		(16)		21	(20)	20	21
Financing[j]								
Contributions	63.2		(59.8)		60.7	62.2	62.8	65.0
Public allocations	33.9		(37.2)		37.0	35.7	35.0	33.0
Sources								
Employers' contributions	34.5		(31.2)		31.1	31.9	30.9	32.4
State, all levels	43.5		(46.6)		41.6	41.1	40.5	38.4
Private households	20.6		(20.9)		26.6	26.2	27.8	28.4
Other	1.4		1.3		0.7	0.8	0.8	0.8

Source: Sozialbericht (1983). Data before 1976 from earlier editions of *Sozialbericht* (Social report).

a Since 1975 change in calculation and definitions.

b Minus deductions, plus children's benefits.

c Net pension after forty-five years of contribution in percentage of last net earnings.

d Compensations for war-related losses.

e Resocialization, family consulting, pregnancy interruption, etc.

f Income compensation in case of sickness, company pensions.

g Compensations for war-related losses and war-related pensions.

h Poverty relief, housing relief, public health service, youth services, educational stipends, savings incentives.

i The difference to 100 percent is made up by other monetary benefits and general services.

j The difference between contributions and allocations to 100 percent is made up by income from private organizations and security institutions themselves.

( ) Figures for 1970.

Table 6.4. A Systematic Scheme of German Social Politics

---

1. Public social politics as protection politics
   a. Workers' protection policies, "protection of earning capacity"
      Working hours regulation (female, child labor)
      Work injuries protection
      Regulation of hiring/firing protection
      Earnings protection
   b. Social insurance policies, "protection of income"
      Risks insurance: old age, invalidity, injuries, survivors, sickness, unemployment
      Prevention: cures, preventive checkups
      Rehabilitation
   c. Labor market policies, "protection of employment"
      Full employment policies
      Job training, registration, mobility
      Wages policies within the bargaining system
   d. Codetermination policies, "protection of participation"
2. Public social politics as compensation and redistribution politics
   a. Social policies of housing
      Subsidized home-building
      Housing allowances
   b. Family policies
      Tax exemptions
      Children's allowances
   c. Educational policies
   d. "Property for workers" policies (e.g. profit sharing, company shares)
   e. Special groups social policies
      Farmers', small self-employed subsidies
      Youth
      Old age
      Marginal groups (handicapped persons, etc.)

Source: Adapted from Lampert (1980: Part III); schematic presentation extracted from the text.

The bargaining system is normally peaceful and effective, the strike level low, and civil service wage increases comparable to industry. Codetermination provisions in one form or the other are widespread. After the war, large programs of property compensations and subsidized home-building have been successfully carried out. On the other hand, family policies (besides tax exemptions and children's allowances) play a much lesser role than might be expected given political rhetoric. Educational policies started later than in other countries and have led since the 1960s to an enormous expansion, even though secondary schools have not become completely comprehensive. The promotion of shareholding by workers has attracted much attention, but policies, in practice, have achieved only limited results compared to intentions. Special groups such as farmers, the small self-employed, and the handicapped have, due to their strong lobbies, much more success in getting consideration and cash subsidies than the unorganized categories such as youth.

The two predominant areas of social policy are old age and health. Two-fifths of all social expenditures go to old age/invalidity/survivors, and one-third goes to health. The old age pension system is still separate for blue-collar workers, white-collar employees, and civil servants, and the benefits differ. The blue-collar/white-collar split depends on earnings differences as well as on differences inherent in the private and public sectors. For instance, the average pensioner who earned DM3000 monthly and worked for thirty-five years, gets a net pension of 63 percent of his wage if a civil servant, 72 percent if he was a manual or clerical worker in the public sector, and only 39 percent in the private sector—often, however, adding an additional pension from company funds (Globus-Kartendienst, 1983). The big achievements in old age insurance were the connection of pensions to the general wage level *(Dynamisierung)* in 1957, and the introduction of the flexible retirement age in 1972. The German pension formula combines the equivalence principle with the participation principle: a pension is determined by personal income, years of contribution, and the overall development of the standard of living as measured by the average wage increase. Because the system is organized on a pay-as-you-go basis, the system is quickly getting into financing trouble, as economic growth declines and unemployment rises. Thus, the automatic adaptation of pensions to the average wage increase had to be halted several times to ensure liquidity and ensure that pensions, which are untaxed, would not rise faster than working income. Even more severe, however, are the long-term problems stemming from the demographic disequilibrium and the opening of the system to new groups of members in the 1970s. The most dramatic formulation of the problem is that, everything else remaining equal, contributions must double by the year 2030 to one-third of the earnings if the present level of payments (about 65 percent of final net earnings) is to be maintained (Grohmann, 1981: 343).

The German health system is neither private nor public, neither a market nor a comprehensive national bureaucracy. Technically, Germany has different types of compulsory or voluntary membership in public or private health insurance organizations. Institutionally, the system at large is a "triangle" of insurance organizations, the medical profession, and the clients. Politically it is a bargaining system with the medical profession in the driving seat. The medical doctors practice as a profession without open competition. Their organizations bargain with public health insurance organizations about the yearly total health budget and the doctors' compensation for each particular service. Since the doctors decide about therapies and medication, however, they at once determine supply and demand. Most patients, with the exception of the minority of private patients, have no say about prices or even information about costs, because the services are remunerated according to the agreed-upon tariffs rather than being paid for directly. That system has led to a cost explosion, to several cost control laws, and to the requirements that patients make some payment. Concerted action by the public insurance system, medical organizations, and government has succeeded in slowing down the cost increase in some years (e.g. 1981–82), but costs still are rising. The long-term problems of the health care system are similar to those of the old age security system. At the core of the problem are the rising costs of the highly technical medical services and hospitals. Less severe are the problems of income compensation in case of illness. In that field, blue-collar workers, in 1969 won equality of rights with white-collar employees (i.e., six weeks sickness benefits without waiting days), and that has become an undisputed standard of the system (Lampert, 1980: 225).

THE PRESENT CONTROVERSIES: SOCIAL DISMANTLING VERSUS CONSOLIDATION

The present situation of the German social state can best be described by discussing the recent controversies over the political efforts to consolidate the social security system. The end of the Socialist–Liberal (SPD–FDP) coalition, in the fall of 1982, was in good part determined by the FDP's demand for a change of course and by the SPD's refusal to back their own chancellor for a revision of the budget and social policies. In the election compaign of 1983, the controversy over social dismantling versus consolidation played a decisive role, and it can be assumed that the majority of voters opted for consolidation. But that election did not end the controversy.

The budget of the Christian Democratic–Liberal (CDU–FDP) coalition provides for a slowdown in the growth of public expenditures, a slower expansion of social expenditures below the rate of economic growth, stabilization of the social expenditure ratio, a reduction of the public debt, a major tax reduction, and the stimulation of private and public investments. Promised also is a major effort in family policies (see Table 6.5).

The strongest critics in trade unions and among Social Democrats (Adamy and Steffen, 1983, 1984) call the government plans a social dismantling and redistribution policy that would amount to about 3 percent of GNP and 4 percent of total wages, and would cause—given the present

Table 6.5. Public and Social Expenditure in the Federal Republic of Germany, 1983–87

	1983	1984	1985	1986	1987
Federal budget (billion DM)	253	258	265	273	281
Increase (%)	3.5	1.8	2.8	3.0	2.9
Net debt increase (billion DM)	41	37	33	28	23
Social budget (billion DM)[a]	537	559	581	603	625
Social expenditure ratio (% GNP)	32.3	31.7	31.1	30.5	29.9

Source: Sozialbericht (1983). Data for 1984–87 are projections.
[a]Total social expenditures of all levels and institutions.

economic stagnation—a decline in the standard of living in real terms because of public cuts. Between 1981 and 1983, the SPD and the CDU governments issued more than 250 new bills and regulations that resulted in increased burdens on the population, in tax reductions for business and in regroupings in social security toward higher contributions by private households.

The critics detect behind particular measures a systematic dismantling of the existing social security system reflecting a class struggle from above. The 1982 reforms of unemployment benefits had, it is claimed, restricted the principle of solidarity by putting the burden onto the unemployed. The reforms of 1983, with the delay in the increase of public wages and pensions, were seen as an attack on the insurance principle. The reforms of 1984, finally, would undermine the equivalence principle by enlarging the gap between wages and social security compensations. By wage cuts in the public sector the government would put pressure on the overall labor force. The critics point out striking parallels in the contribution increases and wage cuts at the end of the Weimar Republic (1930–33), concluding that "The present 'restoration and consolidation' policy is aiming at a fundamental restructuring of the societal make-up of the Federal Republic beyond the financial redistribution . . . " (Adamy and Steffen, 1984: 6).

The present CDU–FDP government, on the other hand, argues that a change of course is inevitable for the long-term stability of public finances and the societal order at large. That was conceded also by the SPD government, which, however, was unable to decide on and implement the necessary policies. What is needed is a package of policies that bring about a revitalization of the economy, a shift from consumption to investment expenditures and a reduction of the public debt, and the beginnings of a long-term structural reform of social security. Since a flourishing economy is still the best social policy, social expenditures will continue to increase, but not as quickly as the estimated economic growth. The cuts and new burdens are exaggerated because the level of expenditures is higher than the average of the 1970s; only the extraordinary cost explosion of recent years has been stopped. Government decisions have the backing of the majority of voters. Moreover, public opinion polls demonstrate that the majority of citizens are prepared to limit their demands for benefits in accord with the available resources.

The government further argues that the criticized cuts have been implemented exactly in accordance with the necessities of a long-term structural reform. Thus, the delay and restriction of pension increases and the new health insurance contribution from pensioners correspond to the reform principle that pensions should not grow faster than net working income. The increase in contributions for unemployment insurance and monetary fringe benefits is justified on the ground that increased commitments must be covered by measures that put the burden on everyone. Furthermore, the delay in wage increases in the public sector fits in with the generally accepted view that civil servants and public sector workers should make a special sacrifice for their high job security. Finally, the government argues that its policies are also justified because they demand more from the higher income groups (cuts in children's allowances, reduction of tax privileges), because they discourage misuse and free riders, and because the successful fight against inflation has already saved part of real income (*Sozialbericht,* 1983).

If we put this controversy into perspective, we come to the conclusion that the critics' standards are in some respects unrealistic but that, at the same time, government policies bear the signs of short-term crisis management. The critics suppose that there are alternative policies available, namely the old anticyclical demand management by public expenditures, and they deny that basic structural changes in demands and benefits are unavoidable. The government has as yet to offer long-term concepts that do more than balance the budgets.

Among the most needed long-term concepts are formulas that cope with demographic imbalance (e.g., in the pension formula) and with broad new risks (e.g., sick and invalid nursing) that may require completely new insurance systems. Also, government policies are violating some basic rules of symbolic politics in that they cut benefits for some of the weakest groups (e.g., poverty relief) at a time when the promised cuts in subsidies (e.g., for farmers) are not implemented, and in that they save a little money on families at a time when family policies are high on their own agenda. Large-scale privatization, as demanded by conservatives who point to the possibility of self-insurance, is out of the question, as are fundamental system changes that would combine basic security through national, comprehensive schemes with private supplements. In sum, the present consolidation is crisis management on the lines of classical German social policies.

WELFARE, WELFARE STATE, AND WELFARE PRODUCTION

The problems of the welfare state—and its German version, the social state—must be analyzed in a broader framework in order to get a better idea about future developments and workable solutions. This section outlines such a frame of reference in four subsections. We define markets, state, associations, and primary groups as the central production, allocation, and guidance mechanisms of modern societies that produce the core values of peace, order, freedom, growth, and welfare. These mechanisms have been historically and institutionally developed in the West as mixed economies, competitive democracies, and affluent societies with mass consumption and the welfare state. Welfare state institutions are therefore but one of the organizational achievements of modern democratic societies. We develop the concept of welfare production in order to investigate the interplay of basic mechanisms and basic institutions. Welfare will be defined as the combination of objective living conditions and subjective well-being, which, by definition and by experience, implies that the role of the welfare state in welfare production is limited.

Peace, Order, Freedom, Growth, Welfare

These five values are indisputably goals at the core of modern democracies. *Peace* here refers to the external security that today is attained in supranational defense systems. *Order* refers to internal peace and the role of law. There is some conflict with respect to *personal freedom:* order versus freedom was an essential political issue in the nineteenth century and still is in the twentieth century, together with the new debate about the appropriate relationship between *growth* and *welfare.* This list excludes equality and ecological balance. Whereas welfare has become a generally agreed-upon goal in industrial and postindustrial development—that is, an empirical and practical concept of progress by which the achievements of modern democracies can be evaluated (Dahrendorf, 1979: 44)—equality, in the sense of equal rights, is disputed and has majority support only in the sense of equality of opportunity. Ecological balance, as preservation of natural resources and environment, is a new and challenging goal that may regroup political cleavages in postindustrial politics.

Objective and Subjective Welfare

It can be demonstrated that individual welfare, as value and goal, has entered only lately into the evolutionary process of modern democracies. The early nation-states, based on external security and order, pursued individual welfare only indirectly by maximizing material production for the wealth of nations. With the establishment of civil and political rights, welfare (social rights) then was conceived as the sum of individual utility. With the emergence of mass consumption and the welfare state, the demands of redistribution and reduction of inequality were formulated, but modern welfare economics has dropped the idea of cardinal utility measurement, intersubjective comparability, and the definition of a social optimum. The rapid increase of the standard of living after World War II has revitalized welfare discussion with respect to the notion of quality of life. Now, distribution and preservation problems are considered just as important as growth: reduction of inequalities between social classes and groups (vertical inequality); approximation of living conditions between different areas, stages of life, and between regions (horizontal disparities); devaluation of material values in favor of such intangible values as satisfaction, belonging, and self-realization; and the long-term precaution for the living conditions of future generations (i.e., the natural environment, economic infrastructure, and cultural facilities).

In the new welfare research, operating with quality of life as a goal, using social indicators as tools, and developed largely outside of welfare economics, initially there was a controversy between objectivists and subjectivists. The former school, mostly in the Scandinavian tradition, emphasized observable living conditions, resources, and accessibility, which can be politically planned and guided: the satisfaction of basic needs and the elimination of poverty in a general sense of insufficient resources. The second school, in the tradition of mental health and satisfaction research, emphasizes that ultimately "the quality of life must be in the eye of the beholder, and it is there that we seek ways to evaluate it" (Campbell, 1972: 442). There is now sufficient consensus that the objective and the subjective approach can be combined: living conditions and resources are related via individual aspiration levels, with subjective well-being (satisfaction, subjective competence) that, in turn, influences the activities by which life conditions can be changed. Thus, we might define individual welfare and quality of life as the joint function of objective and subjective welfare.

But objective and subjective welfare do not coincide. In empirical studies, we find strong relationships on the group level but only medium correlations on the individual level. There are well-to-do people who are dissatisfied (dissatisfaction dilemma) and poor people who are satisfied (satisfaction paradox). We have four welfare constellations:

Well-being: Both living conditions and perceived welfare good.
Adaptation: Living conditions not good; perceived welfare good.
Dissonance: Living conditions good; perceived welfare not good.
Deprivation: Neither living conditions nor perceived welfare good.

For the explanation of these discrepancies there is a voluminous literature and a large set of hypotheses: the pressure to deny dissatisfaction, the resigned lowering of aspirations, cultural definitions of the propensity to dissatisfaction, the role of social comparison and reference groups, the pursuit of new values that implies dissatisfaction with old ones, and also a set of methodological explanations. The social policy of the welfare state is simultaneously originator and victim of these discrepancies. The more universal its benefits, the more benefits go to groups that do not need them and the fewer benefits go to the original target groups, the deprived poor; and in the political process, the well-to-do but dissatisfied normally have a stronger voice than the resigned old and sick people who might adapt individually but are unable to organize themselves collectively.

Welfare Production: Markets, State, Associations, Primary Groups

A welfare concept that combines objective living conditions and subjective well-being might guard us from an overestimation of the welfare state's role in providing individual welfare. Public goods and services are an important part of people's welfare and are, in spite of all criticism, accepted and demanded as entitlements. But overall, welfare is produced by the interaction of markets, state, associations, and primary groups.

Only 45 percent of the German population is in the labor force, and 56 percent of the GNP goes to private consumption. Participation in associations is considerable: of all adults, 55 percent go to church at least occasionally, 47 percent report at least some activity in politics and trade unions beyond election participation, 26 percent are members in sports and leisure time organizations, and participation generally increases life satisfaction. (However, only 9 percent of adults are active in all three areas, 28 percent in two, and 45 percent only in one area.) Families and friends are not only an important primary group source of satisfaction and support but also an important setting for financial redistribution and material production. More than half of households are engaged in some kind of agriculture (own field or kitchen garden), 53 percent regularly or occasionaly do auto repairs, one-third of the homeowners have done part of the building themselves, and 8 percent of households regularly have to care for sick and handicapped. Between 11 and 18 percent support neighbors, friends, and relatives, and 13 percent do volunteer work. More than half of the households, in turn, get private support and are satisfied with kind and amount. The 27 percent of households reporting that they get no private support can very well be defined as a problem group.[4]

Beside theoretical reasons, it is such bits and pieces of empirical evidence that give us an idea how markets, associations, and primary groups, together with the state, can be considered as providers of welfare. The sum of the contributions of those four settings to individual welfare we call welfare production. These four organizational settings differ in their respective allocation and decision-making mechanisms. Each setting produces a certain class of goods, albeit with some overlap: the market setting produces private goods; the state, public goods; the associations, collective goods; and the primary groups, personal goods. The labels public and private goods refer to common terminology and literature. By collective goods one can contrast the outputs of associations like trade unions or churches with the goods and services of the public sector. By personal goods we mean the end products, the commodities of household production (cf. Zapf, 1984).

Welfare production of any period is the total of those four categories of goods, whereas in the established national accounts only the private and public goods are counted. That is why some authors are arguing for the need to redefine the gross national product with a welfare product, by estimating the productive contributions of households and nonmarket associations.

The new theory of welfare production is evolving. Private households are considered as the final production units, using private and public goods in order to convert them, by adding their time and skills (their human capital) into basic commodities or personal welfare goods. To be included also are the process benefits, that is, the welfare that stems from the household activities themselves; and as final reference the resulting satisfaction has to be taken into account. At the same time, a generalized capital account has to be devised. The private households command besides stocks of money and property also competence, skills and traditions (i.e., human and cultural capital), which they use up and renew during the process of welfare production (cf. Becker, 1976; Juster et al., 1981).

The new theory of welfare production also allows for a more thoroughgoing analysis of the production of private goods and public goods. Thus, the critics of mass consumption have tried to explain why "commodities, and the income to purchase them, are only weakly related to the things that make people happy: Autonomy, self-esteem, family felicity, tension-free leisure, and friendship" (Lane, 1978: 815). One reason is that an increase in comfort due to more standardization of products is inhibiting stimulation (Scitovsky, 1976), and that efficiency and mobility often are impairing friendship and belonging. And critics of the policy cycle—the production of political goods—have demonstrated that good planning and decisionmaking alone cannot secure success. Following close on the heels of decisionmaking come the problems of implementation, and even after policies have been successfully implemented, there is no automatic guarantee that those policies will receive positive acceptance or be perceived and honored as real welfare increase (cf. Almond and Powell, 1978).

Competitive Democracy, Mixed Economy, and Affluent Society

Markets, state, associations, and primary groups are the organizational settings for production and control in all modern societies, even in the developed socialist societies. To take a socialist example, the Hungarian development (goulash communism) involves the release to the market of part of agriculture and trade and enormous household production, which have very much improved the standard of living but also demanded very long working hours. In democratic societies we find new innovative combinations, such as the shadow economy (market-households), neocorporatist structures like the concerted action to stop the health cost explosion (state-associations), or public subsidies for private self-help groups (state-households). For an appropriate analysis of developmental trends in modern democratic societies, it is suitable to look at markets, state, associations, and primary groups in terms of historically grown basic institutions: competitve democracy, mixed economy, and an affluent society with mass consumption and welfare state.

In a competitive democracy, even weak groups may be represented by political entrepreneurs in the production and distribution of welfare, and unconventional programs have their chance. But organized interests have a privileged position in a system based on piecemeal change rather than on grand designs. Mixed economies combine growth and social protection, but they are weak in long-term preservation and internalization of external costs. The affluent society is simultaneously based on mass consumption and on the welfare state. That combination has proved to be a historically unprecedented source of mass welfare, but both subsystems have a built-in tendency to ever-growing standardization, anonymity, bureaucratization, and monetarization. These tendencies, however, increasingly contradict the needs for smaller units, more individual care, more creative self-realization. The future of modern democratic societies, the future of the affluent society therefore calls for a new balance, for innovative combinations in the production of objective and subjective welfare.

THE NATURE OF THE RECENT CRISIS AND INNOVATIVE POTENTIALS

The present situation of modern Western democracies is often described by critics as a system crisis involving disturbances of such a scale that only fundamental changes in competitive democracy, the mixed economy, and affluent society can prevent a breakdown. The crisis of imperialism, the legitimation crisis of late capitalism, technocratic, nuclear, and ecological self-destruction are the diagnostic catchwords. The fiscal crisis of the state, caused by politically stimulated aspiration and entitlement explosion, is given as the reason for the bottlenecks of the welfare state.

What also needs explanation, however, is the phenomenon that the Western democracies, in spite of several years of stagflation, high unemployment, and unfavorable job prospects for baby-boom cohorts, do not show extraordinary social conflicts or large-scale political radicalization. On the contrary, conservative governments with rigorous consolidation and reindustrialization programs have won the elections, as in West Germany. The peace movement could mobilize big crowds, but too obviously these crowds consist largely of the younger, better educated "new politics" groups, as is true for other "one-issue" movements. Furthermore, the social dismantling and new poverty theories depict serious problems of minorities but not mass misery.

What we have is not a system crisis but a developmental crisis: *tensions and contradictions stem not from general scarcity but from the very successes of mass consumption and the welfare state over time.* Market failure and state failure disclose many structural transition problems between different spheres of life (production versus reproduction), between different stages of life, and between different life-styles. But they do not lead to hopeless system overload. Recent cumulations of problems—oil price shock, economic structural change, education expansion, "new politics," demographic imbalances—are contingent, not permanent. They are best understood as a developmental dilemma in the sense that previous patterns of mass consumption, the welfare state, the division of labor between markets, state, associations, and primary groups are obsolescent. Innovations—changes in preferences, behavior, and organization—are required, and they are possible with established capacities of society (cf. Zapf, 1983a).

Three arguments back up our interpretation:

1. Current problems do not lead to mass misery but to selection and segmentation processes that discriminate against minorities.
2. The majority of the population, because it has attained a high welfare level and has its material and nonmaterial capital, is a stabilizing factor.
3. There is considerable innovation potential because of individual learning processes and endogenous adaptation mechanisms on the micro and macro levels.

Selection and Segmentation Processes

High unemployment in Germany is less explosive today than in earlier periods because of unemployment compensation (68 percent of net earnings, or 63 percent for unemployed without children), because of other incomes in the family, and because of the waiting, search, and free-rider components in the unemployment ratio. Even with 2.1 million unemployed in 1983, the unemployed definitely have a minority status: yet they comprise several minorities. More than 90 percent of the labor force is working, about seven out of ten unemployed are out of jobs for only a couple of weeks or months, and a small proportion is in some ways "voluntarily" unemployed. Even with mass unemployment, there is considerable movement. For example, in 1981 West Germany had an average of 1.3 million unemployed but 3.0 million exits from unemployment, of which 1.8 million got new jobs, including 1.6 million by help of public employment agencies. However, the dark side of the picture is that the hard core, (i.e., persons unemployed more than one year) is rising, from 200,000 in 1981 to 600,000 in 1983. They disproportionately are under the age of 24 and over 50, have education and health problems, and are in a vicious cycle of repetitive spells of unemployment. A follow-up 1983 Infratest study of people unemployed and rehired in 1977 shows that only one-half could establish a stable career again; the other half is fluctuating or has left the labor force. Thus, we are confronted with a painful selection process in which minorities, in rising numbers are sorted out of the mainstream of social activity.

Such selection processes can also be observed in other areas, from schools to the health system, and even in private social relationships. The result of all selection and segmentation was called by Dahrendorf (1984) the rise of a new underclass, an incoherent subpopulation without class consciousness and class organization. That concept might not be fully adequate, because many in the dropout minorities have low visibility.

But quite clearly the situation of deprived groups worsens as that of the majority improves, and deprived groups grow larger when social competition gets tougher. In this sense, the developmental crises involve selection and segmentation.

Stabilizing Factors

The crisis can be managed by the majority of people because they have attained a considerable level of objective and subjective welfare, because they can cope with normal problems (like ill health or family disputes), because they command a potential of support in their friends and relatives, because negative situations are of only short duration, and, of course, because of social security.

We can monitor and explain some aspects of the objective and subjective welfare of the German population through three national welfare surveys for 1978, 1980, and 1984. Questions about overall satisfaction with life today and projective questions as to life satisfaction five years ago and five years from now show high and stable satisfaction levels; they reveal the change from an optimistic future perspective in 1978 to a less optimistic outlook in 1980; and a slight recovery in 1984, after two years of a real decline in disposable income (see Figure 6.2).

On the 11-point life-satisfaction scale, 67 percent of the respondents in 1978 scored 8 or higher, 61 percent in 1980, and 67 percent in 1984. For working-class respondents the past–present–future curves are at all points somewhat lower than for the middle class. Young people are below

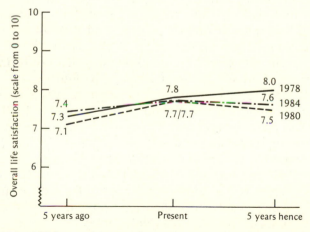

Figure 6.2. Overall life satisfaction of West German population, 1978, 1980, and 1984. Questions: "What do you mean—how satisfied are you at present, overall, with your life?" "And how satisfied were you five years ago?" "And what do you think, how will it be in five years?" (Adapted from Glatzer and Zapf, 1984a: 14; 1984b: 15. Based on representative surveys of German population over 18 years (see note 4.)

old people in their evaluation of past and present in 1978 and 1980, but in 1984 they score higher than old people, not only in the evaluation of the future but also of the present. That does not confirm the image of the young as having no hope for the future, as given in the media. On a happiness scale, we find the overwhelming majority on the happy side; the proportion of unhappy respondents increased from 5 percent in 1978 to 9 percent in 1984, indicating another selection process.

If we compare the satisfaction scores in particular areas of life cross-sectionally and over time, we find marriage, family, housing, and leisure at the top of the list for satisfaction; and the average scores for church, public security, and environmental protection at the bottom. A simple explanation is that people feel responsible, competent, and gratified in their private sphere, but are more critical toward big institutions and public policies. This explanation is supported by the important role that primary groups and networks play for life satisfaction. One noteworthy exception is, however, the rather high satisfaction with social security, which ranks with income and health. The social security system is still a satisfactory institution in West Germany in the 1980s.

It is also noteworthy that our surveys do not reveal overall harmony. Conflicts, quarrels, and worries are often reported as facts of life. There is a significant increase betwen 1978 and 1984 in perceived conflicts between employers and employees and in perceived difficulties in finding a new job, if necessary. But that does not reduce high life satisfaction scores. Satisfaction is determined by comparison with reference groups, in the respondents' social context; it can very well coexist with particular perceived political problems and experienced private problems. Many people have problems, but cumulations are the exception. We have defined four objective and four subjective problem situations.[5] In our 1978 and 1984 samples we find 42 percent (and then 44 percent) in no problem situation, 30 percent (and then 29 percent) with one problem, and only 7 percent with three or more problems. That can be interpreted as another proof of the stability–segmentation hypothesis.

In addition to the representative German samples, we also have a small panel of youth from the large birth cohorts, interviewed in 1980 and 1983 to monitor their placement process. These young men and women, seven years after leaving school and now in their early twenties, are 72 percent employed, 19 percent in further education or in the army, 4 percent not working (females 9 percent), and 5 percent presently unemployed; but not less than 35 percent had already experienced some spell of unemployment. Again the impression is that there are problems but overall a rather well-managed passage into adult life (Noll, 1985).

There are many particular problems reported by a representative sample of the West German population, but no mood of crisis. There is criticism of public institutions, but not widespread system blame. There are private conflicts but also coping mechanisms and sources of support. There is a rather high life satisfaction determined by comparison processes, which mean that limited drawbacks affecting everyone do not reduce satisfaction very much. There is for most people a large objective and subjective welfare capital as a stabilizing factor. And the problem of the disadvantaged and scattered minorities is not that they are threatening the system but that they might be overlooked.

Innovation Potential

Individuals, households, groups, organizations, and institutions have the capacity to adapt because of their existing level of welfare, their reserves in material and human capital, and the established state social security. The people adapt to conditions of temporary economic stagnation, to a slowdown of social expenditures, to new patterns of the life course and social stratification, and to new international and ecological challenges. Our developmental logic is one of long waves with built-in cycles and S-shaped production functions.

On the level of individual preference changes, Hirschman (1982) has postulated a basic expectation–disappointment mechanism that might explain how cyclical preference changes in the private and political sphere are possible at all.

On the level of demographic development, Easterlin (1980) postulates a cyclical sequence of large and small birth cohorts. The large cohorts everywhere find worse relative chances than the small cohorts. They are exposed to increased social stress in school, family and work; they restrict their own birth rate. Over time that leads to a relaxation in the education and job markets, to better income and promotion chances, and eventually again to a change in generational behavior.

On the level of economic and societal development, the long-wave theorists accumulate evidence that innovations follow a rather cyclical pattern of bunching and stagnation. They argue that new spurts of growth are possible when economic and social institutions have been reconstructed and new supply and demand forces are working. Applied to our most encompassing institutions of the affluent society—mass consumption and welfare state—we hold that they have surpassed their optimal size and that big technology now has declining growth rates because of its negative side effects and acceptance problems. If so, then strategies of decentralization and increasing autonomy of smaller units could overcome stagnation, open up new innovative potentials, and avoid the present weaknesses of the superstructures—concentration and vulnerability (cf. Giarni and Louberge, 1978; Rostow, 1978; Mensch, 1979; Zapf, 1983b).

Applying the principles of adaptation, preference changes, decentralization, and more autonomy to the basic production and allocation mechanisms leads to the conclusion that underutilized capacities are to be found in associations and primary groups. The increasing role of voluntary organizations like churches, leisure time associations, citizen's

movements, local groups, private networks, families, and family alternatives illustrate that point. This is thinking not in terms of an alternative
culture but rather in terms of complementary functions of associations
and primary groups in relation to markets and state. New productive
combinations are already present in the shadow economy, in bargaining
coalitions, or in publicly subsidized self-help.

Basically it is the concentration and vulnerability of big organizations
that bring about market failure and state failure. The satiation of mass
consumption, the obsolescence of many commodities, the environmental
damage wrought by externalizing costs, the loss of jobs because of rationalization, and the elimination of weak groups provoke rising resistance.
Some innovation possibilities here include the differentiation of jobs, of
working-time schedules, and of job profiles so as to offer, even with a
stagnating volume of production, reasonable work for more people. The
reactions against the failures of overloaded governments first came from
the protest politics of single-issue movements. Decentralization, devolu-
tion, deregulation, and more responsiveness (*Bürgernähe*) are innovation
possibilities that might prove many present problems to reflect self-
overload.

We must be careful, however, not to overrate the potential of associations and primary groups. Voluntary organizations too are subject to the
law of oligarchy and the selectivity of interest representation. It is the
well-to-do dissatisfied who organize, not the resigned. Private networks
and primary groups might lessen the anonymity of markets and bureaucracies, but they are not self-sufficient. Under modern conditions, the
subsidiary principle cannot replace productive markets and responsible
state.

WELFARE SOCIETY: THE FUTURE OF THE AFFLUENT SOCIETY

While competitive democracy and mixed economy will change toward
decentralization and increasing autonomy of smaller units, what about
the affluent society based on mass consumption and the welfare state?
Will standardized mass production be replaced by more differentiated
markets and more home production, in a zero-growth, steady-state economy? Will the welfare state be reduced by comprehensive privatization
and self-help?

Our scenario is different. In addition to the innovation potentials discussed earlier, we want to concentrate on the innovation realities in the
social structure. Changes in social structure produce new demands, and,
in turn, stimulate new types of supply in mass consumption and the welfare state; these structural changes are to be observed in the individual
life cycle as well as in social stratification (Zapf, 1983b). The average life
course and modal family and household types are already exhibiting new
patterns. There is the new stage of postadolescence, as the prolonged pas-

sage from youth to adulthood, with a youth culture, premarital partner-
ship, and a fluctuating mix of education, work, and breaktime. There is
family postparenthood, "the empty nest" between the children's leaving
home and the parents' retirement; ten to twenty years in which many
women look again for jobs if they have been out of the job market. There
is postretirement, up to ten years during which many couples experience
rather good health and rather comfortable economic conditions, until the
death of one partner. Finally, for most women (and a minority of men)
there is the phase of widowhood in which many have to live alone, if not
in isolation. The ideal-type nuclear family with two children today in
West Germany includes only one-sixth of households. In half of the
households there are no children or they have already left. One-parent
families meanwhile are nearly as numerous as extended families and families with three or more children.

Social stratification has also changed considerably. Occupational status
and the respective occupational prestige is now only one among several
new status dimensions such as educational status, status in the income
transfer systems, and ethnic status. In West Germany half of school leav-
ers now have secondary diplomas. One-fourth of the electorate is living
mostly on pensions and other transfers: 8 percent of the German population are foreigners, the majority *Gastarbeiter* (guest workers) who form
an important part of the new underclass.

Changes in life cycle and social stratification occur gradually but not
spontaneously. They are at least in part produced by the policies of the
welfare state and emphasized by the incentives of mass consumption.
The educational expansion and the prolongation of training result from
political decisions, as does the lower retirement age. Postadolescence is
subsidized by provisions in kind and money. The declining birth rate has
many causes, including the absence of pronatalist family policies. The
increase in the employment ratio of married women also has many
causes, including the growth in service sector jobs, rising consumption
aspirations, and education expansion. All those changes result in a plur-
alization of life-styles and in a differentiation of value patterns, which
open up new life chances and, at the same time, new problems. Traditional behavior patterns and solutions have become obsolete; the individual person is now under heavier pressure to make his or her own
decisions.

On the societal level, there are new opportunities for and new loads on
the affluent society. Postadolescence, postparenthood, and postretirement produce enormous new demands for goods and services that might
stimulate new sectors of mass consumption. Thus, social structural
changes are another endogenous innovation mechanism. The ageing of
the population, beside pension problems, brings about huge demands for
preventive and curative health care. The inability to live self-sufficiently
is a new risk in modern societies. There are 3.6 million people over the
age of 75 living in West Germany, of which no less than 2 million are

widowed. They cannot all be taken care of by public institutions, nor have private households the ways and means to care for all elderly people privately. A comprehensive family policy is needed in order to counteract the demographic imbalances, respond positively to the declining birth rate, and improve combinations of work and parenthood for men as for women. We sense enormous pressure for such social innovations as new patterns of support and more flexible schedules of education, work, and leisure.

There is no alternative to functioning markets for mass consumption and an efficient welfare state. The new needs and demands cannot be satisfied simply in the small-is-beautiful worlds of associations and primary groups. On the other hand, an increased role for those associations and primary groups seems inevitable, because the new differentiated needs and pluralized life-styles are clashing with the trends toward further standardization, bureaucratization, and anonymity. Therefore, it is our prognosis that the affluent society will be rebuilt into a welfare society (cf. Rose, 1984)."Affluent" society always has had that double meaning of wealth and waste, and so had mass consumption (consumption for all versus junk consumption) and welfare state (public benefits versus public dependency). The welfare society would be a society in the framework of competitive democracy and mixed economy with a better division of labor among markets, state, associations, and primary groups, and with more stimulating mass consumption and a more responsive welfare state. The possibilities for such a welfare society exist: the vision, the challenges, the capacities, the individual preferences, the institutional innovation capabilities. To speak of "no future" for modern democratic societies is absurd. But these are only necessary, not sufficient conditions, and they are hidden among daily conflicts, habits, trial and error, and hopes and fears.

NOTES

1. This chapter is a continuation of the author's work on welfare development and on the theory of welfare production, of which two articles and two working papers are available in English (Zapf, 1979, 1981, 1983a, 1984).

2. The best analyses of European welfare state development are in the insightful work of Peter Flora and Jens Alber (Flora, Alber, and Kohl, 1977; Flora and Heidenheimer, 1981; Alber, 1982; Flora, 1983). Jens Alber (1980) also gives an excellent review of postwar social politics in the Federal Republic. The comprehensive textbook on German social politics by Lampert (1980) has aided my work considerably. On the history of German social politics see Henning (1977), and for a sociological perspective, see Tennstedt (1981) and Tennstedt (1983). Good discussions of the most recent problems appear in Helberger (1982), Albers (1983), and Lampert (1983).

3. The volume by Koslowski et al. (1983) gives the best overview of the recent German discussion of the *Sozialstaat* including statements of leading politicians from government and opposition.

4. The empirical data on objective and subjective welfare in Germany, as presented here and in the next section, are taken from three representative surveys of the German popu-

lation, 18 years and older, that our research group (Sonderforschungsbereich 3, Frankfurt/ Mannheim) conducted in 1978, 1980, and 1984. The sample size was 2012 in 1978, 2396 in 1980, and 2067 in 1984. Results of these three "welfare surveys" were published by Glatzer and Zapf (1984a, b). All three data sets are distributed by Zentralarchiv für empirische Sozialforschung of the University of Cologne.

5. The four objective problem situations are (1) poverty (below 60 percent of average net household income per capita), (2) no vocational training, (3) living alone and no friends, (4) permanently ill or handicapped. The four subjective problem situations are (1) often lonesome, (2) often anxious and worried, (3) unhappy and depressed, (4) dissatisfied with life.

REFERENCES

Adamy, W. and Steffen, J., "Sozialabbau und Umverteilung in der Wirstschaftskrise." *WSI-Mitteilungen,* October, No. 10, pp. 603–616, 1983.

Adamy, W. and Steffen, J., "Zwischenbilanz von Sozialdemontage und Umverteilungspolitik seit 1982," manuscript, Seminar für Sozialpolitik der Universitat zu Köln, 1984.

Alber, Jens, "Der Wohlfahrtsstaat in der Krise? Eine Bilanz nach drei Jahrzehnten Sozialpolitik in der Bundesrepublik." *Zeitschrift für Soziologie* 9:313–342, 1980.

Alber, Jens, *Von Armenhaus zum Wohlfahrtsstaat.* Frankfurt: Campus, 1982.

Albers, Willi, "Perspektiven der Sozialpolitik," *Wirtschaftsdienst* 6:280-286, 1983.

Almond, G. and Powell, G. B., *Comparative Politics,* 2nd edition. Boston: Little, Brown, 1978.

Becker, Gary S., *The Economic Approach to Human Behaviour.* Chicago: The University of Chicago Press, 1976.

Bevölkerung und Wirtschaft, Statistisches Bundesamt. Stuttgart: Kohlhammer, 1872–1972.

Brockhaus Enzyklopädie, Vol. 17. Wiesbaden: Brockhaus, 1973.

Campbell, Angus, "Aspiration, Satisfaction, and Fulfillment," in *The Human Meaning of Social Change* (A. Campbell and P. Converse, eds.). New York: Russell Sage, 1972, pp. 441–466.

Dahrendorf, Ralf, *Lebenschancen.* Frankfurt: Suhrkamp, 1979.

Dahrendorf, Ralf, "Die neue Unterklasse," *Die Zeit,* February 2, No. 5, p. 32, 1984.

Easterlin, R. A., *Birth and Fortune: The Impact of Numbers on Personal Welfare.* New York: Basic Books, 1980.

Flora, Peter, *State, Economy, and Society in Western Europe 1815–1975,* Vol. 1. Frankfurt: Campus, 1983.

Flora, P., Alber, J. and Kohl, J., "Zur Entwicklung der westeuropäischen Wohlfahrtsstaaten." *Politische Vierteljahresschrift* 18:707–772, 1977.

Flora, P. and Heidenheimer, A., eds. *The Development of Welfare States in Europe and America.* New Brunswick N.J.: Transaction Books, 1981.

Giarni, O. and Louberge, H., *The Diminishing Returns of Technology.* Oxford: Pergamon, 1978.

Glatzer, Wolfgang and Zapf, Wolfgang, eds., *Lebensqualität in der Bundesrepublik: Objektive Lebensbedingungen und subjektives Wohlbefinden.* Frankfurt: Campus, 1984a.

Glatzer, Wolfgang and Zapf, Wolfgang, "Die Lebensqualität der Bundesbürger," Beilage zu: *Das Parlament,* B 44/84, November 3, 1984b.

Globus-Kartendienst, since 1945 (Hamburg: P.O. 70 07 69)

Grohmann, Heinz, "Finanzierungsrechnungen mit dem Gruppensimulationsmodell," in *Alternativen der Rentenreform '84* (H. J. Krupp et al., eds.). Frankfurt: Campus, 1981, pp. 337–363.

Helberger, Christof, "Sozialpolitik in der Wirtschaftskrise oder Krise der Sozialpolitik?" *Wirtschaftsdienst* 6:280–286, 1982.

Henning, Hansjoachim, "Sozialpolitik, III. Geschichte," in *Handwörterbuch der Wirtschaftswissenschaften* (HdWW) 7:85–110, 1977.

Hirschman, Albert, *Shifting Involvements: Private Interest and Public Action.* Princeton, N.J.: Princeton University Press, 1982.

Juster, F. Thomas et al., "The Theory and Measurement of Well-being," in *Social Accounting Systems* (F. Thomas Juster and Kenneth C. Land, eds.). New York and London: Academic Press, 1981.

Koslowski, P. et. al., eds., *Chancen und Grenzen des Sozialstaats.* Tübingen: Mohr/Siebeck, 1983.

Lampert, Heinz, *Sozialpolitik.* Berlin: Springer, 1980.

Lampert, Heinz, "Stabilisierung der Rentenversicherung—mit Einschränkungen erreicht." *Wirtschaftsdienst* 6:323–327, 1983.

Lane, R. E., "Markets and the Satisfaction of Human Wants," *Journal of Economic Issues* 12:799–827, 1978.

Mensch, Gerhard, *Stalemate in Technology: Innovations Overcome the Depression.* New York: Ballinger, 1979.

Noll, Heinz-Herbert, "Sieben Jahre nach dem Schulabgang," in *Berufliche Verbleibsforschung in der Diskussion* (M. Kaiser et al., eds.). Materialien aus der Arbeitsmarkt- und Berufsforschung, 89(1), Nürnberg, 1985.

Rose, Richard, "Oceans of affluence spotted with islands of poverty." *Daily Telegraph,* London, April 2, p. 3, 1984.

Rostow, W. W., *The Stages of Economic Growth.* Cambridge, England: University Press, 1960.

Rostow, W. W., *Getting from Here to There.* New York: McGraw-Hill, 1978.

Scitovsky, Tibor, *The Joyless Economy.* New York: Oxford University Press, 1976.

Sozialbericht, Der Bundesminister für Arbeit und Sozialordnung, Bonn, 1983.

Tennstedt, Florian, *Sozialgeschichte der Sozialpolitik in Deutschland.* Göttingen: Vandenhoeck & Ruprecht, 1981.

Tennstedt, Florian, *Vom Proleten zum Industriearbeiter. Arbeiterbewegung und Sozialpolitik in Deutschland, 1800 bis 1914.* Köln: Bund-Verlag, 1983.

Zapf, Wolfgang, "Modernization and Welfare Development: The Case of Germany." *Social Science Information* 18:219–246, 1979.

Zapf, Wolfgang, "Wohlfahrtsstaat und Wohlfahrtsproduktion," in *Politische Parteien auf dem Weg zur parlamentarischen Demokratie in Deutschland,* (L. Albertin and W. Link, eds.). Düsseldorf: Droste, pp. 379–400, 1981. In English: "Welfare State and Welfare Production," Working Paper No. 25, Sonderforschungsbereich 3 Frankfurt/Mannheim.

Zapf, Wolfgang, "Entwicklungsdilemmas und Innovationspotentiale in modernen Gesellschaften," in *Die Krise der Arbeitsgesellschaft* (J. Matthes, ed.). Frankfurt: Campus, pp. 293–308, 1983a. In English: "Developmental

Dilemmas and Innovative Potential in Modern Societies," Working Paper No. 97, Sonderforschungsbereich 3 Frankfurt/Mannheim.

Zapf, Wolfgang, "Die Pluralisierung der Lebensstile: Neue Muster des Lebens- und Familienzyklus; Alte und neue Linien der sozialen Schichtung," in *Zukunftsperspektiven gesellschaftlicher Entwicklungen,* Landesregierung von Baden-Würtemberg, Stuttgart, 1983b, pp. 56–73.

Zapf, Wolfgang, "Welfare Production: Public vs. Private." *Social Indicators Research* 14:263–274, 1984.

7

The Israeli Welfare System—
A Nation with a Difference

SHMUEL EISENSTADT

The State of Israel, proclaimed in 1948, developed from the Jewish community in Mandatory Palestine, the so-called *Yishuv,* which in its turn crystallized from the movements of the Zionist settlers from about the 1880s. This Zionist rebellion denied that an integrated and viable Jewish life and tradition could be maintained within the framework of a modern society and sovereign state outside of Palestine. Zionist ideology maintained that in the Diaspora Jews would be threatened with spiritual and cultural annihilation, the undermining of their traditional and communal life by modern economic, political, and cultural forces, and physical annihilation due to the inability of modern society to assimilate this alien element. Zionist ideology assumed that only in Palestine could a viable Jewish society be established, and only in Palestine could a new synthesis of Jewishness and universal human culture, of tradition and modernity, be evolved.

THE CHARACTERISTICS OF THE YISHUV

The Zionist movement aimed at providing the opportunity for cultural and social creativity of universal significance within the framework of a free, modern, self-supporting Jewish society. It is this combination that accounts for the tremendous emphasis it placed on sociocultural creativity and for the strong elitist orientations of this society.

The Zionist orientation characterized the first pioneer groups, which consisted mostly of intellectual youth who rebelled against their parental background in the Diaspora (especially in Eastern and Central Europe). They organized themselves into small sectarian pioneering groups that went to the old homeland in Palestine in order to establish there a modern and viable Jewish society.

It was these characteristics of the first waves of immigration *(Aliyoth)* that shaped some of the most important features of the Yishuv. Especially important, it was an ideological society—that is, its basic collective identity was couched in ideological terms—that combined a national renaissance, cultural creativity, and social ideology.

The original ideological-revolutionary impetus of these groups focused on the image of the pioneer *(Halutz)*, a vision that stressed the attempt to develop a society in which social values were closely linked with the national effort, and emphasized that these values were not conceived in utopian terms but rather as an inseparable element in building a new nation, and its institutions.

It was out of the combination of the ideological visions and orientations and of the attempt to realize the vision in a small and relatively undeveloped country—a land new both to the founders of this society and to many generations of new immigrants—and in the framework of a foreign and even hostile environment that the concrete problems as well as the institutional features, specific tendencies, and perennial problems of contemporary Israel emerged.

These problems remained relatively constant during the development of the Yishuv and of Israeli society, even if their concrete expressions did change: (1) the inevitable stresses connected with immigration and the absorption of new waves of immigrants, (2) the worrisome pressures stemming from the constant development of the economy and its ability to meet the problems of development and modernization, and (3) the problems of creating symbols of a collective Israeli identity in relation both to Jewish identity and to the Middle Eastern environment.

The concrete forms in which these problems became crystallized were also greatly influenced by the constant tension between the social and cultural reality of a small and relatively modern society, and its aspirations to be, out of all proportion to its size, a center of social and cultural creativity of importance both for the Jewish people and for humanity at large.

Indeed, one especially important characteristic of Israeli society has been its smallness. How can a relatively small state maintain a general standard of economic and sociocultural life that is more or less on the same level as that prevailing in its international reference group? To intensify this difficulty, the internal market of a small state is too weak to create the economic momentum required for a high level of development.

Small countries often have to orient themselves toward large, highly developed states. As the small states must find outlets for their own products in a very competitive and relatively open global market, they usually have to specialize and to find areas in which they enjoy special advantages stemming either from their special location or from their social and economic structure.

To understand the special characteristics conferred on the Yishuv and Israeli society by their smallness, we need to remember that major external markets have been the Jewish communities in the Diaspora. The major changes that have taken place in the relations between the Yishuv and Israeli society and the Jewish communities in the Diaspora are among the most important causes or indicators of significant transformations in the structure of the society.

The concrete responses to the continuous problems of the Yishuv and of Israeli society later on were influenced initially by the institutional structure created in the early phase of the Yishuv. A second influence was the high degree of centralization in the economy, and especially the concentration of public capital in economic development, alongside the constant growth of private sectors. The coexistence of public and private sectors has been called a "pluralistic" economic system.

It was also in the Yishuv that the unique Israeli form of socioeconomic organization was developed: (1) the major types of settlements—the kibbutzim and the moshavim (the cooperative enterprises in the urban sector); and (2) the most unusual feature of Israeli reality, the integration of most of these cooperatives and settlements within a unified national framework—and in particular that of the Histadrut (General Federation of Labor). It was integration that made possible the evolution of this structure beyond the boundaries of the pioneering groups' early agrarian orientation, and facilitated the development of the major characteristics of the urban social structure of the Yishuv.

A further crucial aspect of the social structure of the Yishuv was the strong emphasis on egalitarianism and some opposition to occupational specialization. This found its expression in attempts to reduce wage differentials between different occupations and to minimize visible social differences, and in the assumption that an easy transition from one profession to another was possible.

Of special importance in understanding of the Israeli welfare system is familiarity with the development of the Histadrut, created in 1920. Although the official name of the Histadrut is the "Federation of the Workers in Eretz Israel," and it was imbued with socialist values and stressed very strongly class consciousness defined in European terms, it actually differed radically from Western trade unions and labor movements. These differences were above all due to the fact that in early Mandatory Palestine there existed only very weak rudiments of a bourgeois class against which it could assert itself.

Hence, the trade union component in Histadrut's activities was, although not unimportant, initially secondary. The chief aim of Histadrut was to build up a modern economic structure in agriculture, industry, and housing. Histadrut, marketing cooperatives, and the like were to be the tools used to *create* a modern economy and the conditions for the development of a working class.

Histadrut also developed a far-reaching welfare system, although it was not referred to as welfare. This welfare system has several components.

Most important is its Sick Fund *(Kupat Holim)*, which has become the major provider of health services up to the present. A second component, widespread housing projects, provide relatively inexpensive housing for workers in Histadrut. The rudiments of pension and unemployment funds are a third factor; however, these were not as highly developed as the health funds and housing.

It is very important to emphasize that these activities were *not* defined as welfare activities but as a part of the pioneering activities aiming at the construction by the settlers of a modern economy. Welfare in the sense of dealing with social problems was not acceptable, the assumption being that in the socialist society envisioned there would not develop special, distinct social problems.

THE STATE OF ISRAEL: SOCIAL STRUCTURE, POLITICAL ECONOMY, AND CLASS FORMATIONS

The characteristics of Israeli society first developed in the period of the Yishuv, but they have undergone far-reaching changes with the establishment of the State of Israel in 1948. These postrevolutionary changes also contained the seeds of further change.

The most important change has been the routinization of the initial vision of ideologically oriented yet pragmatic pioneers, and its transformation into a full-fledged constitutional democratic state. Second has been the concomitant process of demographic expansion and change in the composition, cultural background, and ideological orientations of large parts of the population. Third is economic expansion and modernization. Fourth, the military security problem is one of the most important, continual problems facing Israeli society, and the elites of the society are becoming more and more aware of this. The fifth group of changes are those involving characteristics of Israeli society inherent in its smallness, and concomitantly, Israel's relations with the Jewish Diaspora.

Through these processes of change there has developed the specific Israeli institutional mold. This mold has been characterized as follows: (1) a constitutional democratic system with initially strong restrictive overtones and consociational characteristics, (2) the seemingly natural granting of the principle of access to the center to all sectors of the population (initially mitigated by development of the clientelistic mechanisms), (3) the appropriation by the center of the Zionist and labor pioneering symbols, (4) the continuous economic development within the framework of a mixed yet relatively controlled economy, and (5) a strong emphasis on the construction of an "old" new nation with a very heavy emphasis on cultural creativity oriented to a national and cultural renaissance.

The development of this institutional mold was in many ways a story of great, perhaps incomparable success, and was perceived as such by large sectors of Israeli society, as well as abroad—at least until after the Yom Kippur war of 1973.

First of all, the Israeli success has been great when compared with many other modern small societies, with developing societies with a weak modern infrastructure, or with other countries of mass immigration. From a community of 600,000 people fighting for its independence and for its very life, living in strenuous and relatively backward economic conditions, there has developed since 1948 an independent state of 4.2 million people that has succeeded in developing a relatively modern, at least semiindustrial economy, with a very successful modern agricultural sector. Its political structure, rooted in rather totalistic movements and organized in a semifederative or consociational mold, has developed into a parliamentary democracy, in some respects restrictive, yet continuously evolving with a strong tradition of rule of law and civility.

The development of the state also saw the specific Israeli model of political economy develop, providing a basic framework for the dynamics of the Israeli welfare state. The specific model of political economy has derived from the confrontation between an initial starting point, the economic base as it existed at the end of the Mandate, the processes of economic development that have taken place in the State of Israel, and policies that guided this development.

The distinctive Israeli model grew out of the transformation and concretization of the original visions of Jewish settlement in *Eretz Israel,* and of the power structure that had already developed in the period of the Yishuv. It was further transformed by the continuous modernization and diversification of the economy on the one hand, and the necessity to absorb many new immigrants on the other.

The following data give us a summary picture of the growth and development of the Israeli economy.[1]

1. *The gross national product* (GNP) grew from IS 9.8 billion in 1950 to 27.4 billion in 1960, to 62.8 billion in 1970, and 104.7 billion in 1981, a growth in constant price terms of 1060 percent.
2. *Private consumption* grew from IS 6.9 billion in 1950 to 68.5 billion in 1981, a 990 percent increase.
3. Spending for *general government consumption* grew from IS 2.9 billion in 1950 to 40.05 billion in 1981, an increase of 1348 percent.
4. *Gross domestic capital formation* grew from IS 5.8 billion in 1950 to 23.3 billion in 1981, a growth of 397 percent.
5. Gross national product *per capita* grew from IS 7,820 in 1950 to 26,510 in 1981, a growth of 339 percent.
6. The differential between exports and imports of goods and services, including net factor payments to abroad, grew by 486 percent— from IS 5,591.0 million in 1950, to 6,129.8 million in 1960, to 21,844.8 million in 1970, and 27,176.0 million in 1981.

7. Private consumption expenditure per capita grew from IS 5,464 in 1950, to 8,393 in 1960, to 12,719 in 1970, and 17,356 in 1981, a growth of 317 percent.
8. The number of employed persons grew from 1955 to 1981 by 218 percent. The percentage of unemployed in the civilian labor forces decreased from 7.2 percent in 1955 to 3.6 percent in 1965, then increased to 10.4 percent in 1968, but decreased again to 5.1 percent in 1981.

A crucial aspect of the Israeli economy has been the heavy burden of defense. Thus, the percentage of security spending in the general government budget grew from 19.6 percent in 1965–66 to 49.3 percent in 1973–74, and from then on started to decrease. At the same time the development of the military industry, and of the air industry in particular, has constituted one of the major aspects of economic development—especially sophisticated, science-based industries, with a relatively great share in Israel's export.

The preceding data tell us that in the area of economic structure, the Israeli economy has become very similar to those in many small, relatively modern or modernizing societies. Yet the data also indicate special characteristics of this economy: the relatively high concentration in services, the special place of agriculture, the continuously increasing public expenditure and rising living standard, and the heavy burden of security expenses.

The basic characteristic of the Israeli political economy has been, first, the development of a very strong concentration of economic resources—probably more than in any other noncommunist modern society—in the hands of the state. Yet, second, the state has not become, as in the socialist or communist countries, the major owner of the means of production and of major industrial and financial enterprises. These are distributed among three major economic sectors: the Histadrut and the private sector, which both continued from the *Yishuv* period, and the state sector, most of it developing since 1948, although in part taking over also some Mandate establishments.

The third characteristic is the uses to which the government has put its large regulative power over the economy, policies rooted in the Labor Zionist vision of building a Jewish society in Eretz Israel. But the vision has become transformed since the establishment of the state. The most important aspect of the vision was the decision, following from the very justification for the establishment of the State of Israel, to open immigration to the state to as many Jewish communities as possible and to create a modern economy rather than a small semicolonial enclave in the Middle East.

Fourth was the very continuous heavy burden of defense and security expenditure, the highest among democratic nations.

Of overall importance has been the concentration in the hands of the state (or of the Jewish Agency, the major prestate Jewish organization, which after the establishment of the state became mostly concerned with immigration, settlement, and activity in the Diaspora) of external funds that were important for closing the gap between Israel's own national product and its level of expenditure—a gap that has been a continuous aspect of the Israeli economy. All major external sources of funds—the various contributions from the Jewish communities coming through such agencies as the United Appeal or Israeli Bonds, the public part of the German reparations, and various forms of external aid, above all from the United States—have been concentrated in the hands of the state (or of the Jewish Agency).

Second, control of investments by the state has been reinforced by the very strong regulation by the state of social security and pension funds, one of the major sources of capital formation and investment in the Israeli economy. To some degree, at least, it also regulates the stockmarket.

Government control and guidance was effected through control of the financial and credit system, through systems of subsidies for products and loans, through taxation, and through control of foreign exchange—most of which, in one guise or another, have basically continued even after the so-called period of liberalization in 1978, under the Likud government.

While overall control and regulation have indeed been characteristic of all Israeli governments since the establishment of the state, there was a gradual move from a direct, detailed administrative control characteristic of the 1950s, to more indirect control through subsidies, special credit allocations, foreign currency exchange, and the like.

At the same time, through the extension of the civil service (including teachers), municipal services, government-owned companies, and defense industries (of which aviation is probably the greatest), the state became the greatest single employer in the country. In 1965 there were 54,247 government employees; this number increased in 1975 to 82,576 and to 87,062 in 1981, an increase of 160 percent.

This development has been a part of the continuous increase of the public sector, as illustrated by the fact that 24 percent of the labor force in 1970 was in the public services (i.e., the government, the Histadrut, Jewish Agency, etc.); 27.3 percent in 1975, 28.0 percent in 1977, and 50 percent in 1981. Public sector employment thus doubled in a decade.

THE DIVISIONS OF ISRAELI ECONOMY: THE GOVERNMENT, HISTADRUT, AND PRIVATE SECTORS

While the state has become the major regulator of investment policy as well as the largest employer in the country, from the point of view of ownership of the major means of production the economy continued to be divided into three sectors: (1) the so-called private sector, composed of private enterprises; (2) the Histadrut, which includes the major collec-

tive settlements, the kibbutzim and moshavim, very widespread industrial concerns, its Sick Fund, in which about 80 percent of the population
are insured, and major cooperative boards; and (3) the government, composed mainly of public services and of numerous state-owned enterprises
in the industrial field, such as the Electricity Company and the Potash
Industries of the Dead Sea, making up about 12 to 15 percent of the
industrial labor force.

The share of the sectors in the net domestic product has been relatively
stable for the Histadrut sector; it is about 20 to 22 percent. It has grown
from the 1960s to the late 1970s for the government sector from about
20 to 25 percent, with a parallel decrease in the private sector from about
60 to 55 percent. If one includes the army, the increase in the public sector has been even greater.[2]

The policies of the state have greatly strengthened and diversified the
economy and have helped to create within all sectors new enterprises as
bases of employment and of economic development. The different sectors have each become very strong foci of power, with the government
greatly dependent on them, albeit within the framework of the basic polit-
icoeconomic orientations centered on the state.

Economic developments have weakened greatly the differences among
the sectors. This can best be seen in the Histadrut sector, which is most
highly organized and has a seemingly clear distinct ideology. All the parts
of the Histadrut sector—the kibbutzim and moshavim, the industrial
marketing, construction, and cooperative enterprises—have intensively
participated in economic expansion. The "constructive" activities of the
Histadrut became even more encompassing, and its economic "empire"
grew rapidly and became highly diversified. This has also happened in
somewhat different ways in private and governmental sectors.

On the whole it seems that the basic economic policies of different Histadrut enterprises or groups of enterprises, as well as of the General Histadrut bank (Bank *Hapoalim*), were guided above all by similar economic
considerations—even if with the possible admixture of political ones.

At the same time the growing similarity of the sectors has often
increased the competition between them over scarce resources and access
to the government. Hence notwithstanding similarities between the sectors, these factors, especially the Histadrut, have remained as potential
centers of power. Indeed the recognition of this fact has also given rise,
with the Likud government in 1977, to attempts to weaken these centers,
either through weakening of the central organs of the Histadrut or
through attempts to undermine some of the bases of their power by such
proposals as establishing a national health service, which would weaken
the monopoly of the Histadrut Sick Fund, or by preferential treatment to
other sectors.

The great concentration of resources in the hands of the government
and the concomitant possibility of the regulation of the flow of capital by
the state were rooted not only in the given historical circumstance, but
also in the ideology of a Labor Zionist vision and its socialist compo-

nents. The different components of the vision have influenced the major orientations of the government, giving a sharp push to the development, and the assurance of employment. The state has used external and continuously growing internal resources for a continuation of the far-reaching economic expansion and modernization, which has characterized the development of the Israeli economy, establishing settlements and encouraging many of the enterprises in the industrial sectors.

In the first decade or so the state policies were oriented toward the initial absorption of immigrants and the creation of minimal conditions of employment. From the middle or late 1950s, they were more and more oriented to the extension of the whole economic structure, its growing diversification, and a continuous increase of standard of living.

The stress of development, investment, and the maintenance of high levels of employment have constituted one basic pole of political economy in Israel—providing the momentum for its development. The other such pole consisted of governmental policies oriented to the outcome of these policies, namely, continuously rising public and private consumption, a continuously rising standard of living, and social welfare.

The considerations that have guided government policy were usually a mixture of two closely interconnected components: economic and sociopolitical. The economic one was based on the necessity in any modern economy in general and in Israeli economy in particular, to regulate the flow of money and the accumulation of capital necessary for the implementation of development policy, and also a high level of defense expenditure that characterizes the Israeli economy. The second component was a social and ideological orientation toward the distribution of resources.

Policies were guided beyond economic and organizational considerations (i.e., the needs of various ministries and interest groups) by several sociopolitical considerations. First was the generally strong tendency to regulation of the economy inherent in the socialist aspect of the predominant ideology and its paternalistic derivatives. Second were the strong egalitarian and distributive components of the regnant ideology. These egalitarian orientations were implemented through a whole series of tax measures, bringing the Israeli taxation to be among the highest in the world (about 56.6 percent of the GNP), and wage policies, especially in the different public sectors, that initially aimed at the minimization of wage differentials.

OUTCOMES OF POLICIES: ECONOMIC DEVELOPMENT AND SOCIAL DIFFERENTIATION, AND PATTERNS OF CLASS FORMATION

The primary outcome of government policies and of the struggle between the various forces analyzed was continuous economic expansion and development, a continuous rise in the standards of living, and economic growth—but with potential contradictions.

A second outcome was a continuous process of diversification and differentiation of the occupational structure, closely connected with a transformation of the different sectors' means of production. Of crucial importance in the development of the occupational structure has been the growing demand for educational qualifications to secure entrance to many occupations, in the service sector generally and in the civil service in particular. This is especially true of positions that were created by the expansion of the welfare system.

These developments were connected with far-reaching shifts from the original egalitarian policy orientations, giving rise to rather special types of class formation. While no exact data exist, there can be no doubt that income and capital differentials have been continually growing, eroding above all the lower middle class. Both the tax policies, which set limits on the upper brackets of income, and a de facto wage policy have greatly favored the upper and upper middle groups, often in sectors created by government policies: the managerial sector, and the upper and middle sectors of the professions (especially the lawyers and physicians), and the upper echelons of the agricultural sector (the kibbutzim, moshavim, and private agriculture). The sectors that benefited relatively less from these policies were the working class proper: the industrial, technologically nonsophisticated work force, and various middle echelons, whether salaried, industrial, or private employees.

There have developed continuous tensions between salaried personnel and manual workers on the one hand, and the salaried and independent professionals on the other. Within each of these broad sectors, tensions are found between the higher and the middle and lower groups within them. Centrality has been the role of government in the regulation and structuring of all these developments.

There has indeed developed what could be identified—in rather general and vague terms—as a working class, within which the most prominent element has been a salaried group employed in the public sector, whether as civil servants of central government or as employees of the municipalities or the Histadrut.

The development of a "real" industrial working class was much weaker. Even here larger parts were employed within the government and Histadrut sectors than within the private sector. There also developed, almost for the first time in the history of the Jewish settlement, something akin to a proletariat proper, namely the new industrial workers, as well as lower grade salaried workers. Also developing has been a relatively great concentration of population beneath the so-called poverty line, which in 1963 and in 1975 comprised about 15 percent of the whole population.

The process of economic and occupational diversification was connected with the growing wage and income differentials, and above all with a tendency to a coalescence between class and ethnicity.

A marked change in the composition of the labor force developed after the Six-Day War. There was a great influx of Arab labor, especially from the West Bank and Gaza, taking over most manual labor and thus

enabling the Jewish labor force to move upward to services and specialized labor, thus both undermining the older Zionist premise of Jewish
labor self-sufficiency and also reinforcing some conservative trends in the
economy that resisted growing modernization, and increasing the service
sector in the economy.

In Israel the workers from the West Bank territories are mostly manual
and unskilled workers: 80 percent are in construction, agriculture, and
industry, compared to three-fifths of the Israeli Arabs who work in the
Jewish economy, to about half of the Arabs who do not work in the Jewish sector (i.e., who work in the Arab sector), as compared to only 35
percent of the Jews who work in these three industries.

Arabs constitute approximately a quarter of all workers in greater Israel
(i.e., pre-1967 Israel and the West Bank and Gaza) as of 1980. They are
more than half of the workers in agriculture and construction. In the pre-
1967 borders of Israel, the Israeli Arabs plus the incoming workers from
the territories comprise 15 percent of the labor force, but constitute a
third of the workers in agriculture and more than half of the workers in
construction.

In the development of the occupational structure, of special importance has been the role of women. Their concentration in the clerical,
professional, technical, and related sectors have greatly bolstered the
earnings of families.

All groups compete for their share of the growing income, for access to
economic resources, and for positions of influence on the government,
and competition has become even sharper with growing inflation.

The outcome of these struggles has been greatly influenced by Histadrut. Thus, from a combination of changes in its ideologies and activities
and its relation to the government, Histadrut activities became more and
more oriented to the more established sectors, especially the higher and
middle sectors of the salaried groups in the service sector, and above all,
the public services; and much less to the problems of the "real" proletariat in the private sector or the rising mobile "bourgeoisie" groups from
among the new immigrants.

Among the workers, the Histadrut tended to support very strongly
some of the special stronger groups with monopolistic positions in the
public sector—the two most extreme illustrations being in El Al (the
national airline) and the electricity company—and other government
corporations and select groups of workers who have attained salaries well
above the average in the Israeli economy.

DEVELOPMENT OF THE ISRAELI WELFARE SYSTEM

Of special importance for understanding the development of the Israeli
welfare system have been two facts. First was the tendency to a relatively
high degree of coalescence between class structure and ethnic origin. The
higher strata contain a disproportionately high percentage of people of

European and American origin, while the lower strata contain a high concentration of those of Asian and African origin, the so-called Oriental population.

The second fact is that there exist poverty sectors that have tended to be perpetuated through generations. The poverty sector has constituted about 15 percent of the population, and poor children in 1975 constituted about 22 percent of the child population. About 80 percent of the poverty sector were of Oriental origin. The conditions of the poverty sector were indeed very bad upon the immigrants' initial arrival. Indeed, in order to cope with this fact, the government and the Histadrut have developed a far-reaching emphasis on welfare policies and services that have indeed been continuously expanded.

What is now seen as one of the major problems of Israeli society, despite the relatively great overall success, is the full integration of the so-called Oriental groups of immigrants, as compared with other modern countries of immigration.

In order to understand the roots, as well as the full impact of the development of the welfare systems in Israel, it is necessary to analyze the development of the ideology and activities of the Histadrut after the establishment of the state. There has been a bifurcation of its constructivist socialist and class emphases, between (1) an emphasis on the economic and institutional development, as carried out by government and Histadrut elites, and (2) a strong emphasis on different kinds of distributive welfare policies, social entitlements, and benefits, and a strong emphasis on governmental regulation of the economy and of wage differentials in a seemingly egalitarian direction.

One crucial aspect of the transformation of the Histadrut ideology was the growing identification of its socialist or class components with economic development under the auspices of the government and the Histadrut enterprises. This has occurred without, however, any specification in what ways these enterprises—beyond belonging to the government or being regulated by it, or by the Histadrut—will be shaped according to some such "socialist" orientations. The class or socialist components of the ideology have become increasingly related to welfare policies and the attainment of high standards of living by the workers.

Thus, the regnant social ideology has developed in a broad social democratic direction without any strong class or socialist connotations, but also without any strong emphasis on participation by various groups in institution-building or further pioneering.

The transformation of the regnant ideology was very closely related to three developments of the activities of the Histadrut: (1) growing participation through the expansion of its industrial sector in the process of economic development, (2) the extension of its service organizations—above all the Sick Fund—and a continuous struggle to maintain a monopoly of these services, and (3) the extension of its trade union activities.

With respect to trade union activities, there developed a certain division of labor between different parts of the Histadrut. The struggle over wages, indexing, and so forth, was divided into two parts. One part was the general struggle about the relative wage, estimating cost of living, and the limits and direction of wage policy. The Histadrut, as the federation of trade unions, the employers, including public employers, and paradoxically the Histadrut as the major employer, all participated. The second part of the struggle was that of specific-sector unions (e.g., public employees, industrial groups) and even of specific enterprises, which have often not accepted the overall authority of the central committee of the Histadrut.

There has also been a very strong involvement of the Histadrut in the provision of welfare services. The Histadrut has often been caught in a dilemma between being a major employer of welfare service workers, and being the representative of these workers, especially in the health services.

The rate of growth of expenditures for welfare services in the course of time has differed from one scheme to another. The growth rate depends on a number of factors that affect expenditure, such as demographic factors that change the size of the population included in the schemes; increases in the number of persons benefiting following extension of the conditions of entitlement; and real changes in the level of benefits.

Expenditure in the old age and survivors' field[3] amounted in constant 1980 prices to IS 272 million in 1960, 421 million in 1965, and 1.128 billion in 1970. The real annual increase of the expenditure of this branch during these years ranged from 8 percent to 17 percent, higher than the rate of growth of the aged population. Following the introduction of maintenance allowances for orphans and rehabilitation grants for widows in 1970, expenditure rose significantly, and 1973 was a peak year in the rate of real increase. These changes were also reflected in the relative weight of the old age and survivors branch's expenditure within total social security expenditure. It was 12.4 percent in 1960, 17 percent in 1970, and 21 percent in 1975. In 1977–79 there was a decline and in 1980 a rise again to 17.7 percent.

Real expenditure in the health insurance scheme, which includes spending within the framework of the Sick Fund as well as the maternity branch of the National Insurance Institute, amounted to IS 925 million in 1960 and rose to 2.1 billion in 1970 and 5.8 billion in 1980. The annual real rates of increase were relatively high until the early 1970s. Expenditure increased 17 percent in 1965, 14 percent in 1970, 17 percent in 1976, and 20 percent in 1977–78. But in 1978–80, the rate of increase slowed down. The rise in real expenditure stemmed from the relative price increase in health services, in both the field of wages and that of hospitalization. Moreover, as from 1977 the method of updating maternity benefits has improved, and they are now adjusted in accordance with the cost-of-living allowance paid to wage earners.

Real expenditure on state health services[4] increased from IS 592 million in 1960 to IS 3.0 billion in 1970. Until 1970 real annual rates of increase were 18–20 percent. Since then, however, the rate of growth has slowed down and real expenditure actually decreased.

A considerable expansion took place in family benefits, of which the main component is children's allowances. This lasted from the 1960s to the mid-1970s. Total real expenditure amounted to IS 54 million in 1960 and rose to IS 685 million in 1970 and IS 2.287 billion in 1975. In the period the conditions of entitlement to this type of benefit expanded: an employees' children's allowance was introduced in 1965, as well as payment by the employer for the first three children. In the early 1970s a veteran's allowance was introduced, as was an allowance for the third child. Finally, the income tax and children's allowance reform of 1975 led to the abolition of deductions for children in the direct taxation system, and to the introduction of a uniform system of children's allowances for all families starting from the first child.

The complete integration of benefits for children within the framework of the National Insurance Institute may be regarded as a continuation of the reform in children's allowances started in 1972. The constant increase of real expenditure in the branch continued and in 1975 amounted to IS 2.9 billion, the rate of increase since being approximately 27 percent, reflecting the impact of the reform of 1975. In 1977–79, real expenditure fell continuously and rates of real *decrease* were 3.8 percent in 1977, 6.4 percent in 1978, and 10.3 percent in 1979. The real decrease originated principally in the continuous erosion of the level of benefits paid. The updating of benefits continually lagged behind the rise in the level of prices and average wages. In 1975 a credit point for these allowances was worth about 5 percent of the average wage; in recent years it fell to less than 3 percent. Real expenditure in 1980 did not fall, thanks to a compensation for price increases outside the usual updating. Since the number of children has grown each year, the real expenditure per recipient declines more rapidly than expenditure as a whole. As of January 1981, children's allowances have been updated four times a year and this erosion of value has been reduced.

In government employees' pensions, the prolonged and natural process of the population's aging and the retirement of civil servants has expressed itself in an increase in real expenditure. Real expenditure on government employee pensions rose from IS 34 million in 1960 to IS 257 million in 1970 and IS 1.076 billion in 1980. Its relative proportion of total social security expenditure also rose from 1.6 percent in 1960 to 3.1 percent in 1965, 3.9 percent in 1970, and 5.5 percent in 1980.

Expenditures on public assistance services, including care of families, old people and handicapped, grants and other aid given by the Ministry of Labor and Welfare, are financed mainly by the state budget. They amounted to IS 170 million in 1960, rising to IS 743 million in 1970 and IS 1.286 billion in 1980.

In 1960 public assistance services constituted 7.7 percent of total social security expenditures, and in 1965 their share grew to 17.2 percent. In the

1970s, however, a downward trend set in. They amounted to 11.3 percent in 1970, 8.1 percent in 1975, and 6.5 percent in 1980.

Expenditure of the Rehabilitation Division of the Ministry of Defense, benefits to hostile action casualties, and to victims of the war against the Nazis, in 1960 amounted to IS 54 million and in 1970 to IS 389 million. Following the Yom Kippur war benefits reached IS 925 million in 1975. The annual rates of real increase were high: 18.2 percent in 1970 and 31.5 percent in 1975. After a peak in 1977, real expenditure began to decline. In 1970 war victims constituted 5.9 percent of total social security expenditure; in 1976 the figure was 7.9 percent, after which the decline began until in 1980 it amounted to 6.0 percent.

Real expenditure for other social programs—including employment injuries, disability, unemployment, employees' rights in bankruptcies and corporate dissolution, and equity grants—have increased greatly since 1960, as most of these programs were developed in the first half of the 1970s.

Some additional special characteristics of the Israeli welfare system are also worth noting: (1) the very heavy outlay on war victims, a characteristic closely related to the special security of Israel; and (2) the outlay on survivors of the Holocaust.

THE BASES OF THE ISRAELI WELFARE SYSTEM: THE POLICIES OF SOCIAL INTEGRATION

The Israeli welfare system has some very specific characteristics. It has several administrative offices: the Social Security Authority (formally within the Ministry of Labor but to some degree independent), established in the early 1950s to deal mostly with old age, family and children's allowances, and public assistance of different kinds; agencies dealing with the health services (the Sick Fund of the Histadrut, under which about 80 percent of the population is insured, and other sick funds that cover an additional 12–15 percent); the various pension funds, a large part of which is also concentrated in the hands of the Histadrut; and finally, the education system.

The development of several different agencies has been based on a particular definition of social problems. A good illustration of this can be found in what has gradually come to be perceived as one of the most central internal problems of Israeli society: the so-called ethnic problem. This has usually been defined in terms of the emergence of a great gap between the relative standing of groups from Asian and African origin and other Israelis in terms of education and economy, as well as the political sphere to some degree. Its most important manifestation has been the rise of a sharp division between "Europeans" and "Orientals," or as it has often been mistakenly described, between Ashkenazim and Sephardim.

A large part of social, educational, and to some degree economic policies undertaken from the late 1950s were intended to cope with manifold manifestations of this ethnic problem. Most actions were distributive measures providing more facilities to deprived groups, mostly defined in terms of ethnic origin, as well as being based on the redefinition of standards of achievement in many fields such as education, so as to make them easily attainable by these groups.

As the educational system does not belong to what is often defined as a welfare system, it is well to stress that many of the most important social policies that have developed in Israel, especially for the integration of immigrants, developed in the educational field. The most important among them were the policies of school integration, bringing children from different neighborhoods and backgrounds into the same school, often by busing; wide-ranging schemes of school aid; and free tuition, which in the late 1970s extended to include secondary education.

A second major aspect of such policies aiming at social integration was oriented to the poverty sector from 1969 to 1977. Because of the new reforms in the national insurance policy, which increased various allowances, there occurred a decrease in the size of the population in poverty, although it again started to increase from 1978. Thus, if we look at the income of the poverty population after they receive different state allowances, we can see that in 1963 every eighth person was under the poverty line, but in 1975 only one in twelve or thirteen.

At the same time, however, the far-reaching development of social service and welfare policies has generated a new social sector, a new social stratum characterized by far-reaching dependency on the state's distributive offices, and maturing growing social demands on the government.

As has been the case in other countries, many policies, such as free education, have benefited not only the lower groups in receipt of special subsidies, but also middle and higher income groups who in general have had easier access to most social services. Moreover, the level of education and health services has been much lower in the social periphery, especially the development towns; yet without a doubt they have greatly improved the situation of the poorer sectors.

The outcome of all these policies has been the general growth in the distribution of entitlements connected with the welfare system, and struggles around them as a major aspect of Israeli economic and political structures.

Beyond this, two additional characteristics underline hectic political dimensions of the Israeli welfare system. First of all, there is the peculiar administrative structure of the system. The most crucial aspect of this structure has been the persistence of the Sick Fund of the Histadrut, with the government playing only a very secondary role. It has been the "rightist" parties, various components of Likud, that have advocated the rationalization of the health service in face of opposition from the labor movement.

At the same time the Likud, unlike the European or American rightist parties opposed to the welfare system, has implemented extension of these services. A large part of its support comes from the deprived sectors.

The Israeli welfare system has its roots in the formative pioneering period of the Histadrut, the transformation of the basic institutional features and ideology of that period after the establishment of the State of Israel, the development of new class formations and immigration, political dynamics, and the concomitant persistence of many of the older institutional features and centers of power. These forces explain features of the Israeli system that distinguish it from other modern societies.

NOTES

1. Most of these items, except when otherwise stated, are in 1980 prices. The data presented here are taken from the *Statistical Abstract of Israel*. Jerusalem: Government Printing Office, 1982.

2. These rough estimates are based on Table 317 in the *Statistical Abstract of Israel,* 1981.

3. Expenditure includes old age and survivors' pensions, widows' and orphans' maintenance allowances, special old age pensions, death grants, rehabilitation grants, burial costs, and legal aid.

4. Includes all expenditures in the sphere of health (curative and preventive medicine, hospitalization, etc.) financed by the state.

8

Overcommitment in Pensions: The Japanese Experience

YUKIO NOGUCHI

Pensions policy is one of the most important considerations for the future of the welfare state in Japan, for many reasons. First, pensions policy is the most critical determinant of the future size of public expenditure, because it is becoming the largest program in the public budget. According to an estimate by the Economic Council, the ratio of publicly provided pension benefits to national income will increase from the present level of 5 percent to 17 percent in the year 2010, which is roughly the same as the General Account expenditure in the current national budget. The size of Japanese government in the future will be determined mostly by the growth of pension payments.

Second, the state pension system[1] will face a serious financial crisis in the future. Maintaining the current ratio of benefits to contributions means an inevitable sharp increase in contributions. According to a prediction by the Ministry of Welfare, the rate of contribution of the Employees' Pension will be forced to rise from the current level of 10.6 percent to 24.9 percent in the year 2010 and 38.8 percent in 2030. Since the latter level far exceeds what is politically tolerable, a radical reexamination of the current benefit structure must be undertaken.

Third, state pension wealth has become the greatest wealth of a household, in the sense that the present value of lifetime benefits (or the difference between the present value of lifetime benefits and lifetime contributions) exceeds other forms of household wealth. Equity in pension programs has thus become one of the most important factors for an equitable income distribution.

Fourth, public pension programs could have a strong impact on economic activity, especially through their effects on savings. If people

I am grateful for constructive comments given by the participants of the conference, especially by Richard Rose and Rei Shiratori.

regard a state pension as a substitute for other wealth and save less for their retirement, and if public pension programs do not accumulate enough savings, total savings in the economy will be reduced significantly. Thus it is possible that over time the state pension system distorts the allocation of resources enormously and thereby has serious adverse effects on the long-run performance of the economy.

In this chapter, we first review the Japanese state pension system. The following section discusses the background of the remarkable improvements in pensions that were undertaken in the early 1970s; an increase in tax revenues appears to have been the most important cause, and this change has had a tremendous impact on the deficit of the General Account of the national budget, which is mostly due to increase in social security expenditures. In the next section the benefit to contribution ratio of the present system is analyzed on a lifetime present value basis, showing that most benefits are not financed by accumulated savings but by payments from the current contributors and taxpayers. Such a system creates *intergenerational* transfers from the employed to the elderly. In the Japanese system, *intragenerational* transfers occur as well because of the difference in benefits among different pension programs, and it is argued that the latter transfers are socially unjustifiable. Future problems arising from the impact of pension improvements in the 1970s are discussed in the next section. Tax and social security payments are bound to increase significantly if the present benefit level is to be maintained, and savings may be reduced. The reduction in savings due to an increase in unfunded pensions, and the consequence of this for future economic growth in Japan, are discussed in the concluding sections.

AN OVERVIEW OF THE JAPANESE STATE PENSION SYSTEM

Until the 1970s, social security programs in Japan were by far inferior to those of Western countries: there were subsidies to low-productivity industries, but they were not large-scale social security programs. This situation is the chief explanation for the long delay in growth of the Japanese government after World War II. The social security system underwent a fundamental structural change during the early 1970s, when major improvements in health insurance and public pension programs were undertaken. The improvements made the social security system comparable, and in some respects even superior, to that of European countries. For details of these innovations, see the next section. Here we outline the present system.

The Japanese state pension system consists of eight programs, each covering people of different employment status. The most important programs are the Employees' Pension *(Kosei Nenkin)*, which covers employees of private firms, and the People's Pension *(Kokumin Nenkin)*, which covers the self-employed, including farmers. Since the establishment of

Table 8.1. Number of Contributors and Recipients of Pension Programs in Japan

Name of program	Number of contributors (× 1,000)	Number of recipients of old age pensions (× 1,000)
Employees' Pension	24,714	1,834
Seamen's Pension	211	36
National Government Employees' Pension	1,175	269
Local Governments Employees' Pension	3,192	526
Public Corporations Employees' Pension	798	263
Private Schools Employees' Pension	311	10
Agriculture Corporations Employees' Pension	474	56
People's Pension	27,851	8,191[a]
Total	58,726	11,184

Source: The Secretariat of the Advisory Council on Social Security (1984). Data for March 1980.
[a]Including noncontributory recipients, 3,340,000.

the People's Pension in 1961, all households have been covered by one or another state pension program. The above two programs cover approximately 90 percent of all households (Table 8.1); six other programs account for the other 10 percent.

A fairly radical reform of the system has been proposed by the Ministry of Welfare; a basic pension would be given to every pensioner regardless of the program to which he or she belongs. The new system became effective from 1986.

Under the present system, the benefit to contribution ratio varies from one program to the next. For example, the benefits and the contributions for the Employees' Pension are related to earnings, but those for the People's Pension are not; assessing the earnings of the self-employed is too difficult. The treatment of the spouse (usually wife) is also different; the People's Pension treats her as an independent contributor or beneficiary, but other programs usually treat her as a dependent. Historical backgrounds vary too. Whereas the oldest program—the National Government Employees' Pension—can be traced back to the 1870s, the youngest—the People's Pension—has a history of little over twenty years. In consequence, there are considerable differences in the benefit to contribution levels and in the rates of government subsidies.

The pension programs provide various benefits such as the old age benefit, survivors' benefit, orphans' benefit, and disability benefit. The most important is the old age benefit. A person is eligible to receive an old age benefit by paying contributions for more than a specified period—twenty years for the Employees' Pension and twenty-five years for the People's Pension.[2] The eligible age is 60 for the Employees' Pension and 65 for the People's Pension, and in the case of the Employees' Pension, the recipient must have retired.

Table 8.2. Model Benefits and Their Replacement Ratios[a]

Fiscal year	Model benefits[b]		Earnings[c]		Replacement ratios	
	B_E*	B_P*	Y_1	Y_2	B_E*/Y_1	B_E*/Y_2
1966	10,000	4,000	44,642	35,017	22.4	28.6
1967	10,000	10,000	49,747	38,865	20.1	25.7
1968	10,000	10,000	56,511	43,731	17.7	22.9
1969	10,000	10,000	65,824	50,088	15.2	20.0
1970	20,000	25,000	76,505	57,896	26.1	34.5
1971	21,500	25,000	87,172	66,085	24.7	32.5
1972	21,500	25,000	101,330	76,696	21.2	28.0
1973	52,242	50,000	123,913	91,509	42.2	57.1
1974	52,242	50,000	158,290	115,560	33.0	45.2
1975	72,997	66,657	176,532	131,905	41.4	55.3
1976	90,392	75,000	199,174	148,137	45.4	61.0
1977	98,325	81,116	217,303	162,573	45.2	60.5
1978	104,485	85,850	231,749	174,174	45.1	60.0
1979	107,858	88,884	242,989	181,610	44.4	59.4
1980	136,050	94,000	259,832	193,208	52.4	70.4

Sources: The Secretariat of the Advisory Council on Social Security (1984); and The Statistics Bureau (1984).

[a]Benefits and earnings in yen, ratios in percent.

[b]B_E* and B_P*, monthly "model benefits" of the Employees' Pension and People's Pension. B_P is for a couple. Additional benefits are included in B_P* since 1970.

[c]Y_1, Total cash payments in all industries excluding service industries; Y_2, regular salaries in all industries excluding service industries.

The old age benefit of the Employees' Pension consists of two parts: the fixed-amount benefit and the earnings-related benefit. In the case of the People's Pension, the benefit is a fixed amount. In both cases, benefits are related to the number of years in which contributions were paid, hereafter referred to as contribution years.

Due to the difference in contribution years and past earnings, the benefit amounts differ among individuals. In order to describe the benefit level clearly a model benefit is calculated, which is the benefit that a representative individual can expect. By the latest revision in 1980,[3] the model monthly benefit of the Employees' Pension was raised to Y136,050 (about U.S. $540) and that of the People's Pension to Y94,000 (about U.S. $380), as shown in Table 8.2.[4] The replacement ratio of the model benefit of the Employees' Pension is about 50 percent in terms of total earnings and about 70 percent in terms of regular earnings.[5]

It must be borne in mind that the model benefits for the two programs differ in nature. While the model benefit of the Employees' Pension can be regarded as the benefit of an actual beneficiary, that of the newer People's Pension is only hypothetical because the contribution years of the current beneficiaries are less than those assumed in the model benefit calculation.

The current rate of contribution for the Employees' Pension is 10.6 percent of earnings excluding bonus; it is shared equally between the employer and the employee. In the case of the People's Pension, the basic contribution is currently Y6220 (about U.S. $25) per month per contributor. The rate of subsidy from the General Account is 20 percent of the benefit for the Employees' Pension, and 33.3 percent in the case of the People's Pension. In both cases, the subsidy is granted at the time of the pension payment.[6] Because the pension system in Japan has not reached the mature stage, the amount of subsidy is at present relatively small. In 1984, the amount of subsidies to all public pension programs was Y2413 billion, or 4.8 percent of the total General Account budget.

The revenues and outlays of the two major programs have always been positive (Table 8.3). However, the ratio of surplus to revenue is decreasing, and especially for the People's Pension.

The accumulated contributions are pooled in the Trust Fund (Shikin Unyobu), which is the main component of the Fiscal Investment and Loan Program (FILP). The FILP is a government-operated system whose basic function is to finance various government-affiliated agencies such as the Japan National Railways, the Japan Highway Corporation, the Japan Development Bank, the Export–Import Bank of Japan, and the Housing Loan Corporation. More than forty agencies receive FILP funds. Although the largest source of revenue to the fund is postal savings, the reserve fund of state pensions also contributes an important share. In 1984, the increment in the fund was about Y19 trillion (about U.S. $76 billion), of which the accumulated contributions of state pensions made up more than one-fifth.

The old age benefit is treated in the income tax system in the same way as wages; it is regarded as taxable income. However, because several deductions are allowed, recipients of ordinary benefits are not in practice taxed. Contributions paid by an individual are fully deductible from income for tax purposes, and contributions paid by the employer are

Table 8.3. Revenues and Expenditures of Major Pension Programs

	Employees' Pension (× Y1 billion)			People's Pension (×Y1 billion)		
	FY 1965	1975	1980	FY 1965	1975	1980
Revenue	384	3,137	7,068	50	694	2,992
Contributions	297	2,202	4,700	25	369	1,182
Subsidies	8	174	570	15	213	1,650
Others[a]	79	761	1,796	10	112	159
Outlays	42	988	3,434	2	462	2,722
Balance	342	2,148	3,633	48	231	270
Reserve Fund	1,441	12,286	27,983	195	1,815	2,638

Source: The secretariat of the Advisory Council on Social Security (1984).
[a]Mainly interest revenue.

treated as business expenses of the firm. The earnings-related part of the Employees' Pension may be contracted out to occupational pension schemes in a manner similar to the British system.

THE IMPROVEMENTS OF THE 1970s AND THEIR IMPACTS ON BUDGET BALANCE

The state pension system in Japan was improved significantly in the early 1970s. Figure 8.1 shows the General Account outlays for the three major social security programs in terms of their ratios to national income.[7] While the ratio of public assistance expenditures stayed almost level, health insurance and state pensions increased dramatically during the past decade. As for health insurance, the introduction of free medical care for the aged, increased insurance coverage for the self-employed from 50 percent to 70 percent, and the introduction of subsidies for expensive medical treatments were undertaken.

Pension programs were also improved greatly. First, benefit levels were raised significantly, as was shown in Table 8.2. The replacement ratio of the model benefit of the Employees' Pension, in terms of total salary, jumped from around 20 percent to more than 40 percent in 1973. Although it fell in 1974 due to an enormous increase in wages after the oil shock, it soon recovered to the 40 percent level and is now above 50 percent. An indexation provision to counter inflation was also introduced in 1973. In fact, 1973 was called "the first year of the welfare era," because so many new social security programs were introduced.

Why did such significant improvements occur during this period? One reason is that after years of economic growth the Japanese economy had arrived at a stage at which it could allocate resources for purposes not directly related to productivity increases. Another reason can be found in the surge of welfare-oriented policies in local government. From the late 1960s, nonconservative parties and coalitions succeeded in taking power in many local governments, especially in urban areas. Following their political slogan of improvements in welfare, these nonconservative groups began to introduce various welfare programs. When these programs had spread, there arose pressures demanding that the central government adapt them as national policies. Free medical care for the aged was a typical example.

In addition, the fiscal condition was exceptionally favorable. Economic growth brought about a remarkable natural increase in tax revenues without any change in tax laws, thanks to the growth in the tax base. Natural increases in tax revenues are resources that the government can use without much constraint. In Japan they have often been used to reduce public borrowing. However, the early 1970s were somewhat different, for the borrowing ratio was not high compared to the previous levels and the magnitude of the natural increase was greater than in earlier years. There-

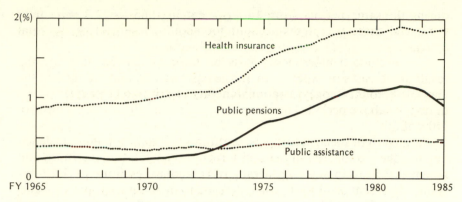

Figure 8.1. General Account expenditures to social security programs in Japan (ratios to national income). (From Ministry of Finance, *Fiscal and Monetary Statistics.* Tokyo: The Government Printing Office, 1984.)

fore, although a portion of the fiscal dividend of growth was used for the reduction of bond issues, another part was used to improve social security programs. At that time, many people, including analysts, did not foresee that the new programs would later cause financial difficulties (cf. Noguchi, 1979, 1980).

The active adoption of welfare programs by many local governments was also made possible by favorable conditions in local tax revenues. We can therefore say that it was fiscal affluence that caused the improvements in social security programs, and that party political influences were not so important as is usually emphasized, because similar increases happened regardless of local political circumstances.

It is, of course, inappropriate to finance long-term commitments such as pension programs by a volatile source of funds such as rapid economic growth. This became apparent when the oil shock of 1973 reduced growth rates, and therefore tax revenues in the subsequent years. The budget deficit was bound to increase, because it was difficult to cut expenditures, especially social security expenditures. The share of borrowing in total revenue for the national budget rose from 11.3 percent in 1974 to 25.3 percent in 1975, and then to a record level of nearly 40 percent in 1979. An increase in social security spending was the most important contributor to the increase in the deficit.

If we examine trends in major expenditures of the General Account of the national budget in terms of their ratio to national income, we find that only two items, social security and debt-servicing cost, show significant upward trends during the past decades. The ratio of the former has risen from 2.0 percent to 4.0 percent, and the latter from zero in 1965 to 3.6 percent at present. The ratio of total expenditures of the General Account Budget to national income has risen by 8.2 percentage points during the same period, from 14.1 percent in 1965 to 22.3 percent in 1984, and these two items account for about 70 percent of the total increase.

If we exclude debt-servicing costs on the grounds that they are the result of increases in expenditure in the past, we find that the ratio of the General Account Budget to national income rose by 4.6 percentage points during the above period. The increase in social security accounts for two-fifths of this.

The growth of social security expenditures enlarged not only the deficit but also the size of government, in terms of both total expenditures and revenues. The ratio of total general government expenditure to GNP was about 20 percent until 1970, when it began to increase steadily to the current ratio of about 35 percent. The share of tax and social security contributions in national income increased from about 23 percent during the 1960s to about 35 percent at present. The ratio of the General Account expenditures of the national budget to GNP has increased from less than 15 percent to nearly 20 percent.

As has been pointed out by Beck (1979), Break (1980), Nutter (1978), OECD (1978), Peltzman (1980), and others, the relative proportion of government activities in the economy has increased significantly in most industrialized countries since World War II, mainly as a result of the growth of social security expenditures. The same phenomenon has occurred in Japan. But while the relative size of government has tended to reach a saturation level in most Western countries, in Japan government is still growing rapidly. The problem of "big government" is a problem that Japan faces in the future.

IMBALANCE BETWEEN BENEFITS AND CONTRIBUTIONS

Because pensions in Japan were improved significantly in the mid-1970s, the Japanese system has become one of the best in the world. If one compares old age pensions in various countries, the level of the Japanese pension exceeds that of most European countries. On the other hand, the rate of contribution is significantly lower than that in the European countries. Thus, it seems as if we have a miraculous system of "high benefit with low burdens."

But there can be no miracles in the real world. In fact, there is an enormous imbalance in the present system between lifetime benefits and lifetime contributions. However, the considerable time lag between the payment of contributions and the receipt of benefits obscures this imbalance. Analysis is further complicated by the fact that benefits and contributions in the future are not definitely determined. Thus, in order to compare lifetime contributions with lifetime benefits, we must make several assumptions.

First, let us evaluate the extent to which benefits are financed from the

Table 8.4. Accumulated Contributions and Net Future Benefits Contrasted[a]

| | Employees' Pension ($\times$ 1,000) | | People's Pension ($\times$ 1,000) | |
FY	Contrib.	Benefit	Contrib.	Benefit
1968	506	2,097	—	—
1969	578	2,466	—	—
1970	672	4,291	—	—
1971	774	4,595	74	1,542
1972	902	4,845	90	1,535
1973	1,033	5,942	110	2,131
1974	1,226	12,109	138	3,762
1975	1,468	14,656	172	4,170
1976	1,778	18,438	214	5,592
1977	2,142	21,889	276	6,927
1978	2,559	24,123	354	7,483
1979	3,007	25,817	452	7,940
1980	3,557	30,327		

[a]Contrib., Accumulated contributions; Benefit, expected net future benefits; both as of age 57. Contributions and benefits of the People's Pension are for couples. Benefits of the Employees' Pension are model benefits, including supplementary benefits and survivors' benefits. Benefits of the People's Pension are average benefits.

recipient's past contributions. Table 8.4 shows the position for a newly entitled representative recipient in each fiscal year. In this calculation, it is assumed that past contributions accumulated at an annual interest rate of 6 percent and that future benefits will grow at the same rate as the discount rate.

If the system had been managed on an actuarially fair basis, and if there had been no improvements in the relative value of benefit as represented by the replacement ratio, then there would be no difference between the accumulated contributions and the present value of expected net future benefits. Table 8.4 shows that this has not been so. For example, in the case of the Employees' Pension, the difference in 1980 was as much as Y27 million (about U.S. $108,000) per beneficiary. For the Employees' Pension, the benefit to contribution ratio in 1980 is 8.5 to 1, and for the People's Pension 17.6 to 1.

The fact that most of the money that current beneficiaries receive comes from current contributors and taxpayers implies an intergenerational transfer. The magnitude of the transfer is greater than the value of household net financial assets, which was only Y4 million (U.S. $16,000) per household in 1980. In terms of the total annual flow, the transfer amounted to nearly Y2.4 trillion in 1980. This was greater than the annual budget for the public assistance program, about Y1 trillion in FY 1980.

The above calculation was for newly entitled recipients. If we consider an individual at the beginning of his or her working career, the result changes somewhat. In this case, assumptions concerning future benefit and contribution become crucial. Let us consider a male who begins work at age 25, retires at age 60, and dies at age 75. Assume that his wage is equal to the average wage, that the present benefit to contribution ratio remains unchanged in the future, and that income and benefits grow at the same rate as the discount rate. If the individual belongs to the Employees' Pension group, the present value of his lifetime contributions is about Y10 million including the employer's share. On the other hand, the present value of his lifetime benefits turns out to be about Y40 million, including survivors' benefits to his wife. Thus, accumulated contributions finance only about one-fourth of total benefits. The difference of about Y30 million must be paid by future generations. In the present system, 20 percent of the benefit is financed by the subsidy from the General Account. Thus, Y8 million must be borne by future taxpayers, and the rest (Y22 million) must be borne by future contributors.

According to the official explanation, the Japanese public pension system employs a "modified funded method." In fact, most people believe that present benefits are financed almost entirely by the accumulated contributions paid in by the beneficiaries. However, the official explanation is misleading, and the public's beliefs are unwarranted.

The present system would not be faulty if the nature of the transfer were only intergenerational. As a matter of fact, state pensions in most countries create this kind of transfer. The problem in the Japanese system is that there is also an element of intragenerational transfer that is quite hard to justify. This arises from the fact that the benefit of the People's Pension is significantly lower than that of the Employees' Pension.

Table 8.4 indicates that the difference between the present value of expected net benefits and accumulated contributions of the People's Pension program is less than one-third that of the Employees' Pension program. If state pensions were managed according to the fully funded method, the difference between the two programs would be justifiable, reflecting the difference in the contributions. However, since most of the benefits are transfers, there is little justification for such a difference. In fact, this difference creates an intragenerational transfer, which is socially inadmissible for several reasons. First, it is a transfer to those people who are relatively wealthy, because under the present benefit structure, those people with higher past earnings receive more transfers. Second, the transfer is not easily perceptible. As mentioned above, many people believe that the current benefits are financed entirely from the accumulated contributions, and that there is no element of transfer in the present system. The present benefit structure in which benefits are related to the number of contribution years and (in case of the Employees' Pension) to past regular earnings tends to strengthen people's belief that the present system is actuarially fair. The use of the term *hokenryo,* which means insurance premium, instead of the term payroll tax or social security tax has a similar effect. Here, semantics is important.

Another problem in the present structure is that it implies a significant increase in the future burden. In spite of the imbalance between the benefit and contribution, the system is presently managed without producing deficits because the number of beneficiaries is far smaller than the number of contributors (see Table 8.1).

However, conditions will change dramatically in the future because of both changes in the age structure of the population and the maturing of the pension programs. According to a prediction by the Ministry of Welfare the number of recipients of the Employees' Pension will increase to as many as 10 million, but contributors will increase to only 31 million in the year 2010. This implies that the burden of contributions by future generations is bound to increase significantly. The magnitude of the increase can be roughly evaluated by assuming a steady-state population. In this case, the present value of lifetime contributions must be equal to the present value of lifetime benefits, excluding the amount financed from general government revenue. Then, it is clear from what has been said that the rate of contribution must be raised from the present level of 10.6 percent of regular earnings to about 30 percent in the case of the Employees' Pension.

A more detailed official prediction by the Ministry of Welfare (1984) states that the rate of contribution must be raised to 24.9 percent of regular earnings in 2010, and to 38.8 percent in the year 2030.

THE FUTURE OF STATE PENSIONS

While the most fundamental change that took place in public finance during the past decade was the growth of social security expenditures, there are considerable time lags between the introduction of a new social security program and the increase in actual outlays. In the case of pension programs, the time lag can be long because the number of beneficiaries satisfying eligibility conditions may be small for many years. This is in fact the case in Japan, because pension programs have a relatively short history and the number of aged people is still small. In this sense, the effect of the improvements in the 1970s has not yet been fully realized, which keeps the *relative* size of government smaller in Japan than in European countries.

In the coming decades, however, the share of transfer payments in national income will grow rapidly as a result of the ageing of the population and the maturing of the pension system. Several attempts have been made to estimate future social security expenditures. Among them, the most comprehensive one is the estimate made by the Economic Council (Economic Planning Agency, 1982). In this report, the increase in the social security burden is regarded as one of the most serious problems that Japan will face.

Social security benefits as a percentage of national income will increase from the present level of 13.7 percent to 25.3 percent in the year 2000,

Table 8.5. Growth of Social Security Benefits and Contributions[a]

	Fiscal year					
	1981	1990	1995	2000	2005	2010
Social security benefits	13.7	18.4	21.3	25.3	29.8	31.2
Public pensions	4.8	8.7	11.1	13.8	17.1	17.1
Medical insurance	5.0	5.9	6.3	7.2	8.2	9.3
Social security contributions	10.1	11.2	11.6	15.6	19.0	21.4
Public pensions	5.4	6.0	6.2	9.7	12.6	14.5
Medical insurance	3.8	4.2	4.4	4.9	5.4	5.9

Source: Economic Planning Agency (1982).
[a]Percentage shares of national income.

and further to 31.2 percent in 2010 (Table 8.5). Most of the increase is brought about by the growth of state pension payments, whose percentage share in national income will increase from the present level of 4.8 percent to 17.1 percent in 2010 (Table 8.5). Social security contributions will also grow rapidly. The share in national income will grow from the present level of 10.1 percent to 15.6 percent in 2000, and further to 21.4 percent in 2010. (The difference between the benefits and contributions corresponds to subsidies from the General Account.) The calculations in Table 8.5 reflect assumptions concerning economic growth rates.[8] However, the effect is not so large because the benefit level is assumed to grow at the same rate as the economy.

The growth of social security expenditures will have a significant impact on the expenditure and revenue of general government,[9] as a rough estimation shows (Table 8.6). The figures for social security benefits and contributions are those derived in Table 8.5. Other figures are

Table 8.6. Expenditures and Revenues of the General Government[a]

	Fiscal year				
	1981	1995	2000	2005	2010
Social security benefits	13.7	21.3	25.3	29.8	31.2
Other expenditures	29.1	29.1	29.1	29.1	29.1
Total expenditures (*A*)	42.8	50.4	54.4	58.9	60.3
Tax revenues (*B*)	24.2	26.8	27.6	28.6	29.4
Social security contributions (*C*)	10.1	11.6	15.6	19.0	21.4
(*B*) + (*C*)	(34.3)	(38.4)	(43.2)	(47.6)	(50.8)
Other current revenues	3.7	3.7	3.7	3.7	3.7
Total revenues (*D*)	38.0	42.1	46.9	51.3	54.5
Deficit (*D* − *A*)	−4.7	−8.3	−7.5	−7.7	−5.7

[a]Percentage shares of national income. Figures are author's estimates.

computed on the assumption that the elasticity of tax revenues with respect to national income is 1.1; the rates of growth of expenditures other than social security and of current revenues other than tax revenues and social security contributions are the same as that of national income. The assumption concerning expenditure has an underestimation bias, since it neglects the fact that debt-servicing costs will increase faster than national income.

The size of the Japanese government, which is still relatively small compared with European countries, will grow dramatically in the coming decades. One reason for this is the growth of social security benefits. Public spending in Japan is likely to reach 40 percent of the GDP (50 percent of national income) by 1995, and it could reach 48 percent by 2010. While Japan's government is not so big today, it is certain to grow bigger in future.

Second, the share of social security programs in public finance will grow. On the expenditure side, the share of social security benefits in total expenditures, currently 32.1 percent, will rise to 51.7 percent by 2010. On the revenue side, the share of social security contributions is assumed to increase from the present level of 26.6 percent to 39.3 percent in 2010. Among the social security programs, the growth of state pensions is the most important factor.

A third point is that the difference between revenues and expenditures[10] will grow in the future. Even at present, the huge deficit in the national budget is regarded as one of the biggest economic problems. The deficit will cause more severe problems in the future, raising the possibility that the savings rate might fall.

Given the enormous increase in state pension payments and tax burdens, to what extent can the benefits and burdens be decreased by modifications to the present system? In Table 8.7, case 1 is that originally shown in Table 8.5. In case 2, it is assumed that the eligible age for receiving old age benefits under the Employees' Pension is raised to 65 by the year 2010. It is also assumed that the rate of contribution of the Employ-

Table 8.7. Effects of Reforms of Public Pensions[a]

Cases[b]	Benefits		Contributions	
	FY 2000	2010	2000	2010
1	13.8	17.1	9.7	14.5
2	12.6	15.3	8.6	11.1
3	12.5	14.7	8.6	11.1

Source: Economic Planning Agency (1982).

[a]Percentage shares of national income.

[b]Case 1, original case shown in Table 8.5; case 2, eligiblity age and contributions raised (see text); case 3, ceiling of 60 percent set for the replacement ratio.

ees' Pension is raised by 1.8 percent every five years from the present.[11] In case 3 a ceiling of 60 percent is set for the replacement ratio, whereas the replacement ratio will rise to 65 percent in the original case. In addition, the provisions in case 2 apply.

It is important to note that even with these modifications, which will not be easily realized, the magnitude of pension benefits will not be reduced significantly. This implies that if we wish to change the future burdens significantly, we must undertake more fundamental reforms.

In 1984, the Ministry of Welfare proposed a "radical" reform of public pension programs. The plan is radical in that it introduces a basic pension that covers everyone regardless of their employment status. It also tries to reduce the effective rate of government subsidies in a somewhat complicated way. However, few revisions in the basic benefit to contribution structure are incorporated in the new plan. Basic revisions such as raising the eligible age or lowering the replacement ratio are left to the future.

EFFECTS ON SAVINGS

In future the burden of supporting public pensions will become enormous. Thus, in order to reduce the burden to a tolerable limit, radical reexaminations of the current benefit structure must be undertaken. However, to think that reduction of benefits is all that is needed would be a serious mistake. The total burden of future generations would remain essentially the same even if benefits were reduced, because the elders would have to be taken care of by individual households or by public assistance programs. Given the changes in the age structure of the population, future generations cannot escape from an increasing burden in some form.

Can we then say that the existence of state pension programs has no effect other than to change the form of burdens? This is not necessarily so, because there is a possibility that economywide savings are reduced significantly (Feldstein, 1974). If people believe that they can obtain sufficient pensions after they retire, they will reduce their saving efforts while working, because the necessity for saving is reduced by the prospect of a pension. As a result, aggregate household savings will be reduced. This is a typical example of "substitution through fiscalization," as pointed out by Rose in Chapter 1. Whether or not the total savings are reduced depends on how public pensions are financed. If the fully funded method is used, total savings will remain unchanged, because the increase in government saving in the form of accumulated contributions offsets the reduction in household savings. On the other hand, if they are managed according to the pay-as-you-go method, such offsetting will not occur because the contributions collected are not saved but used for paying benefits. In this case total savings will be reduced by the same amount as the reduction in household savings.[12]

The actual financing of the public pension program in Japan is far from the fully funded method; it approximates the pay-as-you-go method. This implies a potentially enormous impact on savings. The magnitude of the effect can be evaluated by estimating the present value of net social security wealth, because private wealth would be reduced by that amount if private wealth and social security wealth were perfect substitutes. In order to get a precise estimate of social security wealth, we must calculate present value of net receipts for each cohort, multiply it by the population of the cohort, and then add the results. As a first approximation, we assume that the social security wealth is the same for all cohorts. Thus, we simply multiply the per capita net wealth of Y30 million calculated in the previous section by the total number of contributors of the Employees' Pension; the product is Y750 trillion. If similar calculations are done for other public pensions, the total value of net wealth amounts to about Y1000 trillion, which is more than three times the current GNP. It should be noted that this amount is greater than other forms of net household assets, worth Y850 trillion at the end of 1980.[13]

Other forms of savings may be affected as well. For example, firms will not increase their own occupational pensions if the level of public pensions is high. This will reduce savings because occupational pensions are usually managed according to the fully funded method. Lump-sum retirement payments, which can be regarded as a kind of savings, will also be reduced.

Reduced savings imply reduced investments, which in turn implies a fall in productivity. Therefore, there is a danger that public pension programs will kill the goose that laid the golden egg. Fortunately, household saving propensity is still very high in Japan. However, this does not imply that the Japanese will continue this behavior. The present high propensity to save may be merely due to ignorance of future pension benefits. Indeed this is quite probable, since it was only in 1973 that pension benefits were improved significantly. Household savings may fall considerably in the future as people become more knowledgeable about pension benefits.

There is in fact evidence suggesting a fall in household savings. As noted before, there are various pension programs in Japan geared to employment status, and the benefits provided by them differ considerably. The highest benefit is provided by the Government Employees' Pension, which has also the longest history. Next is the Employees' Pension. The People's Pension has the shortest history and provides the lowest benefit. If one compares the net financial wealth of different types of households with the pension benefits that they receive, there is a strong inverse correlation between the two. In 1980, the average ratio of net financial wealth to annual income was 0.60 for government employees' households, 0.72 for other employees' households, and 1.13 for self-employed households. This can be interpreted as savings behavior being lower where there is an assurance of a good pension.

Therefore, national savings are likely to be reduced significantly in the near future if no changes occur in the present state pension system. From this point of view, the priority should be to convert the present financing structure to a fully funded system. The rate of contribution must be raised sufficiently so that enough funds can be accumulated for future payments. Even if a strictly fully funded system is not achieved, any change will improve the situation by increasing the government savings. It may be argued that this proposal is unacceptable because it imposes too many burdens, yet we must remember that contributions will inevitably increase. Thus this proposal aims merely to shift that burden toward the present.

Another possible solution would be to increase the role of private programs such as occupational pensions. Because these programs are usually managed according to the fully funded method, the reduction in national savings would be avoided.

A REEXAMINATION OF THE ROLE OF GOVERNMENT IN JAPAN

As a latecomer to modernization, Japan has introduced many Western programs to transform its social and economic structure. This is true for the social security system too. When Japan was improving its social security system during the rapid-growth era, there were fairly well-developed social security systems in Western countries that Japan could, as it were, import. At that time it was possible to introduce proposals without seriously examining their fiscal implications or suitability to Japanese society, because the fiscal conditions were favorable and because the number of elderly people was relatively small.

The oil crisis of 1973 has changed the fiscal conditions drastically. Furthermore, the need to prepare for the higher proportion of elderly people in the population has come to be recognized more seriously as their numbers have in fact increased. With this background, many attempts have been made to reorganize the social security system. In this sense, the Japanese welfare state is now at an important turning point.

However, most of the public discussion concentrates on the narrow issue of how to save the system from financial bankruptcy. Obviously, this consideration is important and urgent. However, it must be recognized that even if financial solvency were established, several important problems would remain. It is therefore necessary to consider fundamental issues, and particularly to clarify the reason why government-operated compulsory pensions are necessary.

The justification for a compulsory pension system is presumably paternalistic. In the absence of a compulsory saving system, many people will not have sufficient savings for life after retirement, either because they are shortsighted or because their earnings are insufficient. For this reason, it is necessary to force people to save by introducing a compulsory system and to provide subsidies for low-income citizens.

However, this does not necessarily justify a state-operated pension, because it is possible for private financial institutions to manage a compulsory pension. However, the purchasing power of the benefit must be maintained in the face of inflation or economic growth, and this can be done by private institutions only if interest rates rise in accordance with the rate of inflation. Such economic changes cannot always be anticipated, especially in the case of unexpected inflation. In order to do this, it is necessary to manage the system on a pay-as-you-go basis, which can be operated only by the government.

The above argument suggests possible ways to realize an optimal mix of welfare. First, it is not necessary for public pensions to cover all of after-retirement income; the role of a compulsory saving system can be complementary to the insufficiencies of private savings. The level of compulsory pension benefit may be set at the minimum income for retirement; government's role in securing after-retirement life can be residual, rather than comprehensively generous.

Second, if the role of public pensions is to maintain the real value of benefits via the pay-as-you-go method, it should be regarded correctly as a transfer program rather than as a state-operated insurance program. In this way it is not necessary to relate benefits to contributions. This means that benefits can be financed by taxes. One possible reform is to make the benefit level identical for all individuals. This would solve the problem of the adverse redistributive nature of the present system.

If state pensions provided only a fixed amount, earnings-related payments could be covered by fully funded occupational pensions or by private pensions. If it is necessary for the government to extend assistance to these programs, such policies as tax credits may be used. Increasing the role of fully funded pensions will also mitigate the possible danger of a reduction of national savings.

Finally, it is important to recognize that the problem of pensions cannot be dealt with independently of other economic and social policies. For example, pensions are closely related to the employment conditions of elderly people. If firms employ more elderly people, the need for pensions will be decreased; to accomplish this, however, considerable changes must be made to the present employment system. For example, firms would have to raise the mandatory retirement age, which has already been raised significantly in recent years. The seniority-based wage structure, which has been basic to the Japanese wage system, would have to change too. Even if these difficult changes were made, the productivity of a firm would fall as it employed more elderly workers. A fall in profits of individual firms may be dealt with by providing subsidies or tax reliefs for those firms, but a nationwide problem cannot be resolved by such means. To cope with the macroeconomic problem of falling productivity, it is necessary to increase present capital accumulation. The future of the welfare state in Japan depends on the extent to which these problems can be resolved.

NOTES

1. The term social security *(shakai hosho)* is used in Japan in a much broader sense than in the United States; it includes not only public pensions but also medical insurance, public assistance, unemployment compensations, and other welfare programs. For this reason I use here the term state pension.

2. In the case of the People's Pension, there is a special provision for benefits to those contributors who have paid contributions for more than five years. Noncontributory benefits are provided by the People's Pension program to those people who were over 50 in 1961 and were not covered by other public pension programs. The latter is financed exclusively by the subsidy from the General Account.

3. Since FY 1980, no revisions except for indexation adjustments have been made.

4. An exchange rate of U.S. $1 = Y250 is used throughout this discussion. Reference to a budget year refers to the fiscal year, which in Japan begins on April 1.

5. In the Japanese salary system, bonus payment is important; it increases earnings (here referred to as total earnings) 30–40 percent above regular wage earnings.

6. Prior to 1975, the subsidy to the People's Pension was 50 percent of the contributions and was granted to the People's Pension Special Account at the time of the receipt of contributions. The reserve fund of the People's Pension grew rapidly because of this provision.

7. What should be used as a denominator to represent the relative size of government activity is an unsettled question. In OECD studies, gross domestic product (GDP) is usually used. However, national income is a more natural denominator when transfer items appear in the numerator, as is the case in this chapter. For a further discussion on this problem, see Break (1982). In the case of Japan, national income is about 80 percent of GDP. Thus the ratio to GDP can be obtained by multiplying the ratio to national income by the factor 0.8.

8. Assumptions underlying the projection are as follows: (1) annual growth rate of national income: 1981–95, 7.9 percent; 1995–2000, 6.9 percent; 2000–2005, 6.8 percent; 2005–10, 6.6 percent; (2) basic structure of benefits and contributions is assumed to be the same as at present. However, regarding contributions to the Employees' Pension, a drastic increase is assumed to take place around the year 2000 as a result of the exhaustion of funds. Thereafter, the Employees' Pension is assumed to be managed according to the pay-as-you-go principle.

9. "General government," a concept used in the National Account statistics, includes not only the General Account of the national government but also various special accounts and local governments.

10. This difference is called the "saving–investment gap" in National Account statistics. In most cases it is synonymous with "deficit," but there could be cases in which it is financed by a decumulation of funds, in which case the difference does not become a deficit.

11. Recall that in the original estimation, the rate of contribution is fixed at the present level as long as the fund exists. Note that the rates of contribution in 2000 and 2010 turn out to be lower in case 2. The reason for this is the interest revenue from the fund, brought about by an early increase in the rate.

12. The ageing of the population is itself a factor reducing total savings, because elderly people have in general a lower propensity to save than do younger people; it may even be negative.

13. Gross assets were Y980 trillion, of which land was Y467 trillion and financial assets Y318 trillion.

REFERENCES

Actuarial Division, Ministry of Welfare, *Financing Public Pensions* (Nenkin to Zaisei). Tokyo: Shakaihoken Hoki Kenkyukai, 1981 (in Japanese).

Beck, M., "Public Sector Growth: A Real Perspective." *Public Finance,* 34:3, 313–356, 1979.

Break, G. F., "The Role of Government: Taxes, Transfers, and Spending," in (M. Feldstein, ed.), *American Economy in Transition* Chicago: The University of Chicago Press, 1980.

Break, G. F., "Issues in Measuring the Level of Government Economic Activity." *American Economic Review,* May 1982.

Economic Planning Agency, *Japan in the Year 2000* (2000 Nen no Nihon). Tokyo: The Government Printing Office, 1982.

Feldstein, M. S., "Social Security, Induced Retirement and Aggregate Capital Accumulation." *Journal of Political Economy,* September–October, 82:905–926, 1974.

Feldstein, M. S., "Toward a Reform of Social Security." *The Public Interest,* Summer, No. 40, 1975. Reprinted in *Public Expenditures and Policy Analysis,* 2nd edition. (Haveman, R. H. and Margolis, J., eds.). Chicago: Rand McNally, 1979.

Feldstein, M. S., "Social Insurance," in *Income Redistribution* (Campbell, C. ed.). Washington, DC: American Enterprise Institute, 1977.

Ministry of Welfare, *Explanations of the Pension Reform* (Nenkinseido Kaikakuan no Kaisetsu). Tokyo: Shakaihoken Kenkyujo, 1984.

Noguchi, Y., "Decision Rules in the Japanese Budgetary Process." *Japanese Economic Studies* 7(4), 1979.

Noguchi, Y., "A Dynamic Model of Incremental Budgeting." *Hitotsubashi Journal of Economics,* February 1980.

Noguchi, Y., "Japan's Fiscal Crisis." *Japanese Economic Studies,* Spring 1982.

Noguchi, Y., "The Government–Business Relationship in Japan: The Changing Role of Fiscal Resources," in *Policy and Trade Issues of the Japanese Economy: American and Japanese Perspectives* (Yamamura, K. ed.). Seattle: University of Washington Press, 1982.

Noguchi, Y., "The Failure of Government to Perform Its Proper Task: A Case Study of Japan." *ORDO* 34, 1983.

Nutter, G. W., *Growth of Government in the West, Studies in Economic Policy.* Washington, DC: American Enterprise Institute for Public Policy Research, 1978.

Organization for Economic Cooperation and Development, *Public Expenditure Trends, OECD Studies in Resource Allocation,* 1978.

Peltzman, S., "The Growth of Government." *Journal of Law and Economics,* 23:2, 209–287, October 1980.

Secretariat of the Advisory Council on Social Security, *Social Security Statistics.* Tokyo: Shakaihoken Hoki Kenkyukai, 1984.

Social Insurance Agency, *Outline of Social Insurance in Japan 1981.* Tokyo: Yoshida Finance & Social Security Law Institute, 1981.

The Statistics Bureau, *Statistics Year Book.* Tokyo: The Government Printing
    Office, 1984.

SOURCES FOR STATISTICS

Bank of Japan, *Economic Statistics Monthly* (Keizai Tokei Geppo), Tokyo, Bank
    of Japan (monthly).
Ministry of Finance, *Fiscal and Monetary Statistics* (Zaisei Kinyu Tokei Geppo),
    Tokyo, The Government Printing Office (monthly).
The Secretariat of the Advisory Council on Social Security, *Social Security Sta-
    tistics* (Shakaihosho Tokei Nenpo), Tokyo, Shakaihoken Hoki Kenkyukai,
    (annually).
Statistics Bureau, *Family Saving Survey* (Chochiku Doko Chosa), Tokyo, The
    Government Printing Office (annually).
Statistics Bureau, *Statistics Year Book* (Nihon Tokei Nenkan), Tokyo, The Gov-
    ernment Printing Office (annually).

9

The Future of the Welfare State

REI SHIRATORI

The concept of the welfare state, like the concept of democracy, is extremely vague, and in this vagueness lies its attraction. Nobody can resist the idea of the welfare state, but the idea held is different for each individual. Therefore, although people unanimously agree that the welfare state is good and should be maintained with all its cost, they cannot so easily agree on a specific definition of the optimum welfare state and welfare policy. Despite the ambiguity of the concept of welfare state, all people can agree in principle about the desirability of welfare in society. Defining the welfare state scientifically, using academic jargon, may obliterate its attractiveness to most people.

Even if the concept of welfare state is ambiguous and pluralistic in its meaning, we can certainly classify the various concepts of the welfare state that prevail in the academic world today into several categories.[1]

First, one argument stresses that the welfare state is a particular stage in the development of society. In the process of social development a particular type of society will emerge from the Industrial Revolution, with material abundance resulting from the great expansion of production together with freedom and tolerance, which are caused by political developments. This particular type of society enlarges the capacity of the state, particularly in assuring the material needs of its citizens. Because the welfare state is here defined as having an inevitable connection with affluence and civil liberty, it is only possible in a developed capitalist society. Even if the welfare state appears in socialist societies, it would be incomplete in the sense that civil liberty is not fully developed there.

A second way to view the welfare state is as a way of life. According to this interpretation, the concept of welfare state has more to do with individual behavior in a society. In the welfare state people pursue their own individual way of life, assuming that their fundamental living conditions are secured by society. In spite of the state's broad coverage, they wish to limit its power. They appreciate the value of freedom, equality, and fraternity. The people in the welfare state are tolerant in almost all aspects of life, in religion, in belief, in sex, and in behavior. In the welfare society many people who are healthy, affluent, and enjoy life, give little thought to the meaning of life in society. Rather than contributing, they are often more interested in consuming.

Third, some people emphasize the policy side of the welfare state. They consider the welfare state as a set of social and economic policies, including policies securing the welfare of the citizens such as old age pensions, unemployment benefits, and a national health service. A majority will agree that housing and family policies are legitimate concerns of the welfare state, but there is argument about whether educational policies should be regarded as welfare policies. The interrelatedness of all policies of the state sometimes leads people to include in the concept of welfare state all the policies controlled by the public power, which are considered to form a policy network of the welfare state. If we include all aspects of public policies, then the concept of welfare state in this interpretation will become quite similar to the concept of the welfare state as a stage of development of society.

Fourth, some people place more emphasis on the mode and pattern of government. They consider that during the latter half of the twentieth century governments in almost all industrialized countries expanded their bureaucratic apparatus very swiftly, and the expansion of the bureaucratic system expresses the fundamental characteristic of the welfare state. If we take an extreme view, perhaps every aspect of society will be controlled by political power through the bureaucratic system.

I. CONCEPTS OF THE WELFARE STATE REEXAMINED

Although we can understand that there is some validity in each interpretation, we must formulate an integrated concept of the welfare state to include all aspects of the characteristics described in the four categories, and at the same time achieve a proper balance among the characteristics of each.

The concept of the welfare mix, developed by Richard Rose in Chapter 1 of this book, stresses the necessity of integrating welfare across a broad front. The welfare state is not only a product of government action but also a type of society where families fulfill an important role. A high material stage in the production of goods is achieved, and a degree of redistribution of income is realized. It might be appropriate to discuss the future of the welfare society rather than to discuss the welfare state.

It is also necessary to admit the possible development of varied models of a welfare society. The types that exist at present, whether American, Scandinavian, British, German, or Japanese, are closely linked with respective national histories, cultural traditions, and dominant ideologies. If existing welfare states are the products of past histories, future models of the welfare state are diversified. The role of government as the

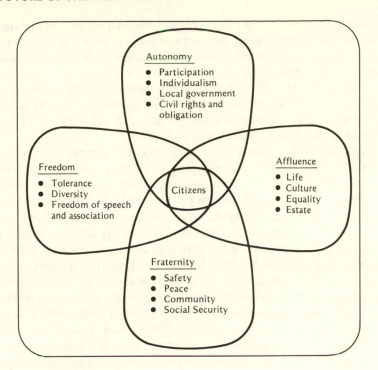

Figure 9.1. Values of citizens.

producer of welfare products will remain large and important in the British model of the welfare state. The bias in favor of welfare programs for what are conceived to be independent individuals (welfare in Nathan Glazer's definition; see Chapter 2) against the welfare programs for the dependent ("welfare" in Glazer's sense) will continue to characterize the American system even in the 1990s. The family will continue to play more important roles in welfare production in Japan than in other industrialized countries.

The concept of the welfare state exactly coincides with the values of citizenship in the modern state, including freedom, tolerance, fraternity, affluence, and autonomy in a citizen's life. The concept of citizenship in the modern sense can be found in the overlapped area of those four clusters of values, represented by autonomy, affluence, fraternity, and freedom (Figure 9.1). These values, if we call them by a single collective noun, can be expressed as the welfare of people today.

It is interesting to know that the Beveridge plan, which established fundamental principles to develop the British welfare state, clearly stated a social philosophy that covered the whole of society, although the report itself had the title *Social Insurance and Allied Services*. Some analysts called Sir William a neoliberalist or "the reluctant collectivist."[2] In his ideal society the state would intervene in citizens' lives to secure their subsistence, but the state intervention should not extend beyond the "national minimum." Some democratic socialists or Labour party supporters advocate more intervention of the state to achieve a higher degree of realization of the social values shown in Figure 9.1; however, the important fact is that the concept of the welfare society is almost equal to the concept of civilized society, because welfare in modern society is in its essence the secure existence (or at least subsistence) of citizens expressed in the words "national minimum."

We can advocate various types of the welfare society by emphasizing one set of values; freedom is certainly one of the most important aspects of the welfare society. It is not a rare coincidence that, when Sir William Beveridge stressed the elimination of poverty in 1941, President Roosevelt also declared four freedoms, which included freedom from want. It is also natural that the concept of a welfare society constantly advocated the necessity of communal fraternity and altruism, because society will become only an accumulation of human beings without them.

In the same way the concept of the welfare society as a civilized society presupposes the existence of modern citizens who identify themselves as autonomous individuals who are independent of state control. It is natural in this respect that the concept of the welfare society is regarded by some scholars to be a corollary of the concept of democratic society. The welfare society, certainly, can be compatible with the concept of the participatory democracy.[3]

Another important component in the concept of the welfare society, affluence, is a matter of the quality of life rather than the quantity of products. The society that produces abundant manufactured goods but has many people who suffer from poverty might be called a fully developed welfare society only with difficulty, as Glazer indicates in Chapter 2 of this book. The expansion of production does not necessarily improve the quality of life.

Figure 9.2 shows the result of the quantitative analysis of cross-national data carried out at the end of 1972 in order to examine the relationship between GNP per capita in 1970 while the horizontal scale indicates the quality of a citizen's life *(life quality indicator)* generated by a principal-component statistical analysis of sixty-eight social indicators.[4] Apparently we can classify two patterns in the combination between the expansion of production and the improvement of the quality of citizens' life. An interesting fact is that Japan was situated where the production-oriented and the welfare-oriented development started their different paths of development. Since 1970, as Maruo shows in Chapter 3, Japan achieved the climax of the rapid growth of GNP policy and started vigorously the development of welfare policies to catch up with the welfare standard in Western industrialized countries. In 1970, Japan also had to deal with a large number of victims of emission gas pollution in Tokyo.

Because of the catchall nature of the welfare society as a highly civilized society, the welfare state is not an exclusive product of democratic social-

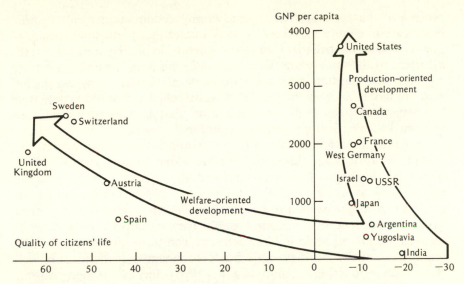

Figure 9.2. Two types of development: production-oriented and welfare-oriented. (From Rei Shiratori, *Nihon Okeru Hoshuto Kakushin,* Tokyo, 1973.)

ists, although this group contributed enormously toward the development of the welfare state in almost all European countries.[5] For example, the British welfare state was jointly built by Conservatives (the Butler Education Act, 1944), Liberals (by Beveridge: National Insurance Act, 1946), and Labour (by Bevan: National Health Service Act, 1946).

II. REEVALUATING WELFARE PROVIDERS

Even if we insist that the fundamental concept or goal of the welfare state is the civilized society, it does not solve the problems the welfare state is facing today, and even if we stress the necessity of flexibility in the conceptualization of the ideal welfare state in various societies, this will not suggest the future pattern of the welfare state in a particular society. It is certainly necessary to examine variations in existing welfare societies.

When we consider the production side of welfare, we find that four kinds of institutions are producers of welfare: the state, private and profit-oriented enterprises, private but nonprofit associations, and families or households. It is necessary to recognize all four kinds of institutions as significant producers of welfare. The state is not the sole institution to provide welfare in society.

On the contrary, families are the main and basic institutions providing meals, personal care, and fundamental socialization, albeit these services are considered to be personal and private ones, and are not listed as products of the market economy. The state is confronted today with problems

because of the decline of traditional family systems that formerly provided care to elderly members in families and that performed socialization functions on behalf of younger generations in the past. If elderly
members of the society are taken care of by families inside their home,
as in the past, the state need not send home helpers to lonely old people
who live alone. Because the state provides public care for old people who
live separately from younger generations, the younger generation can
more easily leave their parents' home and make the old people live alone.

I have no intention of saying that it is not necessary for the state to
provide public care for old people who live alone. What is suggested here
is that, on the whole, by sustaining the family system in more positive
ways and by assisting families to take care of old and infant members,
government might be able to construct a more humane welfare society
with less cost than initiating more public care systems for the elderly or
establishing more public nursery schools. The traditional theory of the
welfare state views families (households) unilaterally as the units of welfare consumption; this is definitely wrong. Providing care to aging parents
by a member of the family, with all its difficulties, can be more humane
than just paying the cost of caring for them. Although we cannot reverse
the progress of history, we can reevaluate the potential contribution of
the family system to welfare in society actively, and this could lead to
changing public policies of government.

The former Japanese Prime Minister Masayoshi Ohira once proposed
a "welfare society Japanese style." He explained his idea by saying: "I
would like to build up a welfare society in the following way while retain-
ing a traditional Japanese spirit of self-respect and self-reliance, human
relations which are based upon the spirit of tolerance and the traditional
social system of mutual assistance. I should like to add the public welfare
system to a fair degree to them."[6]

When Ohira talked of the welfare society, Japanese style, although he
mentioned public assistance programs and public services, he talked
more about self-reliance in families, and welfare facilities and services
carried out by the local community and private organizations, such as
business enterprises.

Although it might be easy for any scholar to repudiate Ohira's idea of
"the welfare society Japanese style" from a radical point of view, it is true
that the Japanese rate of taxation and governmental social security disbursement to national income is comparatively low, while the Japanese
are enjoying a standard of living almost equal to European countries (see
Appendix Tables C, D). It is also true that the Japanese family system has
a more solid bond among members than in Western industrialized countries (see Table 9.1), and the Japanese community system has a more stable sense of fraternity, as shown in the low crime rate (see Table 9.2).
These factors contribute to a low rate of taxation and small government
social security disbursement. It is necessary for us to exploit first the welfare functions of families and communities by preserving their virtues

Table 9.1. Marriage and Divorce Rates[a]

Country	Marriages	Divorces
Japan	6.2	1.38
France	5.5	1.71
Germany	6.0	1.92
Sweden	4.3	2.40
United Kingdom	7.1	2.94
United States	10.5	5.04

Source: United Nations, *Demographic Yearbook, 1983.* Ministry of Health and Welfare, Japan.
[a]Annual rate per 1000 people.

rather than to destroy families and communities first and then try to patch up the deserted societies by starting social welfare policies.

It would also be wrong for us to consider that private enterprises have nothing to do with providing welfare in society. If affluence is one of the goals of the welfare society, private enterprises are certainly contributing to the total welfare of society by producing goods. Employment in the market economy will give employees a recognition of the value of their existence in society, as well as an income.

Even if the private enterprises are organized and managed to obtain profits, it does not necessarily mean that they will be uninterested in creating welfare in society. They may make more efforts to create some forms of welfare (e.g., better working conditions for their employees), which will secure the well-being of their employees as well as achieve high quality in their products or high productivity of their production systems. Good working conditions can contribute to the quality of products and to productivity as well. This is certainly a common belief in Japan.

Workers in large private enterprises in a free capitalist market economy can enjoy better payments or better working conditions than workers in a centralized and state-controlled socialist economy. Democratization of

Table 9.2. Crime and Arrest Rate, 1983[a]

Country	Crime rate per 100,000 inhabitants			
	Homicide	Forcible rape	Robbery	Larceny/Theft
United States	8.3	33.7	213.8	4629
France	5.0	5.2	93.6	3850
Germany	4.5	11.0	48.1	4302
England and Wales	2.8	8.8	44.6	4988
Japan	1.5	1.7	1.9	1117

Source: National Police Agency, Japan.
[a]Because of differences in crime definitions stated by each country, the comparisons between countries are not exact.

the economy (or production) does not mean socialization or the establishment of state control over the economy (production). Historically, democratic socialists who advocated the mixed economy were more enthusiastic to promote welfare policies than communists.

Not-for-profit associations should be paid more attention as producers of welfare in society, as Wolfgang Zapf has argued.[7] New kinds of voluntary organizations need not emphasize the number of members, as did the traditional pressure groups, and may advocate more the interests of unorganized minorities or unorganizable interests, such as the environment, which can play an important role in producing welfare in the future society.

Associations can decentralize the existing conventional centralized production system of welfare to a certain degree, and by doing so they can decrease the power of the state. In some cases they will even become a countervailing power, which resists the monopolization of control over welfare production by the state. These voluntary associations will in the end change even the structure of society by taking over a substantial part of the role of the state, deemphasizing the state's central control through potential coercion by state power. The adjustments of various welfare provisions may take place in local communities mainly between voluntary associations. It is necessary to note that the concept of welfare is remote from the concept of coercion or power.

One of the components of welfare is the concept of autonomy or independence from intervention, because people find the greatest satisfaction when they achieve things voluntarily. Needless to say, the vitalization of associations' activities as producers of welfare will substantially decrease the financial burdens of the government in the welfare society.

Reexamination of the relationship between local government and the central government in welfare production is also necessary. Taking care of an individual can require deliberate and detailed consideration of the person's situation and environment. Welfare does not always fit standardized administration by a central government. It can better fit administration by near-at-hand local governments. This is quite different from the case of the production of consumer goods in a market economy by adopting a standardized mass production system. In the case of welfare production and welfare provision, central government's standardized treatment can create less satisfaction among people who need welfare treatment. If we try to transform our society in the future from a production-oriented society when the financial situation permits, we must appreciate the greater importance of local government and put limits on the role of central government.

It is also necessary to consider changes in the pattern of expenditures of public financial resources by government. At present much money is given directly to the producers of welfare without deep consideration of social need. For example, because in the National Health Service public funds are directly paid to the hospitals or doctors in many countries, they are encouraged to provide more treatments or give more medicine to the patients. More public resources should be given to the consumers of welfare. The consumers know the kind and amount of welfare they need. In private health insurance systems, unlike the National Health Service, the money is usually paid by insurance companies to the patients as consumers of welfare services. By encouraging this system of payment, the private health insurance companies keep their payments to the customers to an economical amount.

Welfare is produced and distributed in society in various forms. Sometimes money will be provided by government or nongovernmental associations, as subsidies, grants, bounties, or payments. Sometimes welfare products take the form of services given by central or local governments (e.g., education), goods (e.g., water supply), or governmental control of behavior of people in society (e.g., traffic control). In some cases the welfare products will be given by ordinary citizens as voluntary activities (e.g., love, personal contacts in society or in families).

When we deal with the present welfare society and future profiles, we can consider many combinations to attain a particular goal in welfare society. For example, in order to secure better lives for old people, we can work out a large-scale old age pension system that can even deal with future inflation. We can achieve the same goal, however, by increasing the opportunities for various kinds of employment for old people. By having some kind of job old people not only acquire better living standards but also confirm their value to society through their work. This is frequently done in Japan.

It is also worthwhile to know that all welfare products do not necessarily cost money. For example, the adoption of the flexitime system for work will cost hardly any money, but it can give many people more freedom, more leisure time, and more satisfaction by enabling them to enjoy their lives more.

Among various types of welfare products, education has a special importance. It brings out, without coercion, the potential ability of individuals and society. More important, by attaining a high standard of education a society becomes able to deal more easily and more quickly with difficult issues, such as the structural change of industry. It is certain that Japan's quick recovery in economy and industry at the end of World War II and the quick and most successful adaptation of Japan after the energy shock in 1973 was possible mainly because Japan has had one of the highest standards of education since opening her society to Western civilization at the end of the nineteenth century (see Table 9.3). It is necessary to invest more public financial resources in education, especially in the years of economic recession. By enlarging educational opportunities to the younger generation, the society can not only reduce the number of unemployed youths but also maintain a high level of morale and increase the society's capability to solve future economic problems. While many welfare products such as unemployment insurance or old age pensions

Table 9.3. Higher Education Enrollment Rates

| | Percentage of relevant age group | | |
Country	Total	Male	Female
United States[a]	45.5	46.3	44.7
Japan[b]	37.6	40.6	34.5
France[c]	27.1	22.8	31.4
Germany[c]	25.0	26.0	23.9
Britain	21.6	24.4	18.7

Source: Ministry of Education, Japan.

[a]New entrants at college level.

[b]New entrants at university level, junior college level, nursery teachers, and senior level of technical colleges.

[c]Qualified students entering college-level education.

secure the present healthy situation of society, education creates future welfare in society.

III. IMPACT OF CHANGING SOCIAL STRUCTURE

When we consider the future of the welfare society, we have to admit the past experience of the welfare state has already changed the structure of existing society, often as a consequence of the state's welfare policies.

First, up to a century of experience of the welfare state has created new social classes in many industrialized nations that have vested interests in existing welfare policies. One of those new classes is the government bureaucracy. The welfare state, which expanded government control from the political arena to economic policies, and from economic policies to welfare administrations, employs a large hierarchical structure of civil servants. In Japan the number of both national and local government employees reached 5.145 million in 1984. Bigness alone is not the problem; a more serious matter is that no other organization exists that can counteract the power of this governmental bureaucracy, because it is so effectively organized as a hierarchical system to carry out policies set by itself.

Under the leadership of this governmental bureaucracy, various business organizations and enterprises constitute another group who also have vested interests in the welfare state. In Japan national health expenditure reached Y14.54 trillion, accounting for 6.6 percent of net national income in the 1983 fiscal year, while national health expenditures were less than half a trillion yen in 1960. We can include in this second group employees and trade unions providing health care. There is also a group of statesmen who get both financial support and votes from private enterprises and workers in the health industry. It is certainly true, as corporatists note,[8] that those groups have an enormous amount of common interests and try to enlarge the policy areas of their vested interests. Although we cannot find any decisive way to destroy these powerful corporations, the financial deficit caused by the energy shocks since 1973 is weakening exploitation by these groups, and encouraging criticisms both from left and right camps against the corporative coordinations of an expensive complex.

A second aspect to consider is that the experience of the welfare state and sustained economic growth from the end of World War II to 1973 increased the number of middle-class people in almost all industrialized countries. To oversimplify, the structure of society in highly industrialized countries has changed from a pyramid to a diamond shape. In the 1940s the rich were few in number and the poor a majority. Although it is curious to say so, the theory of democracy (i.e., the rule of the majority) worked perfectly in this type of society, as a counterweight to the interests of the minority who were rich. Promotion of the interests of the poor was certainly in accordance with justice, because the poor were a majority and this majority often suffered real poverty.

Welfare state policies started with the support of the majority, although we can observe some perversive influences of war upon the initiation of the welfare policies in the early stages of the development of the welfare state.[9] Because the structure of society was pyramidal, welfare policies were public policies that took care of the poor majority at the base of the pyramid. As the Beveridge plan clearly stated, a "national minimum" should be assured the majority of people at the bottom of society.

Sustained economic growth for almost thirty years since the end of the war and the egalitarian redistribution of income under welfare state policies have jointly raised the standard of living of the majority at the bottom in the 1945 model of society. By the time the oil embargo shocked the world in 1973, the shape of the structure of society in almost all industrialized countries, including Japan and West Germany, had been changed into a diamond. It is important to note that the poor, like the rich, are a minority in the 1973 model of social structure.

The subsequent unfolding of OPEC's oil strategies pushed the whole industrialized world into panic. The Western industrialized countries, after having enjoyed a long period of sustained economic growth, now faced stagnation plus inflation. A sense of insecurity about the future standard of living, created by the changed economic condition, has permeated to the depths of the consciousness of the middle class who had climbed from the bottom to the middle. Maintaining the vested interests and the level of living they had secured during the preceding period of welfare state building, the members of the new middle class changed their attitude from liberalism into conservatism without hesitation, abandoning welfare and other liberal causes in egoistic pursuit of their own interests.

This is the background to the crisis of the welfare state in Western industrialized countries today. This "revolt of a majority" or "middle-class uprising" helps explain the landslide election of Ronald Reagan as American president. President Reagan as a presidential candidate called for tax cuts, cheaper government, and strengthening the military and national security. The same temper drove the British Labour government out of power in 1979 and gave a majority to Margaret Thatcher and her hard-line Conservative colleagues who preach "self-help before welfare." In Japan the attitude of the middle class in a diamond-shaped society also caused the overwhelming victory of the ruling conservative Liberal Democratic party in simultaneous elections to both House of Representatives and the House of Councillors in June 1980.[10]

When we consider the economic situation in the 1980s, which shows no sign of improving substantially in the near future, and the seriousness of the financial deficit in industrialized countries, at the risk of oversimplification, only two solutions appear possible: either ensuring revenues by tax increases or reducing expenditures by administrative reforms. Increasing tax rates, especially direct taxations, will not be permissible, considering the majority that is determined to protect its interests. If the middle-class majority continues to seek a lessening of its tax burden, the only possible options under such circumstances would prima facie seem to be the reduction of social security, health, and education budgets, or defense expenditures. For these are the programs that claim most public money.

If we examine the shape of the social structure more closely, however, we can have a more optimistic view about solving the present financial crisis of the welfare state in industrialized countries. Because the shape of the society is now a diamond and because the poor who need desperately the welfare services and goods are relatively small in number in comparison with the pyramidal society in 1945, the cost of welfare policies need not endlessly expand if we concentrate to a certain degree the goals of the welfare policies on that limited number of people who are at the bottom in this diamond-shaped society in the 1980s. The number of poor people who absolutely need welfare at the bottom of the society will further decrease in the future in accord with the increase of the majority middle class as a result of the achievements of welfare policies.

A corollary of this is that people who are able to share the cost of the welfare state policies are now relatively numerous, due to the expansion of the middle class, and enjoy a fairly high standard of living in a diamond-shaped society. In theory, it is certainly possible and more easy for the present diamond-shaped society to share the burden of financial costs of aiding the minority, who are really poor. The middle-class majority who are egoistically sticking to their vested interests, faced with an uncertain future, might be successfully persuaded to share the cost of the welfare state, at least by allowing the increase of indirect taxes in some forms because they are now enjoying a fairly high standard of living.

The future of the welfare state becomes a matter of persuasion or decision making in a new type of society, rather than just an economic or financial matter. A democracy supported by a middle-class majority is vulnerable to problems such as the maintenance of the welfare society when this majority is intent on its egoistical pursuit of its vested interests. While majority rule is undoubtedly one of the fundamental principles of democracy, when the majority is driven to cling egoistically to vested interests, it may justifiably be questioned whether democracy can withstand the pressures.

The crux of the matter is that the evolution of the welfare state in the highly advanced industrial countries has been such that the middle class with their vested interests have come to command a majority, while the handicapped, the old, children orphaned by traffic accidents, and others who are afflicted by poverty and can only maintain their living standard and their membership in society through social welfare systems have been relegated to the position of a minority. The poor mass who promoted the welfare state policies in the pyramidal society are now split into two classes, the affluent majority and the poor minority.

If we consider that the welfare state and democratic decisionmaking are both worthwhile to retain in the future, and if we consider the need of the welfare of the weak minority to be assured, we must find the way to overcome the vulnerability of a democratic society to an egoistic middle-class majority. Opinion leaders and social elites who support the values the welfare society tries to realize have an important role in persuading an egoistic middle-class majority. At the same time, the role of opposition parties in political decisionmaking is important, because they themselves are minorities and represent the interests of minorities. The activities of the voluntary associations are important because they are not wholly captured by the vested interests in industrialized societies.

When we consider the problems of decisionmaking in the present welfare societies, it is also important for us to cultivate fraternity between present and future generations. In the case of decisionmaking regarding old age pension systems, the decisions made by the present generation restrict future generations. Without transgeneration fraternity, the future generation will resist decisions made by the present generation.

It is also necessary to consider the crisis of the welfare state in a global perspective. Interdependencies among industrialized countries are so strong that it is impossible to solve such problems as the financial deficit of government by a country considering only its domestic economy. At the same time, the situation since 1973 has shown that industrialized countries cannot enjoy the fruits of welfare state policies without taking into consideration the situation of developing countries. Perhaps what has been lacking in the corporatist criticism of the present welfare societies in the West is a global viewpoint of the future of welfare societies. One of the strong points of the concept of the welfare state has been its advocacy from the start of universal human values such as freedom, autonomy, affluence, and fraternity.

All contributions in this book recognize the importance and the necessities of welfare policies in principle. All contributors also agree on the necessity of further development of welfare in human societies. Perhaps what we now need to explore theoretically is more democratic, more flexible, more effective, and more integrated welfare policies to be carried out in a more decentralized way.

NOTES

1. Concerning the various concepts of the welfare state, see the following books: D. C. Marsh, *The Welfare State, Concept and Development,* 2nd edition. London and New York: 1980; P. Flora, "Solution or Source of Crisis, the Welfare State in Historical Perspective," in *The Emergence of the Welfare State in Britain and Germany 1850-1950* (W. J. Mommsen, ed.). London: 1981; A. Briggs, "The Welfare State in Historical Perspective." *Archives europeennes de sociologie 2,* 1961; R. M. Titmuss, *Essays on "the Welfare State,"* 3rd edition (with introduction by B. Abel-Smith). London: 1976.

2. *Social Insurance and Allied Services.* A report by Sir William Beveridge, (Cmd 6404, 1942); refer to V. George and P. Wilding, *Ideology and Social Welfare,* London: 1976, Chapter 3.

3. See R. Hadley and S. Hatch, *Social Welfare and the Failure of the State, Centralised Social Services and Participatory Alternatives.* London: 1981.

4. See R. Shiratori, *Nihoni Okeru Hoshu to Kakushin* (Conservatives and progressives in Japan). Tokyo: 1973, pp. 135 ff. Using the conceptual model in Figure 1, I classified them into four categories, seeking the common factor among these four categories (i.e., autonomy, freedom, affluence, and fraternity) by using principal-component analysis, which would indicate the overall concept of citizenship. I scaled the scores of the quality of citizens' life by country on a horizontal axis.

5. Concerning the contribution of democratic socialists, see R. Mishra, *The Welfare State in Crisis.* Brighton: 1984, especially Chapter 5; R. C. Birch, *The Shaping of the Welfare State.* Harlow: 1974, p. 64; T. H. Marshall, *Social Policy in the Twentieth Century,* new edition. London: 1975, p. 95.

6. Prime Minister Masayoshi Ohira's speech in Japanese National Diet, 25 January 1979.

7. Wolfgang Zapf, "Welfare Production: Public versus Private." Paper presented to Conference of the Committee on Comparative Political Sociology, Bad Homburg, Germany, May 1981.

8. Concerning the corporatists' criticism against the welfare state, see, for example, Alan Cawson, *Corporation and Welfare: Social Policy and State Intervention in Britain.* London: 1982.

9. See R. M. Titmuss, "War and Social Policy," in *Essays on "the Welfare State,"* 3rd edition (with introduction by B. Abel-Smith). London: 1976, p. 75 ff.

10. See R. Shiratori, "Revolt of Middle-Class Majority—Reflections on Double Election Returns." *The Oriental Economist* 48(838), August 1980.

Data about Major Industrial Nations

Appendix Table A. Population Statistics

Country	Area (× 1000 sq km)	Population Total (millions)	Population Density (per sq km)	Birth rate per 1000	Infant mortality per 1000 births
United States	9,363	234	25	15.5	11.2
Canada	9,976	25	3	15.1	9.1
Japan	372	119	320	12.9	6.2
Britain	244	56	231	13.0	10.2
France	547	55	100	13.7	8.9
Germany	248	61	247	9.7	10.3
Italy	301	57	189	10.6	12.4
Sweden	450	8	19	11.0	6.8

Source: OECD, *Observer,* March 1985.

Appendix Table B. The Labor Force

Country	Labor force (× 1,000)	Females participating (%)	Unemployed (%)	Take-home pay as % gross wage[a]
United States	113,226	61.7	7.4	78.1
Canada	12,258	60.1	11.2	87.6
Japan	58,886	57.2	2.7	92.0
Britain	26,776	58.1	13.2	72.9
France	23,283	52.2	8.9	85.3
Germany	27,445	49.7	8.1	72.8
Italy	23,185	40.9	10.1	80.1
Sweden	4,375	76.7	3.1	66.6

Source: OECD, *Observer,* March 1985.

[a]Average earnings in manufacturing for one-wage family with two children, after exclusion of income tax and social security contribution.

Appendix Table C. The Economy

Country	Gross domestic product (GDP U.S. $billion)	Change real GDP % per annum 1978–83	Purchasing power per capita (U.S. $)	Net rate savings (% GDP)	Consumer price index annual % increase 1979–84
United States	3,627	1.1	13,969	2.2	7.4
Canada	334	1.3	13,803	7.3	8.7
Japan	1,233	4.1	10,739	15.7	3.9
Britain	426	0.8	9,802	6.0	9.5
France	496	1.5	11,276	6.6	11.1
Germany	616	1.2	11,447	9.2	4.5
Italy	352	1.4	8,711	6.9	16.1
Sweden	96	1.7	—	4.3	10.2

Source: OECD, *Observer,* March 1985.

Appendix Table D. Public Expenditure

Country	Education	Health	Pensions	Total social expenditure[a]	Debt interest	Public expenditure
			(Percent of GDP)			
United States	5.4	4.2	7.4	20.8	4.6	35.7
Canada	6.0	5.5	4.5	21.5	7.2	40.2
Japan	5.0	4.6	4.7	17.5	4.4	30.4
Britain	5.7	5.4	7.3	23.7	4.9	46.6
France	5.7	6.4	11.9	29.5	2.6	48.4
Germany	5.2	6.5	12.5	31.5	3.0	47.7
Italy	6.4	6.0	13.1	29.1	9.1	44.9
Sweden	6.5	8.8	11.2	33.4	7.7	64.0

Sources: For mean, OECD, *Social Expenditure 1960–1990,* Paris: OECD; for debt, OECD, "Fiscal and Monetary Policies," *Economic Outlook,* No. 36, December 1984, p. 32.

[a]Includes unemployment benefit and other social programs.

DATE DUE